Six Moments of Crisis

Gill Bennett was Chief Historian of the Foreign & Commonwealth Office from 1995–2005, and Senior Editor of the UK's official history of British foreign policy, *Documents on British Policy Overseas*. As a historian in Whitehall for over thirty years, she provided historical advice to twelve Foreign Secretaries under six Prime Ministers, from Harold Wilson to Tony Blair. A specialist in the history of secret intelligence, she published a ground-breaking biography, *Churchill's Man of Mystery: Desmond Morton and the World of Intelligence*, in 2006. She was also part of the research team working on the official history of the Secret Intelligence Service by Professor Keith Jeffery, published in 2010. Gill Bennett is now involved in a range of research projects for various government departments.

Praise for Six Moments of Crisis

'Well informed and deeply researched'

International Affairs

'a unique and valuable tool'

Sir Paul Lever, *RUSI Journal*

'Fascinating'

Philip Stephens, *Financial Times*

'Concisely written, authoritative and gripping'

The Tablet

'…impressive. This is a portrait of a formerly great power wrestling with decline.'

Douglas Hurd, *New Statesman*

'[A] masterly study… Besides providing many insights into leading policy-makers, Gill Bennett covers six major 'moments of crisis' spread over a period of more than 30 years in only 175 pages of text without ever oversimplifying. Her book is both a very good read and admirably succinct.'

Christopher Andrew, *Literary Review*

'A wonderful text for the student of international relations, whom it will immunise against infection by arcane concepts and theories that bear little relation to the real world. It is, moreover, beautifully written and an object lesson for academics in history and the social sciences.'

Vernon Bogdanor, *Times Higher Education Supplement*

'Bennett's book is a living example of the importance of history, not just in the context of how and why these decisions were made, but in providing a guide to the complex, and at times misleading phrase: 'lessons of history'.

Keith Simpson, *Total Politics*

Six Moments of Crisis

Inside British Foreign Policy

GILL BENNETT

OXFORD
UNIVERSITY PRESS

Great Clarendon Street, Oxford, OX2 6DP,
United Kingdom

Oxford University Press is a department of the University of Oxford.
It furthers the University's objective of excellence in research, scholarship,
and education by publishing worldwide. Oxford is a registered trade mark of
Oxford University Press in the UK and in certain other countries

Published in the United States of America by Oxford University Press
198 Madison Avenue, New York, NY 10016, United States of America

British Library Cataloguing in Publication Data

Data available

ISBN 978–0–19–958375–1 (Hbk.)
ISBN 978–0–19–870089–0 (Pbk.)

Printed in Great Britain by
Clays Ltd, St Ives plc

Events take place everywhere but the crux is at the centre.

Han Fei: Chinese philosopher, *c.*280–233 BC
(*The Art of Attainment,* trans. Tony Blishen)

Harold Wilson contemplates the burdens of premiership, 1964

Acknowledgements

A great many people have helped me in the writing of this book, either by discussing the issues with me or by commenting on specific chapters. I cannot name them all, but I am most grateful. In particular, I would like to thank Professor Christopher Andrew, Dr Christopher Baxter, Jim Daly, Lord Hennessy of Nympsfield, Professor Keith Jeffery, Professor Roger Morgan, Sir David Manning, Sir David Omand, Professor George Peden, Constance Regnier, Professor Patrick Salmon, Professor David Stafford, Sir Stephen Wall, and Mrs Heather Yasamee for their advice, friendship, and support. I am grateful to the Foreign and Commonwealth Office Historians, and to the Official Histories team within the Cabinet Office Knowledge and Information Management Unit, for facilities and help, and to the staff of The National Archives and Churchill Archives Centre, Cambridge. I could not have done any of it without my agent, Bill Hamilton of A. M. Heath, while my editor, Matthew Cotton, has been unfailingly supportive. Finally, to my two sons, Henry and Dominic, and to those of my friends who have put up with me while I have been writing this book, many thanks.

Contents

List of Illustrations

Abbreviations

BAOR	British Army of the Rhine
CAS	Chief of the Air Staff
CDS	Chief of the Defence Staff (from 1958)
CENTO	Central Treaty Organization (formerly the Baghdad Pact)
CIA	Central Intelligence Agency, US overseas intelligence organization
CIGS/CGS	Chief of the Imperial General Staff/Chief of the General Staff (after 1963)
CNS	Chief of the Naval Staff
CSCE	Conference on Security and Cooperation in Europe
DTI	Department of Trade and Industry
EEC	European Economic Community
EFTA	European Free Trade Association
FBI/CBI	Federation of British Industry/Confederation of British Industry (from 1965)
FO/FCO	Foreign Office/Foreign and Commonwealth Office (after 1968)
FRG	Federal Republic of Germany (West Germany)
GCHQ	Government Communications Headquarters
GDR	German Democratic Republic (East Germany)
GRU	Glavnoye Razvedyvatelnoye Upravleniye, Soviet military intelligence
IMF	International Monetary Fund
IRA	Irish Republican Army
JIC	Joint Intelligence Committee
KGB	Komitet Gosudarstvennoi Bezopastnosti, Soviet security and intelligence service
MI5	Security Service, Britain's domestic intelligence organization

MI6	Secret Intelligence Service (SIS), Britain's overseas intelligence organization
MOD	Ministry of Defence
NATO	North Atlantic Treaty Organization
NFU	National Farmers Union
OEEC	Organization for European Economic Cooperation
PUS	Permanent Under-Secretary
SDP	Social Democratic Party
SEATO	South East Asia Treaty Organization
SIS	Secret Intelligence Service
TUC	Trades Union Congress
UN	United Nations Organization
UNSC	United Nations Security Council
US	United States of America
USSR	Union of Soviet Socialist Republics
WEU	Western European Union

List of Principal Ministers Featured, and their Ministerial Posts since the Second World War[*]

Clement Attlee (1883–1967)

- Lord Privy Seal, 1940–2
- Secretary of State for the Dominions, 1942–3
- Lord President of the Council, 1943–5
- Deputy Prime Minister, 1942–5
- Prime Minister, 1945–51, Minister of Defence, 1945–6

Aneurin Bevan (1897–1960)

- Minister of Health, 1945–51
- Minister of Labour and National Service, 1951

Ernest Bevin (1881–1951)

- Minister of Labour and National Service, 1940–5
- Foreign Secretary, 1945–51
- Lord Privy Seal, 1951

George Brown (1914–85)

- Parliamentary Private Secretary to Minister of Labour and National Service, 1945–7, and to Chancellor of the Exchequer, 1947
- Joint Parliamentary Secretary, Ministry of Agriculture and Fisheries, 1947–51
- Minister of Works, 1951
- First Secretary of State and Secretary of State for Economic Affairs, 1964–6
- Foreign Secretary, 1966–8

[*] Titles given as held at the time they appear in this book.

R. A. Butler (1902–82)

- Parliamentary Under-Secretary, Foreign Office, 1938–41
- President of the Board of Education, 1941–4
- Minister of Education, 1944–5
- Minister of Labour and National Service, 1945
- Chancellor of the Exchequer, 1951–5
- Lord Privy Seal, 1955–9
- Home Secretary, 1957–62
- First Secretary of State and Deputy Prime Minister, 1962–3
- Foreign Secretary, 1963–4

James Callaghan (1912–2005)

- Parliamentary Secretary, Ministry of Transport, 1947–50
- Parliamentary and Financial Secretary to the Admiralty, 1950–1
- Chancellor of the Exchequer, 1964–7
- Home Secretary, 1967–70
- Foreign Secretary, 1974–6
- Prime Minister, 1976–9

Lord Carrington (1919–)

- Parliamentary Secretary, Ministry of Agriculture and Fisheries, 1951–4
- Parliamentary Secretary, Ministry of Defence, 1954–6
- First Lord of the Admiralty, 1959–63
- Secretary of State for Defence, 1970–4
- Secretary of State for Energy, 1974
- Foreign Secretary, 1979–82

Sir Stafford Cripps (1889–1952)

- Lord Privy Seal and Leader of the House of Commons, 1942
- Minister of Aircraft Production, 1942–5
- President of the Board of Trade, 1945–7

- Minister for Economic Affairs, 1947
- Chancellor of the Exchequer, 1947–50

Sir Alec Douglas-Home (1903–95) (*Lord Dunglass, 1918–51; 14th Earl of Home, 1951–63*)

- Minister of State for the Scottish Office, 1951–5
- Secretary of State for Commonwealth Relations, 1955–60, Lord President of the Council, 1957 and 1959–60
- Foreign Secretary, 1960–3
- Prime Minister, 1963–4
- Foreign Secretary, 1970–4

Anthony Eden (1897–1977)

- Secretary of State for the Dominions, 1939–40
- Secretary of State for War, 1940
- Foreign Secretary, 1940–5, and Leader of the House of Commons, 1942–5
- Foreign Secretary, 1951–5
- Prime Minister, 1955–7

Denis Healey (1917–)

- Secretary of State for Defence, 1964–70
- Chancellor of the Exchequer, 1974–9

Edward Heath (1916–2005)

- Parliamentary Secretary to the Treasury and Chief Whip, 1955–9
- Minister of Labour, 1959–60
- Lord Privy Seal, 1960–3
- Secretary of State for Trade and Regional Development, 1963–4
- Prime Minister, 1970–4

Sir Geoffrey Howe (1926–)

- Solicitor-General, 1970–2
- Minister for Trade and Consumer Affairs, 1972–4
- Chancellor of the Exchequer, 1979–83
- Foreign Secretary, 1983–9
- Lord President of the Council and Deputy Prime Minister, 1989–90

Roy Jenkins (1920–2003)

- Parliamentary Private Secretary, Commonwealth Relations Office, 1949–50
- Minister of Aviation, 1964–5
- Home Secretary, 1965–7
- Chancellor of the Exchequer, 1967–70
- Home Secretary, 1974–6
- (President of European Commission, 1977–81)

Lord Kilmuir (1900–67) (*Sir David Maxwell-Fyfe, 1942–54*)

- Solicitor-General, 1942–5
- Attorney-General, 1945
- Home Secretary, 1951–4
- Lord Chancellor, 1954–62

Selwyn Lloyd (1904–78)

- Minister of State for the Foreign Office, 1951–4
- Minister of Supply, 1954–5
- Minister of Defence, 1955
- Foreign Secretary, 1955–60
- Chancellor of the Exchequer, 1960–2
- Lord Privy Seal and Leader of the House of Commons, 1963–4
- (Speaker of the House of Commons, 1971–6)

Harold Macmillan (1894–1986)

- Parliamentary Secretary, Ministry of Supply, 1940–2
- Parliamentary Under-Secretary, Colonial Office, 1942
- Secretary of State for Air, 1945
- Minister of Housing and Local Government, 1951–4
- Minister of Defence, 1954–5
- Foreign Secretary, 1955
- Chancellor of the Exchequer, 1955–7
- Prime Minister, 1957–63

Reginald Maudling (1917–79)

- Parliamentary Secretary, Ministry of Civil Aviation, 1952
- Economic Secretary to the Treasury, 1952–5
- Minister of Supply, 1955–7
- Paymaster-General, 1957–9
- President of the Board of Trade, 1959–61
- Secretary of State for the Colonies, 1961–2
- Chancellor of the Exchequer, 1962–4
- Home Secretary, 1970–2

John Nott (1932–)

- Secretary of State for Trade, 1979–81
- Secretary of State for Defence, 1981–3

Emanuel Shinwell (1884–1986)

- Minister of Fuel and Power, 1945–7
- Secretary of State for War, 1947–50
- Minister of Defence, 1950–1

Margaret Thatcher (1925–)

- Parliamentary Secretary, Ministry of Pensions and National Insurance, 1961–4

- Secretary of State for Education and Science, 1970–4
- Prime Minister, 1979–90

William Whitelaw (1918–99)

- Parliamentary Secretary, Ministry of Labour and National Service, 1962–4
- Lord President of the Council, 1970–2
- Secretary of State for Northern Ireland, 1972–3
- Secretary of State for Employment, 1973–4
- Home Secretary and Deputy Prime Minister, 1979–83
- Lord President of the Council and Deputy Prime Minister, 1983–6

Harold Wilson (1916–95)

- Parliamentary Secretary, Ministry of Works, 1945–7
- Secretary for Overseas Trade, 1947
- President of the Board of Trade, 1947–51
- Prime Minister, 1964–70
- Prime Minister, 1974–6

Within the text, the names of these and other ministers appear in bold type when they first intervene in a discussion and biographical information is given.

Introduction

Everyone has a view on what the foreigners are up to.*

It has become increasingly fashionable to invoke history on both sides of any argument about why the British government should or should not have taken certain foreign policy decisions. Politicians seeking to justify their actions (or inaction), in retrospect or in real time, point to historical analogies to show why they took a certain course of action. Experts of all persuasions and special interest groups accuse governments of ignoring, manipulating, or foolishly repeating history. (They are rarely praised for learning from it.) Media commentators pick up and rehearse all these arguments, with the danger that in becoming newsworthy they become distorted or meaningless. How often are 'Munich' and 'Suez' invoked, for example, even when there is little or no comparison between those episodes and current events? As former Foreign Secretary Douglas (now Lord) Hurd says, ignorance of history is foolishness, but the false analogy can be more disastrous than the blank mind.[1]

This book is based on the experience of a long career (well over thirty years) spent as a professional historian working for the British government within the Foreign and Commonwealth Office (FCO). The FCO is now the only major department of state to employ a cadre of full-time in-house historians, whose task is partly to document the official history of British foreign policy, and partly to offer 'historical advice'—happily, a very flexible concept—to ministers and senior officials. The job offers a wonderful opportunity to observe, and to some extent participate in, the workings of government: to get inside history, in fact. It is, as one of my academic colleagues puts it, 'applied' as opposed to 'pure' history,

---

* Sir Percy Cradock, *In Pursuit of British Interests*.

and I was lucky enough to engage in it under six different Prime Ministers and twelve Foreign Secretaries before retiring from the post of Chief
Historian in 2005.

If my experience as a historian working in government has shown
me anything, it is that foreign policy decisions are *always* difficult and
complicated, even if that does not appear to be the case from the
outside. Quite apart from the complexity of the issue on which the
decision is to be taken, those who have to take it are influenced by a
wide range of pressures: domestic, economic, electoral, legal, international, parliamentary, party political, personal, and more. They
may then be criticized, by their political opponents, by the media,
and by the general public for taking decisions that seem hasty, ill-
informed, short-sighted, or just plain wrong. It seems to me that such
criticism often arises because people do not understand fully the context in which the decision was taken. Of course, governments can
make bad decisions, and it is not (nor has it ever been) my job to
defend them. But government ministers do a difficult, important, and
responsible job that affects all of us. If we are going to criticize their
decisions, it should be on the basis of an informed judgement. That
is where history comes in.

This book is in no sense official, and any views expressed are purely
personal. But I am drawing on my experience as a government historian
to try and explain to those who may be interested—particularly those
who may have had little or no contact with policy-making—how British
foreign policy is made. To do this I have chosen six decisions taken by
British governments since the end of the Second World War. Some will
be familiar, such as Suez and the Falklands conflict; others, such as the
decision to withdraw British forces from East of the Suez Canal in 1968,
or the expulsion of 105 Soviet intelligence officers in 1971, may be less
so. But they were all controversial at the time they were taken, and they
all had a profound effect on British policy and Britain's relations with
other countries. My aim is to show how and why they were taken, not to
judge whether they were good or bad. Understanding those decisions
better can help a good deal with understanding how others were taken.
Although none of the episodes I have chosen happened less than thirty
years ago, the reader will soon realize that each has a resonance in more
recent events.

All the chapters in this book have the word 'challenging' in their title,
for three reasons. The first is that because foreign policy decisions are

always complex, they are challenging to understand. We have to work at it. The second is that looking at those decisions from the inside out, studying both the decision-makers and the context of each decision in its broadest sense can produce results that challenge existing interpretations. We may need to change our minds. The third meaning refers to the examples I have chosen, which all involved a challenge by the British government, whether to a person (like the Egyptian President Gamal Abdel Nasser), an institution (like the KGB), or a concept (like Britain's world role).

If we want to understand how and why a decision was taken, the first thing we have to do is to try and forget what we know about its consequences. Of course it is impossible to eliminate hindsight entirely. Most people will have heard of, and may have read about, some or all of the decisions examined in this book. But if we really want to get to the root of things, we have to look at them from the inside: that is, on the basis of what the decision-makers knew, or could have known, at the time, not from the viewpoint of what we now know, or in the knowledge of how things turned out. For example, when Mrs Thatcher's government took the decision on 2 April 1982 to send a naval task force to the Falkland Islands, they did not know yet that they were going to be fighting a war, still less that it would end in victory. Of course, they considered the possibility of fighting and hoped in that case to be successful. But they could not see into the future, and it is important not to let our assessment of the decision be coloured by our knowledge of what happened afterwards.

The second key element to every decision is the context, in the broadest sense. Books, sometimes a great many of them, have been written about the subject of most of the decisions considered here. But nearly all of them focus—naturally enough—on the episode or crisis itself, and few take full account of the broadest context in which decisions were taken. Yet without that context, it is impossible to understand fully how ministers arrived at their conclusions. For example, both the Suez and the Falklands crises need to be set against the background of European federalism; the Korean War against events in central Europe; Britain's application to the European Economic Community against decolonization in Africa; the decision to withdraw from East of Suez in 1968 against American involvement in the Vietnam War; and Operation FOOT against quadripartite agreements on Berlin. At the same time, domestic factors such as the state of the British economy (which encompasses everything from unemployment to globalized commerce), the size of the government's parliamentary majority, and likely media reaction are equally important.

This means that a lot of questions have to be asked about every decision, no matter what its subject. Here are just a few of them. How long is it to the next significant elections in the United Kingdom *and* in the United States? How unified is the governing political party, and is there a powerful interest group involved? What is the current economic situation, and future prospects? Are any of the key ministers under particular pressure from personal factors such as newness to the job, health, or personal relationships? Who is talking to whom on this issue, and how are their views being fed in? What is the likely media, parliamentary, and public reaction to alternative courses of action? What do government officials, the military, and coordinating bodies (like the Joint Intelligence Committee) make of the available intelligence? And most importantly, in foreign policy: what is going on in Europe and in the rest of the world that may have a bearing on the issue at hand, even if it is apparently unconnected? It is not always possible to discover the answers to all the questions, but it is important to ask them.

Decisions are taken by people, and to understand how foreign policy is made we need to look closely at those who took them. In each of the six decisions examined in this book, the focus is on a specific meeting, usually of the full Cabinet but always of Cabinet ministers (in 1968 there are several linked meetings). The choice of meeting is inevitably somewhat arbitrary, and doubtless some will argue with my selection. I am also well aware that in choosing meetings of Cabinet ministers I lay myself open to criticism from the school of thought (a very large one) that believes ministers are not the ones who take the decisions. The real decisions, this argument goes, are made elsewhere, by a combination of officials, advisers, and other more shadowy interest groups. I do not accept this. After long years of going through the archives, as well as dealing professionally with officials, advisers, and ministers, I believe firmly in two golden rules of governmental decision-making.

The first is that government policy is made by government ministers, not by officials, special advisers, Brussels, or Washington, though all these, and many more, have an input. Only ministers, for example, have the authority to mobilize the armed forces. Politicians, civil servants, military commanders, intelligence agencies, industrial leaders, special advisers, and trade unionists may, and do, have views on policy, which may be fed in to the decision and may be very influential. But ministers are ultimately, and collectively, responsible for policy and therefore they are the decision-makers, whether it is in full Cabinet or in Cabinet Committee. The Cabinet, in Walter Bagehot's words, is 'a *hyphen* which joins, a *buckle* which fastens the legislative part of the State to the executive part of the State'.[2] Cabinet ministers, not their advisers, take the decision and the responsibility. Naturally, a great deal of preparatory work is involved, and in the examples chosen here I have tried to reflect the range of opinion and advice on which ministers based their approach to the question in hand. But to reflect it comprehensively would require a book-length study of each decision, so it must be taken as read that I understand that the advice of officials and others will have played an important part.

My second golden rule is that even in times of crisis, ministers always think about more than one thing at a time, even if at the meeting in question they discuss a single issue. This may seem obvious, but most people writing about foreign policy focus on a particular issue, and tend to assume that ministers do the same. Of course most ministers have a particular departmental responsibility and, with their officials and advisers, are to an extent preoccupied with that area. And in times of crisis, ministers focus on the urgent matter in hand. But at Cabinet level, no decision is taken in a vacuum. Even in cases where a foreign policy issue is handled by a small group of ministers, they must bear in mind other considerations, whether it be the views of their constituency and party, or the current electoral position or budgetary restrictions on their department, not to mention what might be going on elsewhere in Britain or in the world. And despite what a lot of people think, it is impossible for ministers to be unaware, in one way or another, of history.

What is true for ministers is doubly so for Prime Ministers. By nature of their office they are responsible for the whole spectrum of policy, domestic and foreign, for the security of the realm, and for the reputation of the government they lead. Whether they took over from a member of the same party or from a political opponent, they are aware of precedent and the need to do better than before. And in the end, the final responsibility for the government rests with them: as Tony Blair wrote, the difference between everyone else and the final decision-taker is that everyone else can debate and assume, but only one person can decide.[3] While they rely on their ministers to carry specific policies forward, they have to be sufficiently on top of every one of the Cabinet portfolios in order to assess the national interest, the relative merits of the policy proposed, and its potential effect on the government as a whole. As the doyen of historians of government, Peter (now Lord) Hennessy, puts it, 'The dilemma of the job of Prime Minister is that its holders must be selective in their detailed interventions yet constantly sensitive to virtually the whole range of government activity.'[4]

Not surprisingly, Prime Ministers tend to be exceptional people. The former diplomat and Downing Street adviser Sir Stephen Wall, who has worked closely with a number of Prime Ministers, writes that those who make it to the top in politics are 'almost invariably extremely bright, exceptionally hard-working and of superhuman stamina…I do not believe that anyone who has not experienced the life of a top politician at first hand can appreciate the relentless pressure and the constant stress which those politicians endure, in the midst of which they are expected to perform at the top of their game and to make good judgements based on careful and wise thought.'[5] Another distinguished foreign policy adviser with personal experience in Downing Street, Sir David Manning, points to the influence of 'decision fatigue': by the time decisions reach the Prime Minister, they are by definition very difficult, or they would already have been taken by someone else. All Prime Ministers have to take too many decisions on too many things.[6]

Each of the six Prime Ministers featured in this book, from Clement Attlee to Margaret Thatcher, was bright and hard-working with exceptional stamina, though each was quite different. Some were, of course, more successful than others. All had their own way of dealing with the pressures of the job, of managing their Cabinets, and of safeguarding both their personal position and the authority of their governments. But all government ministers are under a lot of pressure, some of it subconscious. Patrick Gordon Walker, briefly Foreign Secretary in the Wilson government 1964–5, wrote that 'ministers are very conscious of the interconnection between issues: one reason why they may not clearly detect the interconnection between various factors affecting an isolated issue is that they connect them all together in a living and continuous nexus.'[7] I would go further: to understand why a decision was taken, it is necessary to look *outside* the interconnections that ministers themselves make, and take into account the connections made by others, as well as the things that do not look as if they are connected at all. For in foreign policy the world is truly a global village, and was so before the term 'globalization' was thought of.

My starting point for each of the decisions has been the formal Cabinet minutes, which at the time of writing are all in the public domain except for the 1982 decision on the Falklands. These minutes are written by the Cabinet Secretary and his team, and are not a verbatim record of the proceedings. The Cabinet Secretary may write part of the record and other members of the Secretariat the rest; but he (so far it has always been a he) signs them off, and they are then circulated to ministers who do not see them in draft. Lord Armstrong, who as Sir Robert Armstrong was Cabinet Secretary 1979–87, says that he tried to write his minutes in sonata form, with an exposition, development section, recapitulation, and coda. They should, he said, be a tool of government, not just the record of a meeting.[8] Cabinet minutes do not include every element of a discussion, do not normally ascribe remarks to individual ministers, and summarize much of the argument under the name of the Prime Minister. But they are still the right place to start. It is also important to look at what else was on the agenda at the meeting, and at other meetings leading up to the one at which the particular decision was taken.

For the first three of my decisions, taken in 1950, 1956, and 1961, the Cabinet Secretary's Notebooks are also available. A rolling programme has been under way since 2006 to transfer to The National Archives these bound volumes of handwritten notes by the Cabinet Secretary. Although they are not complete, can be difficult to decipher, and vary considerably according to the identity of the Cabinet Secretary, they are tremendously interesting for the historian of government. They tell us who said what on what subject, and give a flavour of the discussion in a way that the formal Cabinet minutes cannot. The detail they include can be significant: for example, the discussion of 'unseating' Nasser at the beginning of the Suez crisis is included in the Cabinet Secretary's notebook, but is not mentioned in the formal minutes. They have to be treated with some caution—we cannot know if the Cabinet Secretary was interrupted, or left the room at any point, for example—but they are still extremely useful.

I have also made extensive use of the published diaries and memoirs of ministers. The former have been particularly helpful. One has to be careful with them, since they are a personal, and possibly prejudiced account. Clement Attlee, in retirement, was scathing about the historical value of a diary. By its nature, he said, it represents 'a point of view limited by time, place and emotion, if not by knowledge...If a diary is to enable tense minds to let off steam in private, it cannot be regarded as a safe historical source; and if it is written for use as a future historical document, it is suspect for the opposite reason. One cannot have it both ways.'[9] Of course, he was right. But diaries have a value just by being written at the time. Even if what a minister wrote was biased, or wrong, it represents a point of view. And in cases where a number of ministers kept diaries covering the same period, as was the case in January 1968 when the decision was taken to withdraw British forces from East of Suez, it is particularly valuable to be able to compare their recollections and opinions.

Memoirs are rather different. If written shortly after being in office, they tend to be self-exculpatory; if written much later, they tend to be forgetful. But they are still a valuable source, particularly when based on a minister's contemporary notes and diaries. Memoirs by officials, too, are valuable, as are the memoirs of foreign statesmen and officials who have a different perspective on their British counterparts. The best memoirs can be extremely perceptive and informative. But it is unwise to rely on them for factual information. No matter how clear a former minister's recollection, it may well be inaccurate. There is a natural tendency for ministers (and officials) to inflate their own role in any given incident or decision. If the subject matter is sensitive, as in the case of Operation FOOT in 1971, then it may not be mentioned in memoirs at all, or only in passing. Biographies of key figures, especially if written with the cooperation of the subject and/or access to their papers, are also an important source.

Finally, there is the archival record, in the form of departmental files kept at The National Archives and elsewhere. This is a huge resource, and an essential component of any study of foreign policy-making. But as Peter Hennessy says, the archive is 'frozen history': it needs historians to 'make it twitch and warm it up a bit'.[10] It would have been impossible, and indeed undesirable, to give extensive archival references for all the decisions featured in this book. Again, I must ask the reader to take it on trust that those archives have been consulted, selectively if not comprehensively, and references given where appropriate. Anyone wanting to look further must delve into the archives themselves, or read the scholarly works based on them. In my comments on the decisions and the people who took them, I make no claim for infallibility. My aim was to twitch back the curtain to reveal the backstage apparatus of policy-making, not to reveal the whole plot. Foreign policy is one of the most tightly controlled areas of government activity, never delegated and rarely subject to consultation. Yet it is one of the least well understood by those in whose name the decisions are taken. In the twenty-first century people are more aware of what is happening in the world than they have ever been: much of it seems frightening, confusing, or even inexplicable. What is British foreign policy, and why? People want, and need, to know: and looking inside history is a good way to find out.

Clement Attlee (*right*) and Ernest Bevin (*left*), 1945

1

Challenging Communism
Britain Sends Land Forces to Korea, July 1950

Militarily not very desirable. Psychologically inevitable.*

On the morning of Tuesday, 25 July 1950, the British government led by Labour Prime Minister Clement Attlee agreed to send a Brigade Group (about 9,000 men) to serve under American command in the war that had broken out when Soviet-backed North Korean forces invaded US-backed South Korea on 25 June.[1] The significance of the decision was political rather than military. Taken at the very beginning of a conflict that was to escalate considerably and last until 1953, the decision was of minor importance in the overall context of the war (except, of course, to those who did the fighting). But it was of considerable symbolic significance, and provides an illuminating snapshot of Britain's national and international position five years after the end of the Second World War. It is also a very good example of the complexities of foreign policy-making. Many of the issues raised still have resonance sixty years later.

On 6 July 1950 the Defence Committee, chaired by the Prime Minister, had accepted the Chiefs of Staff's advice that it would be 'militarily unsound to make available any land or air forces for the Korean campaign'.[2] Most of Britain's armed forces were already deployed overseas, in the Middle East and in the British Zone of Germany as well as in Asia, fighting a communist insurgency in British-administered Malaya, and protecting Hong Kong. But American pressure to announce that land reinforcements would be sent had become irresistible. The British Ambassador in Washington, Sir Oliver Franks, warned that failure to

---

* Defence Minister 'Manny' Shinwell's view on sending British troops to Korea, as noted by Cabinet Secretary Sir Norman Brook on 25 July 1950.

offer troops would cause long-term damage to transatlantic relations. The Americans, he said, needed to feel they could count on Britain, seeking a reassurance as much psychological as practical: 'The Americans in Korea will be in a tough spot for a long time. They look round for their partner.'[3]

None of the ministers present at the Cabinet meeting on 25 July was in any doubt that the United Kingdom was the partner the Americans sought. And the British needed the Americans, whose support was fundamental to their defence, their prosperity, and their position in Europe and the world. Relations in the previous few months had been prickly, with the US reluctant to allow Britain the place at the atomic top table she felt was rightly hers, and some resentment on both sides at Britain's failure to respond positively to the Schuman Plan for a European coal and steel organization.[4] But in global strategy, as the Chiefs of Staff had stated in June, 'Full collaboration with the United States in policy and method is vital.'[5] So despite doubts about US policy in the Far East; despite warnings that military resources could ill be spared; despite fears that higher defence spending would derail social programmes; ministers in a government best known for establishing the welfare state acknowledged the centrality of the Anglo-American relationship and agreed to reverse their previous decision and send troops to Korea.[6]

Yet this was no knee-jerk response to an American demand. Rather, it reflected a complex set of domestic and foreign policy issues. Attlee, a deceptively mild-mannered but terse and decisive Cabinet chairman, was well aware that July morning of the conflicting pressures on his ministers, a number of whom were newly appointed following a general election on 23 February when the Labour majority had been reduced to five. Although Attlee had determined to continue in office, there was a general perception—encouraged by a resurgent Conservative Party, still led by the ageing Winston Churchill but with a promising new intake of MPs—that Labour was in decline. Exhausted by five years of reconstruction and a major legislative programme, the government sought a second term to consolidate its achievements, but instead was faced with the need to increase defence spending at a time when the British people were looking for a long-delayed improvement in their standard of living.

The Korean peninsula, occupied by the Japanese since 1910 and divided at the 38th parallel when Soviet and American troops drove them out at the end of the Second World War, was not a foreign policy priority for the United States in 1950, let alone for the United Kingdom. The government of North Korea, led by Marshal Kim Il-Sung,[7] was seen as little more than a Soviet puppet.[8] South Korea, led by the ageing and autocratic President Syngman Rhee, received US support as a bulwark against communism. Though relations between North and South were fractious, the North Korean attack had taken the West by surprise, despite reports that something was brewing. The attack was assumed to be Soviet inspired.[9] Neither the British nor the American government thought that the Soviet Union wanted a general war (yet). But the Korean conflict seemed to be symbolic of the power struggle that had developed since the Soviet Union had metamorphosed from a wartime ally into a post-war threat to the West. The swiftness of the US response, securing within three days a UN Security Council Resolution to support South Korea and moving forces to the area, seems equally to have surprised the Soviet leader, Josef Stalin. The Soviet Union had walked out of the United Nations in January 1950 in protest at the exclusion of Communist China, and so could not use its veto. The British government was quick to support the resolution, and agreed to place British naval forces in Japanese waters at the disposal of the US Commander.[10] The stage was set for an East–West power struggle by proxy in which neither side was quite sure what the other intended, producing global instability and uncertainty that led directly to the Cabinet's decision on 25 July.

No one at the meeting on 25 July argued against the decision to send troops to Korea. A number of ministers resented diverting money to defence that should be used to continue and consolidate the government's welfare and nationalization programmes. This feeling was certainly prevalent in the wider Labour Party, where the Korean War was a deeply contentious issue. Some thought that the United Nations was being misused by the US to intervene in a civil war.[11] After five years in office, however, government ministers had developed an understanding of the constraints of national security and geopolitical realities. They knew that an exhausted and bankrupt Britain needed support both to ensure domestic recovery and to fulfil worldwide obligations; that peace had brought an end to hostilities but not to danger. An increasingly threatening Soviet Union, made powerful by victory in the Second World War and vengeful by the scale of its suffering, now dominated Eastern Europe. It must be balanced by a strong Western bloc; and the only power with the necessary economic and military muscle to create that strength was the United States of America.

This was certainly the view of Attlee and his Foreign Secretary, the formidable but now ailing Ernest Bevin (represented in Cabinet by Minister of State Kenneth Younger while issuing instruction from his hospital bed). Together, Attlee and Bevin dominated defence and foreign policy. Their service in Churchill's wartime Cabinet and a series of testing postwar crises had turned them into accomplished cold warriors. Both were convinced of the importance of Anglo-American solidarity in a world threatened by a newly atomic Soviet Union and a newly communist China.[12] Though the Cold War front line lay in Europe, it had a global dimension, and East Asia was one of the fault seams. A Soviet-backed attack on South Korea provoked worrying memories of Hitler before 1939—memories still very fresh in 1950, when another world war did not seem unlikely. Bitter experience of early Cold War incidents in Iran, Czechoslovakia, and Berlin suggested Korea might be the thin end of the wedge.[13] The Chiefs of Staff drew a parallel—as did US President Harry S. Truman—between Hitler's challenges to the League of Nations in the 1930s and Stalin's to the UN since 1945.[14] For Bevin, the telling analogy was the Berlin airlift crisis of 1948–9 when Anglo-American solidarity had forced the Soviets to back down.[15] What if this were not a local crisis, but a curtain-raiser to further Soviet aggression, perhaps in the Middle East or Berlin? At worst, the Korean conflict might, as the President of the UN Security Council warned, mark the prelude to 'a third world war, with all its horrors'—a war in which both sides now possessed atomic weapons.[16]

In Britain, the last week in July 1950 was unseasonably wet and windy: on the 23rd, torrential rain and gale force winds had brought lifeboats into action round the south and east coasts and forced the cancellation of a naval exercise, codenamed 'Seaweed', in Portsmouth Harbour. On the 25th, however, bad weather did not prevent the West Indies from beating England by ten wickets in the third Test Match at Trent Bridge, with the legendary Ramadhin and Valentine bowling a record 1,040 balls and taking eight wickets between them. (The Prime Minister, very keen on cricket, would check on the score, rather gloomily, throughout the day.) At 11.30 that morning, seventeen ministers, together with Cabinet Secretary Sir Norman Brook, sat round the Cabinet table in Downing Street to tackle a potentially divisive agenda. Before Korea, they were to discuss an increase in defence expenditure, another issue that aroused strong feelings in the Labour Party as a whole as well as in the Cabinet. After Korea came another potentially tricky agenda item, 'Interference with Military Supplies', a discussion on how to respond to a series of communist-inspired strikes and sabotage incidents designed to prevent the dispatch of supplies to British forces overseas.

The weather was bad on 25 July 1950 in Korea as well as in London, at least if you were an American pilot trying to fly a B29 bomber through thick cloud over mountainous territory to identify targets. A month into the war, victory over North Korean forces who were familiar with the terrain and were led by well-trained officers was proving much more difficult than President Truman or his Supreme Commander General Douglas MacArthur had anticipated. At least 75 per cent of US troops in Korea had no previous battle experience, and though they fought well they were heavily outnumbered and their anti-tank weapons made little impression on the heavy Russian tanks used by the North Koreans.[17] Indeed, as the Cabinet met in Whitehall, MacArthur was reporting to the Security Council that North Korea had 'resources far in excess of their internal capabilities', by which he meant they had help from the Russians and possibly the Chinese. A few days earlier General Omar Bradley, chairman of the US Chiefs of Staff, had made clear during Anglo-American staff talks that land reinforcements were needed in Korea to support US forces.[18]

The Americans certainly welcomed military assistance, but they wanted moral support even more. Technically, the campaign to support the South Koreans was a United Nations operation, and the Americans were anxious that it should look like a coalition effort rather than a US crusade. As Franks told the Foreign Office on 23 July, 'the United Nations character of American action is essential to their relations with the new nations of Asia and as a refutation of imperialism'. He also warned that a British refusal to send troops was likely to produce a 'deep and prolonged reaction'. 'I believe', the Ambassador wrote, 'that because of the rational and irrational elements in the American mind about this for them unparalleled undertaking to act as a policeman in the world, a negative decision would seriously impair the long term relationship.' (Harold Macmillan, then a prominent Conservative MP, put it rather less diplomatically in his diary. The Americans, he said, were 'for the first time experiencing the burdens of world responsibility. Being unaccustomed to reverses, they are irritable and impatient. They are also beginning to regret all they did to help break up the British Empire in Asia.')[19]

The argument that a British military contribution in Korea was needed to help reassure Asian governments that the US was not pursuing an imperialist agenda might have stuck in the throat of a Labour government that since the Second World War had been harangued regularly by Washington on the subject of its imperial ties, and put under considerable pressure to dismantle the sterling area and imperial preference. But Franks's somewhat veiled warning was quite clear to British ministers. Britain depended on the United States for financial and military support and for the development of its atomic capability, underpinned by an intimate security and intelligence relationship. It also depended, as did the rest of Western Europe, on US leadership in the Cold War power struggle with the other emergent superpower, the Soviet Union. Underlying all this was the British government's desire and determination to continue to be treated as a great power, even as the post-war US–Soviet power struggle threatened to freeze them out; as well as the struggle to maintain their trade and commercial presence worldwide in the face of competition with powerful American corporations. This was the situation that faced Attlee and his colleagues on 25 July 1950.

Sixty years on, the Labour government of 1945–51 is still considered to have been one of the most successful of the post-war period, containing an array of ministerial talent that has rarely if ever been surpassed. It included the so-called 'Big 6': Attlee, Bevin, Stafford Cripps, Aneurin (Nye) Bevan, Hugh Dalton, and Herbert Morrison. Coming to power in a landslide in July 1945 when the British electorate rejected Winston Churchill, the man who had 'won the war', it was the first Labour government ever to win a general election outright and to serve a full term. The Cabinet was almost evenly divided between working-class men of scant education who had risen through trade union or local government politics, and middle- or upper-class activists for whom socialism was a matter of intellectual choice and moral commitment. Their common objective had been to build a better and fairer society in a Britain exhausted and bankrupted by six years of war.

In the past five years, the Attlee government had presided over the creation of the modern state, not just in terms of health, welfare, and education, but also in agriculture, criminal justice, transport, and nationalized industries.[20] Most people today think of its achievements in terms of domestic policy. Yet in fact those years after the Second World War were equally important in respect of the government's contributions to decision-making and institution-building on the international front.

It was intimately involved in the creation of the Western security and intelligence structures, like NATO, that still underpin Britain's foreign relations today; in the development of the US-funded European Recovery Programme (the Marshall Plan); in meeting the challenges of the early Cold War, including facing down the Soviet Union in the Berlin airlift crisis of 1948–9; and participating in new multilateral organizations like the United Nations, the World Bank, and the International Monetary Fund. In all of these developments Britain worked closely with the United States, which had emerged from the Second World War as a military and economic superpower. Though the British and American governments did not always agree, each regarded the other as its closest partner. The Anglo-American relationship was—as it remains—symbiotic: 'intimate, but not exclusive'; not always harmonious; not balanced in terms of money or might; but fundamental.[21] It was almost unthinkable for Britain not to support the United States in a conflict affecting both their interests and, potentially, the interests of world peace.

This view was held by both Attlee and Bevin, though each man reached it by a slightly different route. Although the Foreign Secretary was not present at the meeting on 25 July, his opinion was crucial and provides important context to the decision on Korea. **Ernest Bevin**, a former trade union leader of little formal education but formidable intellect, and a big man in every way, considered himself unique ('I'm a turn up in a million', he said).[22] As Foreign Secretary since 1945 he had not only dominated British policy but had been the major player in the development of Western security policy and institutions. The workload and pressure were prodigious, and Bevin was not one to spare himself. When Roderick Barclay became Bevin's Private Secretary in March 1949, he was told by the Foreign Office, by Buckingham Palace, and by the Chief of the Imperial General Staff that his first duty was to keep the Foreign Secretary from working himself to death.[23]

By 1950, however, Bevin—now aged 69—was debilitated by heart and circulatory problems and between March and July spent more than half the time in hospital or convalescing. Kenneth Younger, appointed Minister of State at the Foreign Office in February 1950, felt thrown in at the deep end. He found himself in charge of the Foreign Office in Bevin's absence and with access to the Prime Minister. It was, he noted in his diary, 'a considerable opportunity, though rather a strain while it lasts'. Younger admired Bevin greatly, but thought it a scandal that he remained in post when he was 'not in a fit state to do a good job'.

He admitted, however, that the Foreign Secretary retained 'a firm grip on realities in most respects and an ability to make up his mind'. As far as Attlee, and indeed most Foreign Office officials, were concerned, even a seriously ill Bevin had more knowledge and better judgement than anyone who could have taken his place.[24]

Bevin had identified Korea as a likely trouble spot late in 1949, and had warned Commonwealth ministers at their meeting in Colombo in January that Western successes in Europe were being offset by an adverse power shift in South East Asia.[25] He argued that the Americans were wrong to think of 'Europe' as a separate entity, and suspected they had no coherent policy in Asia. Washington, in his view, needed to do more joined-up thinking and realize that the Cold War in East and West was the same fight. When the Korean conflict broke out in June Bevin had no doubt that the British must support the Americans fully. From his hospital bed, he argued against his colleagues when they wanted to restrict British support for a second UN Resolution widening the scope for US military action. They had been alarmed by Truman's announcement on 27 June that the US 7th Fleet would be deployed to prevent any attack on Formosa (Taiwan), and that military aid to the Philippines and Indo-China would be increased.[26] Nothing must be done, Bevin warned, that might discourage the Americans from supporting Britain in Malaya or the French in Indo-China.

For Bevin, ensuring a continued US commitment, not just to Europe but to what he called the Free World, was worth far more than a brigade in Korea. He was also quite sure of Britain's importance to the Americans and to the West as a whole. Britain, albeit weakened and impoverished by the war, remained a global power in a key position, central to what he regarded as the prime objective of creating an Atlantic community that transcended Europe. Though he was one of the principal architects of the European security apparatus, Bevin had little faith in the ability of Western Europe to stand up to the Soviet Union, telling Younger it would 'not even attract the loyalty of Europeans or impress the Russians unless it is very solidly linked to North America'.[27] Anglo-American cooperation was to him of paramount importance, and if that meant compromising some British positions and ignoring policy differences with the US administration, he was prepared to do it.

Bevin certainly did not agree with US foreign policy in all respects. He argued vigorously with his US counterpart, Dean Acheson, on a range of issues, including policy on American-occupied Japan, the future development of NATO, and the possible rearmament of West Germany. In May 1950 he had been enraged by what he regarded as Acheson's collusion with the proposal for a supranational European coal and steel organization, put forward in May 1950 by French Foreign Minister Robert Schuman and rejected roundly by the British government.[28] Most of all, the two governments disagreed fundamentally on policy towards the communist regime in China led by Mao Tse-tung (Mao Zedong). For many Americans, the North Korean attack in June 1950 represented another advance for the evil doctrine of communism, after the shocking victory by Mao's forces in 1949. Like General MacArthur, they did not care if Chiang Kai-shek was corrupt and incompetent: 'If he has horns and a tail, so long as he is anti-Communist we should help him.'[29] The British government, however, regarded the Chinese Nationalists as a lost cause and worried that US support for them endangered British interests in mainland China and Hong Kong.

Hoping to salvage its commercial interests as well as to draw China away from the Soviet orbit, the Attlee government had recognized the People's Republic in January 1950. The Americans, less ready to accept Mao's victory as permanent, refused to agree that the People's Republic, rather than the Nationalists, should represent China at the United Nations, leading to the Soviet walk-out in January 1950. Though this meant that subsequent Security Council resolutions were not subject to the Soviet veto, it also produced considerable unease among developing nations. The Foreign Office warned of the danger that the UN could be seen as 'merely an anti-communist alliance' that would 'throw all Asia on to the side of the communists'.[30] Bevin had intended to support Communist Chinese representation on UN bodies until the Korean War led him to put the issue on ice. He did not wish to undermine the US war effort, and knew how strongly the Americans felt about it.

For the US administration, China was a domestic as well as a foreign policy issue. President Harry Truman was already under attack from Republicans still sore about their unexpected defeat in the 1948 presidential election, and in particular from Senator Joseph McCarthy (raving about 'Communists and queers' who had 'sold China into atheistic slavery').[31] Korea might not be a US priority, but Congressional and public pressure made it so. Bevin and Attlee understood this, up to a point. The British government also saw communism as a threat to both domestic and national security. Although ideological fervour on American lines was not a feature of British life, there was considerable distrust and dislike of communism among the general public. John Lewis employees, for example, faced dismissal if they would not sign an anti-communist declaration.[32] George Orwell's futuristic novel *1984*, published in 1949, provided a powerful warning of the dangers of totalitarian rule. But to Bevin and his colleagues, basing foreign policy on opposition to communism as a matter of principle was not only fruitless but potentially harmful to British interests. In their view, the best way to ensure that China was steered away from the Soviet orbit and dissuaded from aggression towards the West was to engage with it.

It may seem perverse to explain at length the views of a sick man who was not present when the Cabinet took its decision on Korea. But Attlee trusted his Foreign Secretary to direct British foreign policy ('If you've got a good dog, you don't bark yourself').[33] When Bevin was out of action the Prime Minister spoke to him at least once a day and usually visited him as well. From a foreign policy perspective, Bevin's views informed Attlee's approach to the meeting on 25 July. The two men usually presented a united front, although the Prime Minister's own take on the fundamentals of British policy was rather different. Attlee believed strongly in placing foreign policy in a global context, and had a particular interest in Commonwealth and former colonial territories. His approach was far more detached than that of Bevin, and deliberately so. Nye Bevan's complaint that the Prime Minister treated world affairs 'like a piece of fretwork, when it is really a passion play' would probably have struck him as a compliment. It was, indeed, his job as Prime Minister to work out the intricate patterns of British interests against the only too solid background of Cold War tension on a global scale. It was also his job to consider the domestic implications of foreign policy decisions, in terms of the economy, industrial relations, and parliamentary and public opinion.

Clement Attlee was in many ways the most extraordinary figure in an extraordinary government. Small, neat, unassuming, a man of few words either spoken or written, he seemed an unlikely figurehead for an administration that set out to do no less than transform British society. His rise to the Labour premiership was an enduring source of surprise (and sometimes disappointment) to some of his outwardly more charismatic and talented contemporaries. Coming from a comfortable middle-class background, Attlee became a committed socialist as a young graduate working with boys' clubs in the East End of London. He had joined the national government in May 1940, and was the only minister, except Churchill, to serve in the War Cabinet from its first to last day, including as Deputy Prime Minister from 1942. He had already been living in Downing Street for five years when he became Prime Minister at the age of 62, and remained there until he left office in 1951. He made time for family life with wife and children (Mrs Attlee, known as 'Vi', had no interest in politics but supported her husband by driving him round London at hair-raising speed).

Attlee placed a high premium on sound judgement, and was the embodiment of his own recipe for it: 'an equable temperament, a strong constitution and freedom from excessive appetite of any kind'. He took regular exercise, had considerable stamina (a prerequisite for all Prime Ministers), and devoured official papers 'like a boa constrictor', as one observer put it. But his modest manner concealed an ambitious and sometimes ruthless core.[34] Attlee saw himself as a coordinator, organizing government business and his occasionally temperamental colleagues with military precision. He held strong views on the management of Cabinet meetings, considering it his job to 'collect the voices', but also to stop people (including himself) talking too much. Cabinet, in his opinion, was no place for eloquence ('some men will be ready to express a view about everything. They should be discouraged'). It was judgement that was required, he said, in order to 'make important decisions on imperfect knowledge in a limited time'.[35]

The Prime Minister's keen appreciation of Britain's global responsibilities and of how a threat in one area might impact on another was important to the decision to send troops to Korea. Attlee saw that the Korean conflict might look quite different from the perspective of Britain's closest Commonwealth partner, Australia, whose troops were involved in the occupation of Japan and which was vulnerable to regional instability. His old friend Robert Menzies, the Australian Prime Minister, had attended a Cabinet meeting on 17 July during a visit to Britain. Discussing the need for extra troops in Korea, Menzies pointed out that Australian forces currently serving in Japan were needed at home to form the nucleus for Australian national forces. He also reminded ministers that it had been agreed at the strategic level, first that Malaya was the No. 1 priority, and second that in any major war it was in the Middle East that Australia could best contribute to Commonwealth defence. It would, said Menzies, be 'playing into Russia's hands if we allowed our immediate preoccupations in the Far East to deflect us from our long-term strategy'.[36]

The Korean War also looked different from India, whose government took a keen interest in any Asian area of conflict. Attlee had long had a strong personal involvement with Indian affairs, and as Prime Minister had been a driving force in the process that led to India's independence and partition in 1947.[37] He remained keenly interested in developments on the sub-continent, and in 1950 was particularly worried about tension between India and Pakistan. Indeed, talks between the two countries about the demilitarization of Kashmir broke down on the day of the Cabinet meeting, 25 July. Like other newly independent and developing nations, India was wary of any Western interference in Asian affairs that might cause dangerous instability while provoking unwelcome reminders of imperialism. From June 1950 India also held the chair of the UN Security Council.

The Indian Prime Minister, Pandit Nehru, had approached Stalin on 12 July seeking cooperation in finding a way to settle the Korean issue through a deal on Chinese representation at the UN. The Americans were inclined to be impatient with such efforts, but Attlee encouraged them, warning that the US must not 'get into a position where whites could be represented as contending against coloured races'. Initially supportive of the US intervention on behalf of South Korea, India and other Asian countries were alarmed by Truman's declaration on 27 June of the intention to defend Formosa. As Kenneth Younger put it, if the Korean conflict were to spread to Formosa, 'that would at once bring in China, and would antagonise nations like India & Pakistan who would never support an American war against an Asian power'.[38]

These are just two examples to illustrate Attlee's awareness of the global context of Korea. Others could be given. Nevertheless, Attlee shared American alarm at the spread of communism, and believed that Britain, however impoverished, still had an important role to play, individually and in partnership with the United States, in defending freedom and resisting aggression. He was committed to opposing the spread of Soviet influence and oppressive government whether in East or West. But he also believed the atomic bomb had produced 'not a quantitative but a qualitative change in the nature of warfare' and in the post-war international landscape, reducing the importance of national boundaries and increasing that of global organizations.[39] For Attlee, a strong supporter of the United Nations, the UN action in Korea represented the first significant test of the collective security apparatus set up at the end of the

Second World War. He considered this a cause for which it was worth fighting.

Attlee followed his predecessor as Prime Minister, Winston Churchill, in taking a personal interest and exercising his authority in certain sensitive policy areas, particularly atomic energy and defence. Both were relevant to the decision taken on 25 July. At the end of the Second World War Attlee was one of the very small circle admitted to the secret of the development of the atomic bomb by British and American scientists, and was Prime Minister when the dropping of the bombs on Hiroshima and Nagasaki on 6 and 9 August 1945 brought the war in the Far East to an end. In government, he continued to take a close interest in policy on 'Tube Alloys', the codename for nuclear matters. While he believed in working towards the international control of raw materials and atomic research, he also believed that it was essential for Britain to have its own nuclear capability for deterrent purposes. This belief was confirmed by the successful Soviet atomic test in August 1949. As Air Marshal Sir William Elliot (who also attended the Cabinet meeting on 25 July) wrote on 10 February 1950: 'How does it come about that, knowing all that we did in 1945, we are still without an atom bomb, by contrast with the Russians who, starting from scratch, have apparently already passed us?'[40]

But British nuclear development depended on US technical cooperation as well as money, and Attlee had spent a good deal of time as Prime Minister trying to overcome American resistance to sharing their atomic know-how and to persuade them of the importance of working with Britain and Canada in order to ensure the West kept ahead of the Russians.[41] Tripartite talks began in September 1949, but were suspended by the Americans following the unmasking and arrest in February 1950 of Klaus Fuchs, a Soviet spy working at the UK Atomic Energy Authority. It provoked a major investigation into the British security and intelligence establishment and, in the words of the official historian of MI5, led to a 'crisis in the Special Relationship'. It was also a serious blow to the British nuclear programme.[42] Attlee was anxious to find a way of persuading the Americans to resume negotiations. At an informal meeting in May 1950 with Dean Acheson and Canadian Foreign Minister Lester Pearson, Attlee had stressed his government's anxiety to speed up atomic cooperation. Acheson's response was not encouraging. A refusal to send troops to Korea could only make things worse.

The other policy area that the Prime Minister dominated was that of defence. In addition to his overall responsibility for the defence of the realm, he was interested in military manpower and organization and in budgetary matters too. Attlee was in general very sympathetic to the military. His own record was a distinguished one, having served throughout the First World War and risen to the rank of major. George Mallaby, who was part of the Cabinet Secretariat at this period, observed that Attlee disliked it when his Labour colleagues referred to the armed services with contempt, and was apt to 'burst out' in their defence.[43] The Prime Minister knew that in 1950 British forces were overstretched and undermanned, and understood how hard it was for the Chiefs of Staff to admit that when it came to readiness for war 'the peace-time forces maintained by the United Kingdom were hardly more than bluff'.[44] But he also understood why spending money on defence and armaments instead of improving living conditions at home was unpopular with some of his ministerial colleagues, as well as the wider Labour Party and the public. At the Cabinet meeting on 25 July, the discussion of defence expenditure that preceded the item on Korea was an essential component of the decision to agree to the US request for land reinforcements.

Opening the meeting, Attlee explained that in the light of the Korean situation, the Defence Committee proposed that the Cabinet authorize an additional £100m for 1950–1 to meet immediate deficiencies and prepare for emergencies. £30m of this was to be spent in the current year. Even without Korea, there would need to be large increases in the defence estimates for 1951–2, to meet commitments to NATO and elsewhere. Though the Europeans were 'showing signs of getting a move on', and the Americans might be willing to help, that would not be enough. He proposed to announce the increase during the debate in the House of Commons scheduled for the following day, 26 July, with some reference made to the need to remedy the manpower deficiencies in the services. There was a severe shortage of air crew and tradesmen, and recruitment overall needed to be stepped up. It might even be necessary to consider extending the period of National Service, although this would be difficult politically as well as administratively.[45]

At this point the Defence Minister, **Emanuel 'Manny' Shinwell**, intervened. The two words most often used to describe Shinwell, a self-educated Glaswegian of Polish-Jewish extraction, are 'vigorous' and 'pugnacious', not least because he struck a Conservative MP during a House of Commons debate in 1938. They also indicate that his relations with ministerial colleagues (particularly those who had been to public schools) were not always smooth.[46] He had made an important contribution to the 1945 election victory and to the first Attlee administration, steering through the nationalization of the coal industry and negotiating the miners' charter with the unions. But in 1947 he lost his job as Minister for Fuel and Power after mishandling the coal shortage, and served in a non-Cabinet post as Secretary of State for War before returning to the Cabinet at the age of 65 after the February 1950 election.

On 25 July 1950 Shinwell reminded his colleagues that the extra £30m proposed for defence only bridged the gap between the original estimate of £810m and the £780m to which the Cabinet had cut it on a previous occasion.[47] It was, therefore, hardly an increase, and there must be a 'big figure next year'. Even if precise figures could not be given, Shinwell favoured a bullish approach in the forthcoming defence debate. He thought the government had a good case in arguing for increased expenditure. Parliament, and indeed the general public, were aware that British forces were overstretched and faced obligations and threats all round the world. Unlike Attlee, he thought there was no point in expecting any help from European allies, though the United States might help with aircraft.

Shinwell disapproved of US policy in the Far East, not least because it distracted American attention from the vital European theatre, but understood the reasons for agreeing to the request to send British troops to Korea. Not only would the US public fail to understand a refusal, as Franks had explained, but the Americans might also be less inclined to help the French, struggling to maintain authority in Indo-China, which would have consequences for Britain in Malaya. And Shinwell was more aware than some of the potential Soviet threat. As Defence Minister, he had access to secret intelligence about the strength of Soviet armed forces, and told his colleagues on the morning of 25 July that the Russians had forty fully equipped divisions that could mount an immediate attack; he favoured passing this information on to the House of Commons. Hard facts, he thought, should not be withheld and could strengthen the government's case.

Attlee tended to agree, commenting that if Shinwell did not make the information public, Churchill would. (Attlee was doubtless remembering the 1930s, when Churchill had frequently embarrassed the government by publicizing German rearmament.) But **Viscount Alexander**, now Chancellor of the Duchy of Lancaster, disagreed: 'If you disclose in detail, our intelligence sources will dry up.'[48] Alexander was another remarkable Labour figure, who had started work at 13 and progressed through the Cooperative Movement to serve three times as First Lord of the Admiralty between 1929 and 1946 and then as Defence Minister. Like Attlee, Alexander could draw on instructive memories. He had been an MP in the 1920s, when on two occasions in 1923 and 1927 evidence of Soviet espionage and anti-British propaganda produced by the government in the House of Commons resulted in the loss of vital intelligence sources.[49] The published Soviet budget figures, Alexander told Shinwell on 25 July, gave sufficient information to indicate the threat.

Shinwell, like his predecessor Viscount Alexander, found it difficult to exert his authority when the Prime Minister took such a close interest in defence matters and the Chiefs of Staff reported personally to him.[50] He also held conflicting opinions on defence and on Korea, not a comfortable position for a Defence Minister. He thought that Britain was spending too little at a time when it needed to improve war readiness, but also that money should not be diverted from the government's domestic programme. He believed that extending National Service was 'neither right nor politically acceptable' because it took manpower away from 'rebuilding Britain'; on the other hand, he knew how important it was that national servicemen should be induced by better pay and conditions to stay on. If troops were to be sent to Korea these men would be needed, as they would if the Korean War led to wider hostilities, or the Chinese communists attacked Hong Kong. He was wary of American dominance—he had been the only minister to vote against acceptance of the US loan in December 1945—but understood the need for US support, as well as the American desire for Britain to show support in turn. It was he who on 25 July summed up the Cabinet's position on sending troops to Korea: 'Militarily not v[ery] desirable. Psychologically inevitable.'

Attlee had already made his mind up before the meeting that the Defence Committee's recommendations for extra defence spending, agreed by the Treasury, must be accepted. But he understood the reservations expressed on the morning of 25 July by the Minister of Health, **Aneurin Bevan**, who had grown impatient during the talk of raising estimates, remedying manpower deficiencies and increasing service pay. A miner's son who had worked in a colliery himself from the age of 13, Bevan had been elected MP for Ebbw Vale in 1929 and was married to another Labour MP, Jennie Lee. He was a major figure on the left wing of the Labour Party, and the creation of the National Health Service in Britain was his crowning achievement. But his political position had been undermined by a remark made in 1948 that Tories were like 'vermin', which damaged both the government's electoral prospects and his own reputation. Though still a powerful figure, and younger at 52 than some of his ministerial colleagues, he was not, as Younger put it, 'a member of the inner circle who really decide things'.[51]

On 25 July Bevan pointed out that the extra expenditure proposed on defence would absorb all increases in industrial productivity over the next few years—increases on which the government relied to sustain Britain's dollar balances. The Chancellor, Sir Stafford Cripps, had already told the Defence Committee that any increase in defence spending would involve spending cuts, additional taxation, a reduction in capital investment, 'or a combination of all three'.[52] That was all very well, said Bevan, but it would be civil departments who paid the price. The government would have to choose between a lower standard of living and ensuring that any additional munitions production conformed to their existing economic plans. Otherwise, Britain must accept continued dependence on the United States. In common with some of his ministerial colleagues—including Cripps—Bevan found this dependence uncomfortable, even humiliating, though he had to agree that the economic realities meant there was no alternative.

Bevan worried that the government's assessment of the Korean conflict was based too much on US sources, and since the outbreak of hostilities had asked some probing questions. In Cabinet on 17 July he wanted to know whether there was any evidence that the civilian population in the South had welcomed their Northern comrades when they crossed the 38th parallel, or that China was sending an International Brigade to Korea. The Chief of the Imperial General Staff replied in the negative to both questions. Bevan also asked what the evidence was that the Soviet Union had a military mission helping North Korean troops. The evidence came, replied the CIGS, from captured prisoners of war, although there was nothing at present to indicate Russians were actually fighting with North Korea. Bevan was also concerned—as indeed were Bevin and Attlee—about what would happen if fighting should break out over Formosa. Britain could not follow the US in any conflict with Communist Chinese forces. The Cabinet agreed on 20 July that the British government's position must be made clear.[53]

Nevertheless, the Minister of Health had no hesitation five days later in supporting the decision to send British ground troops to Korea. In fact, he thought it would be worth sending a larger force. The aggressor, he said would 'always have advantage if we spread our forces over all soft spots, in small packets'. No one else supported this idea, however. **Hugh Dalton**, the former Chancellor of the Exchequer now serving as Minister of Town and Country Planning, said that while he agreed with sending troops to Korea it must be a token force only. Dalton, who had refused the post of Colonial Secretary in February 1950, favoured a limited British engagement and thought it important to remind the Americans that the British were already making a contribution by sea and air. Attlee, well aware that any British land contribution would be a small one, observed that the Americans were in a position militarily to hit the enemy 'very hard'.[54]

Bevan's real objection on 25 July 1950 was to an increase in defence spending at the expense of domestic requirements, not to the decision to send British troops to Korea. In agreeing to the higher figures he asked for an assurance that extra defence production would create more jobs, for example for unemployed shipyard workers. Attlee agreed to work some reference to these questions into the defence debate the next day. The Cabinet also agreed to support the Defence Committee's recommendation that £136m should be spent over the next four years on essential civil defence measures. But in line with his general argument that all spending must be considered in the context of an overall economic strategy, Bevan urged that this money should be spent with reference to the effect on economic recovery and improving the country's capital equipment.

This was not out of line with the Prime Minister's own approach to the integration of foreign and domestic policy. During the Second World War Attlee had irritated Churchill by insisting, even at the height of the armed struggle, on the importance of planning for the future housing, education, and employment of those who were currently fighting the war. But making Britain a better place to live in was a very expensive business, and the Labour government had had a rocky road financially, from being forced to accept the American loan in 1945—with many strings attached—to the devaluation of sterling in 1949. For all the government's achievements since 1945, life for most British people still seemed hard in 1950. Rationing was in place on a range of goods including petrol, a continuing reminder of the recent conflict—as were the many war-damaged buildings still to be seen around the country. The historian David Kynaston quotes the author Doris Lessing, recently arrived from Southern Rhodesia, who wrote that 'The war still lingered, not only in the bombed places but in people's minds and behaviour.' It was, as Kynaston terms it, 'Austerity Britain'.[55]

Austerity was, however, a condition that Chancellor of the Exchequer **Sir Stafford Cripps**, another key figure at the meeting on 25 July, considered to be admirable, indeed desirable, both personally and for the people of Britain. The son of a Labour peer and nephew of social reformer Beatrice Webb, Cripps was ascetic and eccentric, an insomniac plagued by ill health. He was also a brilliant barrister, an able and ambitious politician whose belief in the virtues of hard work and self-sacrifice many found surprisingly inspiring. The young Labour politician Hugh Gaitskell, with some admiration, called it Cripps's 'martyr complex', while American diplomat Averell Harriman noted drily that according to Cripps's intimate friends 'he thinks he is the messiah'. Certainly, photographs of the tall, attenuated Cripps reveal a somewhat messianic gleam in the eye behind the thick lenses. Many thought him a crank, but he was also brilliant, charismatic, and capable, a major figure in the Attlee government if an awkward one.[56]

Cripps was regarded by many (including himself) as an intellectual giant in a Cabinet well endowed with brains. He resented Attlee's position and disliked the dominance exercised by the Prime Minister and Foreign Secretary over foreign policy. In 1947 he organized a campaign to get rid of Attlee, who responded with typical deftness by putting Cripps in charge of economic planning, then appointing him to succeed Hugh Dalton as Chancellor when the latter was forced to resign later that year after leaking budget details. Though Cripps did an exceptional job at the Treasury—his grasp of economic planning has led some to call him the 'first modern chancellor'—his spirit as well as his health was broken by the devaluation of sterling in 1949, a decision taken in his absence and in contradiction of his public assurances that it would not happen. Seriously ill, he had wished to retire at the February 1950 election at the age of 60, but was persuaded to stay on in view of the government's tiny majority.[57]

Cripps held decided views on overseas affairs, including a strong sympathy for the Soviet Union, and did not hesitate to express them. Since 1945 he had opposed any further British overseas commitments, arguing against the introduction of National Service in 1946 and the decision that the UK should develop its own atomic bomb. He also believed that the government should have ensured Britain's economic recovery before attempting to build the welfare state. He and his Treasury officials were constantly at odds with Bevin and the Foreign Office, arguing that Britain simply did not have the resources to maintain both the living standards of its population and its position as a world power. These differences had been thrown into sharp relief in May 1950, during preparations for Anglo-American talks in London. Cripps and the Treasury thought that the Americans should be told frankly that Britain's external problems could not be separated from its internal financial policy, and that Britain could not just fall into line with the United States, which was bigger, richer, and took a fundamentally different approach towards economic policy. The Labour government believed in a planned economy, in which trade discrimination and the non-convertibility of sterling were essential instruments. The US government, on the other hand, believed in a free economy and was constantly pressing the British 'to pursue economic policies which they would not and could not accept'. Cripps looked forward, he told a meeting of ministers on 4 May 1950, to 'the day when this country could free herself from the hegemony, political and economic, of the United States'.[58]

Not surprisingly, this approach did not recommend itself to the Prime Minister or Foreign Secretary. Britain could not just stop being a world power. Its overseas obligations might cost money, but they also contributed a lot to the standard of living of the British people, through trade, supplying essential raw materials, and military support. If Britain declined, then the other Western powers would decline as well.[59] In order to prosper, Britain needed US help. As Bevin put it, Cripps seemed to think 'that we can arrange our own affairs as we please, in our own little circle, and that the Americans can adapt themselves to our ideas if they so wish'. Attlee agreed: it was hardly good tactics to stress the differences between US and UK economic policy. It was better to cooperate as far as possible, while 'losing no opportunity of pointing out that the United States Government were quite ready to adopt the methods of the controlled economy when it suited their domestic purposes'.[60] But though there were genuine differences here, they were more of style than of substance. As Attlee knew perfectly well, Cripps was far too good a politician to place his more ideological opinions ahead of British self-interest.

Initially Cripps had argued against any British contribution to the Korean War other than the naval support already pledged. But on 20 July, when the Cabinet had discussed President Truman's message to Congress asking for $10,000m for the armed forces and foreshadowing further requests to NATO powers, the Chancellor observed that the British government, while taking care not to commit itself to any unspecified increase in spending, should take equal care not to give American public opinion a chance to grumble that 'we are leaving it all to them'.[61] If the US wanted British military help, though, Cripps wanted to make sure that they were prepared to give financial help in return. This was a view shared by most of his colleagues, even if on the whole they expressed it less stridently.

During the discussion on 25 July Cripps did little more than warn against the government's committing itself publicly to future spending on defence: the proposals Attlee put forward when the meeting opened had, of course, originated in the Treasury. In respect of Korea, he understood how important it was to tie the US into continued support for the security apparatus (such as NATO) to which Britain was also committed financially as well as politically, and to ensure the continuance of Marshall Aid. Even without other factors, this led Cripps to accept that Franks's arguments in favour of agreeing to send troops to Korea were persuasive, despite the costs involved. At the same time, Cripps displayed impatience with US policy in the Far East, remarking that the 'key to present difficulties is Western attitude to nationalist upsurge in Asia and failure to appreciate that Communism is much less offensive to the Asiatics than colonialism'.[62]

The decision on 25 July to send British ground troops to Korea affected a number of other ministers, apart from the Prime Minister, Foreign Secretary, and Minister of Defence who were naturally most concerned. **James Griffiths**, Colonial Secretary, and **Lord Ogmore** of the Commonwealth Relations Office were both very aware of the potential implications, both political and military, for Britain's handling of the Malayan insurgency, for Hong Kong, and for Commonwealth members like Australia and India for whom turmoil in the Far East was a local as well as global problem. The introduction of substantial American military resources into the area could lead to increased pressure on British forces, and perhaps even make a Chinese attack on Hong Kong more likely. It was important that existing British forces in the area not be diverted to Korea. They were also concerned about the possible effect of the war on Chinese populations in British-controlled territories.

The potential disruption of trade, and a possible increased requirement for scarce British food supplies to be sent to British dependencies in the region, worried **Tom Williams**, Minister of Agriculture and Fisheries, and the young President of the Board of Trade, **Harold Wilson**. Meanwhile, the Lord Chancellor, **Lord Jowitt**, remained unimpressed by the legal arguments invoked by the US to justify the intervention in support of South Korea. Although the Cabinet had decided on 4 July that such intervention conformed to the principle, if not the letter, of Article 51 of the UN Charter, Jowitt—like Younger—felt that the Americans should be reminded that it was UN endorsement that legitimized their military operations. Attlee, however, welcomed the fact that the UN Security Council wanted to 'avoid fettering the discretion of the United States Commander', although the difficulty of obtaining up-to-date information on what was actually happening on the ground made it difficult for the UN to exercise much control over what was being done in its name.[63]

After the decision on sending troops to Korea had been taken, the Cabinet moved on to the rest of the agenda, including the question of interference with military supplies. The discussion on this issue gives a further insight into the complexities that faced ministers in connection with the Korean War. **George Isaacs**, Minister of Labour and National Service, was worried about the possible extension of conscription at a time of industrial unrest and serious worries about communist-inspired sabotage and civil defence. The *Daily Worker* was campaigning openly against the dispatch of either equipment or troops to Korea, and there had been a number of worrying incidents recently, including a large explosion on 14 July at Portsmouth Dockyard that was clearly intended to stop a ship sailing to Korea. Similar industrial and criminal action had been reported in France and Australia.

The Home Secretary, **James Chuter Ede**, had been disturbed to discover that the scope for legal action against those inciting or carrying out acts of sabotage was limited. As the Attorney-General, Sir Hartley Shawcross (not present on 25 July but represented by Lord Advocate **John Wheatley**, KC), had pointed out at a previous Cabinet meeting, Britain was not formally at war. Acts that could be regarded as treason in wartime had to be treated differently in peacetime. New legislation might be needed. **Herbert Morrison**, Lord President of the Council, favoured an Order in Council making it an offence to do anything that interfered with supplies to HM forces engaged in operations, or which was calculated to assist those opposing them. However, as the Home Secretary pointed out, it was difficult to prosecute someone for assisting the enemy when there was no proper definition of who that enemy was.[64]

The issue was a political as well as a legal minefield. While Attlee condemned the sabotage strongly in the House of Commons and promised that perpetrators would be 'prosecuted with the utmost vigour of the law', the government had to be wary of taking action that could restrict legitimate trade disputes, alienate the trade union movement as a whole, and cause difficulties with civil liberties campaigners. A number of ministers, including both Cripps and Shinwell, felt that new legislation could be difficult to pass in the House of Commons and might also fail to achieve the desired result. Attlee felt it would be necessary to consult the Trades Union Congress before going ahead. The TUC's reaction, the Cabinet was told on 25 July, was that legislation to forbid certain strikes was 'psychologically unnecessary'. Morrison's verdict was terse: 'Lost psychological moment. TUC is uncertain. Drop this now and keep it for next Session.'[65]

Although, as the above discussion shows, the decision to send troops to Korea had the potential to cause the Attlee government difficulty on a number of fronts—political, economic, and industrial—no one in the Cabinet suggested that any of these difficulties should prevent them from agreeing to the American request. They understood, as Franks had put it, that although the power and position of the US made it paradoxical that they should feel vulnerable without support, that feeling was 'real and a reality in the Korean situation'. It was one more demonstration of the view held by most British politicians, and a constant in government policy since the Second World War, that Anglo-American relations were paramount. The arguments put forward by Oliver Franks, which proved so persuasive, were very similar to those that had been used earlier by Franks's predecessor Lord Halifax in favour of British forces taking part in the invasion of Japan.[66] Only in extreme cases would the wishes of the US government be disregarded on a foreign policy issue: the decision to withdraw British forces from East of Suez, examined in Chapter 4, was one such example.

An announcement that Britain would send land forces to Korea would, the Cabinet minutes for 25 July 1950 recorded, 'have a valuable effect upon public opinion in the United States', and 'give a useful lead to other members of the United Nations'. It did not matter that it would take a considerable time for those forces to be assembled and dispatched.[67] General Omar Bradley, Chairman of the US Chiefs of Staff, had explained during staff talks that no advance in Korea was anticipated for several months. It was the psychological effect of the announcement that mattered. The Cabinet agreed to endorse the Defence Committee's recommendation, made the evening before, that a Brigade Group should be formed, without reducing the strength of the forces available in Hong

Kong and Malaya, and sent out as soon as possible to operate under US command.[68] That night, Younger told the US Ambassador, Lew Douglas, of the decision. He seemed 'gratified'. Attlee had an audience with HM King George VI, and informed him.

Some might argue that the decision to send British ground troops to Korea represented only a very small part of Britain's involvement in a conflict which was to escalate dramatically later in 1950 with the American decision to cross the 38th parallel and the entry into the war of Communist China. There is some truth in this, certainly in military terms. It is also true that the arguments about the costs involved were only part of a much bigger debate about the financial implications of British rearmament. As the official historian of the Korean War put it, the cost of sending a brigade to Korea was 'fractional and brief, an unexpected but essential expense in resisting expansion by the communist powers'.[69] It was already apparent that a major review and modernization of British armed forces was necessary, in the context of Britain's changing world role and its commitments to European defence. The Korea decision hastened developments that were already in train, and forced both the military and the politicians to face difficult issues such as the future of National Service and the general shortage of manpower.[70] It also sharpened government thinking on the relative priorities of the domestic economy and defence.

Similar difficulties were indeed being experienced by other NATO members, too; and indeed to some extent indeed by the two competing superpowers, the United States and Soviet Union. There was a general feeling of uncertainty and threat, combined with a great desire to get back to 'ordinary' life after the disruption of the Second World War. There is also force in the argument that for US foreign policy, the Korean War was not so much a turning point as a milestone on a continuum that included the Soviet atomic test, the communist conquest of China, the rising costs of Western security arrangements, and the need for greater European integration to meet them.[71] Britain's unwillingness to engage too closely in Franco-German moves towards greater integration is also part of this story, and was another irritant in Anglo-American relations in the summer of 1950. Although the decision to send troops to Korea was taken in deference to American wishes, it did little to mitigate the considerable policy differences between the two governments. In June, the Chiefs of Staff had stressed in their Global Strategy paper that after the stabilization of the European front, 'the next most important object should be to secure an agreed Allied military strategy in the Middle East and Asia theatres—and the machinery to implement it'. At the same time, they said, 'the key to the problem in the Far East is China'.[72] On none of these key areas was much harmonization of views evident between London and Washington.

But the decision taken on 25 July is, nevertheless, instructive by illustrating the wide range of problems faced by the Attlee government in 1950 and the difficulties of the foreign policy decision-making process. Contemporary evidence suggests a considerable degree of consensus among ministers, aided by skilful handling from the Prime Minister. To an observer like Kenneth Younger, new to Cabinet but plunged into the policy-making fray by Bevin's illness, there seemed too little principle and too much pragmatism, and a lack of leadership in the face of American pressure. He complained to Bevin on 6 July 1950 that the United Kingdom did not seem to be following a clear path, either towards effective defence (which must involve rearming West Germany), or towards increasing trade and economic prosperity. Younger also noted what he considered to be a fundamental difference of view between the British and the Americans, who seemed to have decided that a war with 'the communists' was inevitable and that 'the main problem is how to win the war when it comes'.[73]

This was not, Younger protested, the view of Attlee and his colleagues, despite the recognition of the need to rearm and increase readiness for war. The British government, 'despite growing pessimism', did not believe war inevitable and was therefore 'unwilling to prepare uninhibitedly for an early war if by so doing we make war more likely or seriously impair our ability to raise our own & other living standards over a longer period of years'. If, Younger said, 'our main effort was to be military and everything else becomes almost stagnant, it is hard to see how our policy can differ from the Tories except perhaps in ensuring somewhat greater equality of sacrifice…It is doubtful whether we can in such circumstances maintain national leadership for more than a limited period.'[74] Younger was right: the Attlee government was replaced by a Conservative administration led by Churchill in October 1951, when the war in Korea was still going on. But in July 1950, ministers had to take a difficult decision at a time when the war had only just broken out, and no one knew what it might lead to. They did this quickly and unanimously, thereby fulfilling one of Attlee's requirements for good government: 'It is essential for the Cabinet to move on, leaving in its wake a trail of clear, crisp, uncompromising decisions. This is what government is about.'[75]

Anthony Eden and Selwyn Lloyd, 1956

2

Challenging Nasser
The Suez Crisis, July 1956

It is either him or us, don't forget that.*

'Suez' has become shorthand for post-imperial decline, ministerial duplicity and incompetence, humiliation, and failure; the lowest point of British government in the twentieth century which must never be repeated. Everyone thinks they know what Suez means, even when the events of more than fifty years ago have been obscured by time, prejudice, and hindsight. Certainly, things went badly wrong in 1956: a British Prime Minister, in an attempt to restore international control of a waterway in a Middle Eastern country and get rid of a man he regarded as a dangerous dictator, was involved in a secret plan to collude with an Israeli attack on Egypt so that Anglo-French forces had a pretext for invasion to 'separate the combatants' and protect the Suez Canal. Less than twenty-four hours after that invasion, international pressure—notably from the Americans—forced a ceasefire and withdrawal.[1] It was a fiasco that ended Anthony Eden's career. So far, the facts seem to fit the perception.

But behind this now infamous sequence of events lies a far more complicated story, rooted in the global nature of British overseas interests, fierce Anglo-American rivalry in the Middle East, and Arab nationalism set in a Cold War context, as well as a host of personal and political considerations. What became known as the Suez crisis had its origins in events and decisions taken long before Eden's 'collusion' with France and Israel in the autumn of 1956. To show this, a good place to start is with the decisions taken on the morning of Friday, 27 July 1956, at a

---

* Anthony Eden to Evelyn Shuckburgh on 12 March 1956, talking about Colonel Nasser.

meeting held at 11.10 a.m. in Prime Minister Anthony Eden's room at
the House of Commons.[2] There the Cabinet agreed that essential British
interests in the Suez Canal area must be safeguarded, by force if necessary, and instructed the Chiefs of Staff to prepare a plan and timetable
for military operations. They had two aims: to reverse the Egyptian government's nationalization of the Suez Canal, announced the previous
day; and to get rid of President Gamal Abdel Nasser—regime change, as
it would now be known.[3] These twin objectives sowed the seeds for
everything that happened thereafter, and are essential to an understanding
of the crisis as a whole.

It may seem surprising that Nasser's announcement, in a speech on
26 July, that he was nationalizing the Suez Canal Company came as
such a shock to the British government. Egyptian resentment of the
long-standing arrangement whereby an Anglo-French company controlled and derived most of the profit from a waterway that was an
integral part of Egypt meant that the canal was bound to become a
target of nationalist agitation.[4] Many Egyptians worked for the company, helping to run and maintain the canal, but senior posts were
held by well-paid and privileged Europeans—mainly British. (There
was a widespread misconception, significant in the Suez crisis, that
Egyptians were incapable of operating the canal by themselves.)
Though an agreement had been reached early in 1956 for the transfer of substantial company reserves in the next few years to the Egyptian government, there had been growing signs, including violent
incidents in the Canal Zone and inflammatory speeches by Egyptian
leaders, that what the latter wanted was to take control of the company, and get rid of the British, altogether. The Canal Base agreement signed in October 1954 had set an end date to British military
occupation of the Canal Zone (in fact the last troops left only six
weeks before the canal was nationalized in 1956) but it clearly did not
go far enough for Nasser.

The Egyptian President, who had first come to prominence after the
Young Officers' coup in 1952, saw himself as the natural leader of the
Arabs at the intersection of the African and Islamic worlds.[5] While the
Western powers saw his dealings with the Soviet bloc as a potential invi-
tation to the extension of Russian influence in the Middle East, Nasser
saw himself, as the Joint Intelligence Committee concluded in April
1956, as maintaining a balance between West and East. Though he upset
the former by buying arms from Czechoslovakia, and generally flirting

with the Soviets (thereby demonstrating that he 'possessed the nerve to defy the West and to sup with the devil'), he continued to rely for advice and expertise in security and intelligence matters on a close relationship with both British and Americans.[6] His ambitious plans to dam the waters of the Nile at Aswan required substantial funding from either East or West, with the prospect of increased influence for whoever supplied it. Anglo-American willingness to supply such finance was based on political as well as economic grounds, as was the US decision to withdraw the offer, announced to the Egyptian Ambassador on 19 July 1956, and seen by many as precipitating Nasser's nationalization of the Suez Canal Company.[7]

The British government also saw the Middle East in terms of inter-secting spheres: a 'land bridge' between Europe, Asia, and Africa that was key to British strategic interests, important to Commonwealth com-munications, the source of oil supplies, and a base that could be used to counter Soviet influence. During the Second World War the Middle East had been a key supply and transit zone, and its importance to British military capability continued into the post-war period.[8] Britain had close links with many countries in the region, including treaty obligations, and considered itself to have a special position and influence there on histori-cal, commercial, and political grounds. One thing Nasser and the British government could agree on was the importance of Egypt, a large and dominant power in the Middle East, even if the long history of British involvement there as an occupying and later a 'protecting' power was seen as an irritant by one and an asset by the other.

Of course, Egypt was also particularly important to Britain because the Suez Canal ran through it (just as Clarissa Eden later felt it ran through her drawing room). Its nationalization seemed to pose an existential threat. Most of Britain's oil supplies from the Persian Gulf travelled through the canal, and trade routes to the southern hemisphere and Far East depended on its passage. So did the ability to deploy British forces to Africa, Asia, or the Far East: while it was possible to transport troops by air, supplies and stores, ammunition, artillery, and armour would still have to travel by sea—through the canal. In addition, until the drawdown agreed in the Anglo-Egyptian treaty of 1954, the Canal Zone was Brit-ain's largest military base.[9] It is not surprising, therefore, that the control of the canal by a potentially hostile or at least unpredictable power was seen as dangerous, particularly when that power had close ties to the pri-mary Cold War adversary, the Soviet Union.

News of Nasser's announcement reached the Prime Minister on the evening of 26 July, as he and senior Cabinet colleagues were entertaining the young King of Iraq and his uncle, together with veteran Iraqi Prime Minister Nuri es-Said. Eden later wrote that his guests saw the nationalization of the canal as 'an event which changed all perspectives',[10] a judgement that was certainly true for him. To Eden it was, simply, unacceptable that Nasser should be permitted to destabilize an already turbulent region and hold Britain and other powers to ransom by threatening free passage through the Suez Canal. Later that night, the Prime Minister spoke to the French Ambassador and the US Chargé d'Affaires, leaving them in no doubt that he and his government took a most serious view of the situation. The following morning, after a brief statement to the House of Commons, the Cabinet met to decide what to do about it. Seventeen ministers gathered in Eden's room, plus the three chiefs of the armed services. There was only one item on the agenda: 'Suez Canal'.

While the nationalization of the canal proved the 'inciting incident' (as screenwriters say) for a crisis that was to dominate British foreign policy for the rest of the year, it is important to remember that the conflict with Nasser and Egypt was only one of many serious problems facing the government in the summer of 1956. In the Middle East alone there were multiple challenges. The government may have seen the region as a useful 'land bridge' for supply and transit, as well as a base from which to exert political influence, but in the post-war period British influence was weaker while the local social and political tensions were greater. Widespread discontent against local rulers led to British troops being called in to quell disorder in Bahrain in March, while both the Yemen and Saudi Arabia were encouraging states in the Aden Protectorate to shake off British links. Countries like Iraq, Jordan, and Libya were torn between long-standing close ties with Britain (and the military assistance they offered), and the lure of nationalism, anti-colonialism, and Arab solidarity. The dismissal in early March 1956 by King Hussein of Jordan of General Sir John Glubb ('Glubb Pasha') as Commander of the Arab Legion was symptomatic of the instability caused by this uneasy balance of competing pressures.[11] At the same time, the fallout from Israel's decisive military victory against the Arab countries in 1948 continued to cause tension and resentment across the region.

Beyond the Middle East, Britain also faced multiple threats to its global interests and influence. In Cyprus (to which Nasser's covert propaganda activities extended), Malaya, and Singapore, difficult negotiations were ongoing about constitutional change against a background of political instability that also affected Ceylon, Hong Kong, Korea, Borneo, and Indonesia. Other problems included managing the transition to self-government in former African colonies, concern about the costs of maintaining British forces in West Germany and meeting other NATO obligations, and tension with the Soviets over the status of Berlin. Meanwhile there was hard bargaining with the Americans about trade, particularly with Communist China, and the need to balance the pursuit of a reduction in nuclear weapons (and public disquiet at nuclear tests) against the perceived need for the UK to build up its own deterrent. Finally, the British government was concerned at the strengthening of the Franco-West German nexus, manifested in the accelerating momentum towards a European Common Market.

The backdrop to all these problems was the ongoing military and nuclear threat posed by the Soviet bloc, a threat that a faltering economy and stretched military and intelligence resources made it difficult for Britain to counter. In June 1956 a major review was set in train to consider 'what adjustments should be made in Government policy in view of changes in the methods, if not the objectives, of the Soviet Union', taking account of economic and financial circumstances and the need to modify defence programmes. Though not completed by the time the Suez crisis broke, the review had already produced papers recommending a reduction in the defence burden in order to free up resources against Soviet economic offensive measures, and a strategic shift away from a reliance on costly conventional forces towards increasing reliance on a nuclear deterrent.[12]

In 1956 the British government faced all these issues with a large balance of payments deficit and uncertain commercial prospects, and against a background of growing industrial unrest. In the early 1950s the end of a post-war industrial boom, and the rising cost of social measures introduced by the Labour government between 1945 and 1951 together with Cold War defence commitments, imposed great financial strain on Britain. Repayments would soon be required on the loans secured in 1945 from the US and Canada.[13] Though still a world power with extensive (and expensive) global obligations, Britain faced increasing competition from Western European countries whose economies had been devastated in the war but were now booming, as well as from the might of US corporate enterprise. In hindsight, it may seem easy to attribute many of its difficulties to Britain's diminished position in a post-war world dominated by the superpowers, a natural result of the end of empire and (as some see it) a reality check. But this was not how it seemed in 1956, when world war was still a recent memory and a possible future conflagration a very present threat. As Harold Macmillan, Eden's Chancellor of the Exchequer, noted gloomily in his diary on 21 July, 'The Government's position is very bad at present. Nothing has gone well.'[14]

This sense of gloom was not confined to ministerial circles, but was also apparent in the wider political arena, and in popular opinion as reflected in the press. There was a general perception that Britain, despite victory in the Second World War, was not only in decline but seen as being so by the rest of the world. Anthony Sampson, writing only ten years after Suez, encapsulated the cultural and political landscape of 1956 in terms that are perhaps a little exaggerated, but give a good idea of the mood nevertheless. There was, he wrote, 'a current wave of nostalgia for the last war, a sense of the boredom and fatuousness of contemporary Britain: it was the year of *Look Back in Anger*, Colin Wilson, and Rock 'n Roll. Nearly everyone seemed touchy, and when the Canal was seized there was an instinctive feeling that something must be done. There was a mood of almost tribal recidivism, like the moods that sweep through a school, which was not easy to resist.'[15] In such a mood, the difference between Conservative government and Labour opposition seemed to play little part, perhaps because the 1950s was a period in which the middle classes were a 'growth area', despite the country's economic problems, while the increased level of welfare spending eroded the conditions that drew the working classes towards Labour.[16] Despite bitter criticism later in the crisis on both sides, in the early stages Suez was not a party political issue.

While the Cabinet meeting on 27 July may, therefore, have had only one item on its agenda, most ministers present had other pressing issues on their minds and were worried about the possible impact of an international crisis on their own departments and political concerns, as well as on the reputation of the Conservative government and on Britain's broader interests and influence. It was a situation in which the potential loss of the Suez Canal seemed a far more serious threat than it might appear in retrospect. The Prime Minister, in the chair, was probably one of the more single-minded participants at the Cabinet meeting. For him, as he later admitted, the nationalization of the Suez Canal trumped nearly all other concerns, and he opened the proceedings determined that decisive action should be agreed. In many ways **Anthony Eden**, at

59 still an elegant, handsome, and striking figure, with unmatched experience in the conduct of British foreign policy, seemed the ideal person to deal with the Suez crisis. In the 1930s, as the youngest Foreign Secretary of the twentieth century, he had pitted his wits against Hitler, Mussolini, and Stalin; during and after the Second World War, though rather overshadowed by Winston Churchill (a Prime Minister who liked to 'do' his own foreign policy), he had continued to enhance his reputation in international circles. By the time Eden became Prime Minister in April 1955 he was widely regarded (including by himself) as a leading statesman.

He was also an Arabic speaker with a deep knowledge of Middle Eastern history and politics, and had a long association with Egypt. Eden had negotiated personally the treaty of 1936 that recognized the Suez Canal both as an integral part of Egypt and as an international waterway, and allowed for British troops to be stationed in the vicinity of the canal. In October 1954, after persistent pressure from the Egyptian government, he concluded the agreement terminating the British occupation of the Canal Zone in the face of opposition from Winston Churchill and those members of the Conservative Party who found it hard to accept the shrinking of British influence and resented any reduction in Britain's military 'reach'. The flavour of the argument can be seen in the remark made to Eden in 1953 by Lord Hankey: 'If we cannot hold the Suez Canal, the jugular vein of world and Empire shipping communications, what can we hold?'[17] Eden, however, believed that the 1954 agreement was both militarily desirable (in terms of handing over responsibility to Egypt and relieving overstretched British resources) and conducive to the regional stability that the British and other Western governments sought. Good relations with Egypt were, he thought, key to Britain's commercial and strategic position in the Middle East and to the prospects for an Arab-Israeli peace settlement, quite apart from the Suez Canal. To that end he had invested considerable political and personal capital in that relationship and in Nasser in particular.

By 1956, however, this investment looked increasingly insecure, and Eden's judgement was being called into question. Project Alpha, an Anglo-American plan to use Egypt to broker an Arab-Israeli settlement, had collapsed in January 1956, and the Baghdad Pact, which the British government had worked hard to promote, seemed to offer tenuous security, particularly since the US refused to join.[18] Prospects for an Arab-Israeli peace settlement remained remote, while the threat of Soviet influence increased.[19] As Evelyn Shuckburgh, Assistant Under-Secretary in the Foreign Office, wrote to his Permanent Under-Secretary Sir Ivone Kirkpatrick on 10 March, Britain was left 'without a Middle East policy of any kind', faced with equally unpalatable options of fighting Israel if it attacked Arab allies, or supporting Israel against an Arab world backed by the Soviets.[20] Meanwhile, domestic criticism of the government's Middle Eastern policy became increasingly vocal, particularly from the 'Suez Group' within the Conservative Party, who pointed to Nasser's aggressive and, as they saw it, insolent attitude towards the Western powers and demanded robust action to defend British interests.[21] Eden, always sensitive to criticism, took both political and policy setbacks personally. Nasser's intransigence challenged his personal authority as well as that of his government.

Nor did the Prime Minister meet this challenge in a robust physical or psychological state. Churchill had kept him waiting a long time before handing over power: partly because he did not want to give it up himself but also, according to contemporary witnesses, because he did not feel Eden had the strength or stamina to be a successful Prime Minister.[22] The delay put a lot of nervous strain on Eden, exacerbated by poor health following botched surgery in 1953 that had left him weak, in pain, and sometimes dependent on drugs.[23] By the time Churchill finally gave up the premiership in April 1955, Eden was both physically debilitated and vulnerable to stress. All Prime Ministers require great stamina, and even in the 1950s were subject to intense media and public scrutiny as well as parliamentary and party criticism. Eden increasingly resented being challenged and was uncomfortable with a hostile media.[24] He had little appetite for party politics or parliamentary networking, and little interest or experience in domestic affairs. In 1954 Evelyn Shuckburgh, then Eden's Private Secretary, had described him as being 'like a sea anemone, covered with sensitive tentacles recording currents of opinion around him'; two years later, he noted sadly that Eden's response to the dismissal of General Sir John Glubb by the King of Jordan was 'petulant, irrelevant, provocative at the same time as being weak'. Minister of State Anthony Nutting agreed: 'Eden completely lost his touch. Gone was his old uncanny sense of timing, his deft feel for negotiation...he began to behave like an enraged elephant charging senselessly at invisible and imaginary enemies in the international jungle.'[25]

Eden was certainly in no mood on 27 July to take Nasser's defiant nationalization of the Suez Canal philosophically. He made clear to the Cabinet from the outset his view that if the Western powers failed to regain control over the canal the economic and political consequences would be disastrous. As the Cabinet minutes record, the canal was 'a vital link between the East and the West and its importance as an international waterway, recognised in the Convention signed in 1888, had increased with the development of the oil industry and the dependence of the world on oil supplies. It was not a piece of Egyptian property but an international asset of the highest importance.'[26] Nasser must be made to restore international control: Eden was sure the French would agree. As for the Americans, Eden asserted confidently that as 'on previous occasions' the US would 'follow our lead if we took it'. (If this was a reference to the operation to unseat Prime Minister Mossadegh of Iran in 1953 it was a misleading analogy.[27]) The fundamental question before the Cabinet, he announced to his colleagues, was 'whether they were prepared in the last resort to pursue their objective by the threat or even the use of force, and whether they were ready, in default of assistance from the United States and France, to take military action alone'. As the Chiefs of Staff entered the room, Eden began immediately to question Lord Mountbatten about the whereabouts of Egyptian ships and the availability of British naval resources.

All this was very much to the point: how to return the canal to international control. But there was also a sense that for Eden, and for some of his colleagues, the crisis precipitated by the nationalization of the Suez Canal presented not only a threat to British interests, but also a wider opportunity to tackle the problem presented by Nasser: in short, to get rid of him and replace him by someone more 'reasonable', that is amenable to British interests. This idea had been discussed in corners of Whitehall on a number of occasions and with varying degrees of seriousness, but it was new for it to be mentioned in Cabinet. According to Sir Norman Brook's notes it was the Lord President, **Lord Salisbury**, who first raised this possibility on 27 July. The 5th Marquess of Salisbury—the former 'Bobbety' Cranborne[28]—had been a close friend and colleague of Eden's since the 1930s when they were known as the 'glamour boys', and sympathized with those who saw Nasser as an insolent upstart and regretted the loss of empire.

The objective of British action, Salisbury said, should be to 'unseat Nasser', not just to safeguard the canal. It would be better to 'strangle' Egypt rather than to launch a military operation that would unite the Arab world behind Nasser. Failure to act would pave the way for greater disaster later. Eden picked up on Salisbury's comment, stating that military planning should be on a worst case basis, that is, Britain acting alone: 'Object: elimination of N[asser].'[29] The Prime Minister knew from secret intelligence reports that British and American agencies were in touch with groups and individuals who might be prepared to take over in Egypt if Nasser were supplanted. Though none of these schemes looked practicable in the short term, the prospect of getting rid of him was clearly attractive.[30] According to the record, no other minister endorsed this idea, but none spoke against it either.

While no one at the meeting disagreed that Nasser's nationalization of the canal required a strong response, some were more inclined than Eden or Salisbury to consider the potential difficulties, and to question the likelihood of international support if force were used. The first to do so was **Selwyn Lloyd**, who had been appointed Foreign Secretary only seven months earlier, though he had served as Minister of State in the Foreign Office 1951–4 (admitting to Churchill when appointed that he knew nothing of foreign affairs, spoke no foreign languages, had never been abroad except in wartime, and did not like foreigners).[31] Lloyd, a former barrister with a somewhat understated manner, has tended to be dismissed in the Suez context as a rather weak and inconsequential Foreign Secretary, dominated by a Prime Minister who wished, like his predecessor, to direct foreign affairs personally. It is true that Lloyd tended to defer to Eden—Shuckburgh complained that he seemed 'absolutely determined not to take decisions of his own, even on the simplest matters'—but over Suez he displayed a greater awareness of the international dynamics of the situation than his Prime Minister.[32]

Lloyd had his own recent experience of trying to deal with Nasser, having returned exasperated and empty-handed from a visit to Cairo in March 1956 to tell the Cabinet that the Egyptian leader was unwilling to work with the Western powers or curb anti-British propaganda. Nasser was aiming at the leadership of the Arab world and if necessary would accept Soviet help to get it. He had, Lloyd reported, no interest in promoting an Arab-Israeli settlement. Britain should realign its policy and 'do our utmost to counter Egyptian policy in the Middle East'.[33] Though his Foreign Office officials were actively considering options for alternatives to working with Nasser, Lloyd knew perfectly well that this was easier said than done.

There was no obvious alternative to Nasser, and like Eden, Lloyd knew from intelligence sources that the motley collection of monarchists, exiles, and opposition politicians who claimed to be ready to take over were unlikely to be capable of doing so without military intervention from outside. Discussions between British and American intelligence agencies, as well as between certain rather less official representatives, were proceeding, but no one had yet come up with a credible scheme. In any case, a change in policy towards Nasser would be difficult to sell to the US government, who were quick to suspect the British of neo-colonialist motives and tended to think that Nasser, however awkward, was at least the 'devil you know'. As one former CIA officer put it, 'If he had to be "anti" anything...we preferred that it be "imperialism" rather than Israel.'[34] The US, less dependent than Western Europe on oil supplies through the canal, suspected the British attitude towards its nationalization was rooted in outdated imperialist attitudes.

Lloyd understood the uncomfortable fact that on a strategic level, Britain's long relationship with Egypt, however troubled, made that country an important partner in the Middle East, and there were not many promising alternatives. All the Arab countries, even those with close ties to Britain, were affected by nationalist propaganda (much of it spread by Nasser). None was independently powerful or reliable, and the Suez Canal did not run through them. Israel seemed, in some ways, a better bet as a regional partner: it was supported by the US, bought its armaments from the West, and was developing a useful intelligence relationship with Britain. Certainly the Labour Party, led by Hugh Gaitskell, favoured better relations with Israel. But a closer Anglo-Israeli relationship at the political level would alarm and upset Arab countries that already felt threatened, particularly Jordan.

Only three weeks before, Lloyd had told the Cabinet that 'relations between Israel and Jordan had reached a potentially explosive point', and the Israeli Ambassador in London had been warned that Britain was bound by treaty to come to Jordan's aid if attacked. Plans for military action against Israel had been in preparation by the Chiefs of Staff for the past eighteen months.[35] A closer Anglo-Israeli relationship could only strengthen Arab nationalism (and so Nasser) and diminish British influence in the Middle East and further afield, not to mention threatening the security of the Suez Canal. Though sharing with Eden the frustrations of dealing with Nasser and the need to act decisively over Suez, the Foreign Secretary realized that there were no easy answers. When the question of removing Nasser came up, he did not dissent but added quickly that the real objective must be the securing of permanent international control of the canal.

Lloyd agreed with Eden that the first priority was to establish a common position with the United States and France. The French Foreign Minister, Christian Pineau, was due to arrive in London on 28 July, and seemed likely to support a strong line: Nasser's encouragement of Arab nationalism alarmed the French government just as it did the British, particularly in relation to Algeria and Tunisia, and there was a similar degree of domestic pressure towards firm action. President Eisenhower, Lloyd agreed, should be asked to send someone over to London as soon as possible. But Lloyd was much less sanguine than Eden that American support could be counted on. In his experience, and that of his Foreign Office advisers, the US government was much better at agreeing on the need for a coordinated Anglo-American policy in the Middle East than on pursuing one. Discussions in Washington in early 1956 had not proved as reassuring as he and Eden had hoped.[36]

Since emerging from the Second World War as a military and financial superpower the US had pursued its objectives aggressively both in the region and globally, acquiring overseas bases and extending commercial dominance for its oil, airline, and communications companies, a process that undermined rather than supported British interests. In the Middle East, American strategy included encouraging Egypt to believe that the US and UK had different policy objectives, criticizing 'colonial' attitudes, granting military aid to Iraq to reduce that country's reliance on the UK, and supporting Saudi Arabia in its dispute with Britain over the Buraimi oasis. It also included refusing to join the Baghdad Pact, while welcoming its anti-Soviet stance. Lloyd thought the Americans wanted to have it both ways, and their attitude was 'a mixture of anti-colonialism and oil tycoonery'.[37]

The Foreign Secretary also knew, however, that British economic weakness, as well as the close defence and intelligence ties between the two countries and their nuclear partnership, made it essential to work closely with the US and keep the Eisenhower administration on board. Lloyd's sources of information, including the Joint Intelligence Committee, secret intelligence, and diplomatic reporting, left him in little doubt about the wider implications of the crisis caused by Nasser, not least because it was suspected that the Egyptian intelligence services were actively fomenting anti-British unrest in the Mediterranean and North Africa as well as in the Middle East itself. He was not, perhaps, as well informed on the Middle East as he would have wished. British intelligence resources, generally concentrated on the Cold War front line in

Europe, were stretched thinly in the region, and directed towards communism and Soviet-sponsored activities rather than towards Nasser's intentions and capabilities (which might have been more instructive). In a bad year for the British intelligence establishment, intelligence-sharing with liaison partners, particularly the US, was even more important than usual.[38]

As Foreign Secretary, Lloyd appreciated that there was no single 'American' policy. The State Department, Trade, Pentagon, and even the CIA all had their own interests to pursue in the region, and there were, of course, contacts between the British and American governments at every level and on many issues. Secretary of State John Foster Dulles (with whom both Eden and Lloyd found it difficult to get along) was a key figure, but in a crisis it was the President's view that counted, and getting his support for action that could destabilize the Middle East would not be easy, particularly if Nasser took a reasonably conciliatory line and argued that Egypt would respect international interests. In a presidential election year Eisenhower would be very unwilling to take any action that would expose him to Congressional or public criticism. This had been a factor in the US decision to withdraw the offer of funding for the Aswan Dam. Apart from anger at Nasser's arms deals with the Soviet bloc, the administration was sensitive to complaints from southern Congressmen that building the dam would enable Egypt to grow more cotton in competition with the US; and from western Congressmen that they could not get money to build dams in their States, as well as public outrage at committing so much money to someone who had dealings with the Soviets.[39] Eden showed little awareness in July or later in the crisis that he understood such constraints on American policy, but they were certainly on Lloyd's mind.

Lloyd told the Cabinet on 27 July that while it was important to make clear to Egypt that Britain was ready to take economic, political, and if necessary military steps to reverse the nationalization of the canal, it was essential to get the backing of as many other countries as possible, including those like Norway who also had an interest in keeping the canal open, and oil-producing countries such as Iraq and Iran who would want to safeguard passage of their tankers. (The Secretary of State for Commonwealth Relations, **Lord Home**, endorsed this point, stressing that the Dominion High Commissioners in London were keen to bring in canal users on any course of action decided.[40]) While accepting that military action might well prove necessary, Lloyd considered it a last resort.

First, Lloyd favoured referral of the matter to the UN Security Council and possibly a conference of maritime powers; again, Home endorsed this idea on behalf of the Dominion High Commissioners (Salisbury retorted that the only action in the UN would be a Soviet veto). Meanwhile, plans should be made to ensure oil supplies were maintained: according to the Minister of Fuel and Power, **Aubrey Jones**, 60 million tons of the oil passing annually through the Suez Canal from the Persian Gulf were destined for Western Europe, representing two-thirds of European oil supplies. The UK had enough oil to last for about six weeks (though there might need to be some restriction of supplies to industry), and if the canal were closed it would be necessary to ask the Americans to divert some of their supplies. Any interference with free passage would also damage British exports, particularly to India, and increase freight charges.

The Foreign Secretary also raised the question of challenging Nasser's actions on legal grounds, as well as in relation to the government's obligations to British citizens working in the Canal Zone. Had Nasser broken international law? Surely, at the least he had breached the 1954 Canal Base agreement. The Lord Chancellor, **Lord Kilmuir**, addressed these questions. Kilmuir was a notable lawyer who as Sir David Maxwell Fyfe had played a leading role in the Nuremberg war trials, and had served as Home Secretary from 1951 to 1954. He was a man of great energy who had managed to combine successful careers in both the law and Conservative politics. Noted for taking a robust and political approach to the role of Lord Chancellor that he had assumed in October 1954, he had proved a tough chairman of the constitutional conference on Malta in 1955, and the week before the Suez crisis had presented a report warning of the progressively serious implications of uncontrolled immigration into the UK.

Though inclined to take a harder line than the Foreign Office legal adviser, Gerald Fitzmaurice,[41] the Lord Chancellor conceded on 27 July that the fact that the Suez Canal Company was registered in Egypt weakened grounds for protest against its nationalization. From a narrow legal point of view, after all, Nasser's action amounted to no more than a decision to buy out the shareholders, and if Nasser fulfilled his promise of compensation, the UK would not be in a strong position to object. In Kilmuir's view, it would be better to base any challenge on the 1888 Constantinople Convention that guaranteed free navigation of the canal. Such a guarantee required confidence in the management and the collection of reasonable dues, and Nasser could not, he said, be trusted in either respect.

Without what the Lord Chancellor called 'Company organisation' (meaning European managers) there could be no confidence in the technical ability of Egypt to run the canal, and Nasser had announced that he intended to use the profits to fund the Aswan Dam, not to maintain the canal. A few days later, on 31 July, Kilmuir was to submit a memorandum on the international legal position stating that it was contrary to the 1954 Treaty for the canal to be under the control of only one power, as well as contrary to international law for British and French employees to be forced to work under the threat of imprisonment.[42] But the legal argument was neither sufficiently clear-cut nor strong, and on 27 July the Cabinet agreed that the British case would have to be made on 'wider international grounds', enforced by political, economic, or in the last resort military means.

The Lord Chancellor's argument that Egypt could not be trusted, in the sense that it would not be able to pay for, run, or develop the canal, was supported by the Chancellor of the Exchequer, **Harold Macmillan**. He also agreed that any protest must be made on wider international grounds. Yet while the Foreign and Commonwealth Relations Secretaries had drawn the conclusion, from their own consultations as well as from the Cabinet discussion, that the uncertainty of international support and the cost implications of unilateral action meant that the sensible way forward was to adopt a careful and collaborative approach, the Chancellor's views were framed with far less caution and more aggression. Despite the fact that he had been warning the Cabinet of the parlous state of the British economy ever since he took over at the Treasury—telling them on 11 January 1956 that the country had 'reached the same vulnerable position as a private business which persisted in trading beyond its means'[43]—on 27 July Macmillan was one of the most decided advocates of action against Egypt. The canal, he asserted, was an international trust, and Britain would not put up with having it 'monkeyed with'. Whatever it may cost, the government had no choice but to act against Nasser, whom he called in his diary an 'Asiatic Mussolini'. It was, he agreed, a very grave decision, but one that was 'essential to our future' and could not be determined on narrow financial or technical grounds.[44]

Harold Macmillan's motives during the Suez crisis have been the subject of considerable scrutiny and speculation. Some have accused him of a deliberate attempt to undermine Eden so that he himself could become Prime Minister (as indeed he did in January 1957, when Eden resigned). It is true that by 1956 Macmillan was at 62 the dominant figure in Eden's Cabinet. Wartime experience and exposure to the highest levels of decision-making had transformed a hitherto lacklustre political career. A successful stint as Minister of Housing and Local Government under Churchill 1951–4 honed his executive skills and boosted his ministerial prospects. After short spells as Defence Minister and Foreign Secretary in 1954–5, he apparently thought twice about accepting the post of Chancellor, and did so only after Eden agreed to his having a free hand in key policy areas.[45] But it is unlikely he thought very hard: apart from Macmillan's long-standing interest and expertise in economics, the Treasury was a key post for anyone seeking the highest office. As Brendan Bracken commented to Lord Beaverbrook on 1 July 1956, 'The Treasury was the only carrot that would have led Macmillan to go quietly from the Foreign Office.'[46]

As for ministerial competition, by 1956 Eden himself and the former Chancellor, R. A. Butler, were both weakened in political terms, the former by illness and fatigue, the latter apparently struggling to recover his zest for life after the death of his wife in 1954. It is certainly possible, as one of Macmillan's recent biographers has commented, that he saw both Eden and Butler as rivals who could be pushed aside—'both of them had a soft centre'. Robert Murphy, the Under-Secretary for Political Affairs in the US State Department and a wartime colleague of Macmillan's, dined with him two days after the Cabinet meeting, having been sent to London by Eisenhower to discuss the Suez question and 'see what it was all about'. Murphy sensed that although Macmillan was 'well pleased' with No. 11 Downing Street, 'he had aspirations to move some day to No. 10'.[47] Certainly Macmillan, like the majority of senior ministers, aspired to be Prime Minister. But to argue that he advocated an aggressive response to Nasser over Suez, knowing that the government could not afford it, the Americans would be unlikely to support it, and that the consequent failure would clear his path to No. 10, is a judgement that owes too much to hindsight. Macmillan's approach to the early stages of the Suez crisis was based on a more complex set of considerations.

As Chancellor of the Exchequer, former Defence Minister, and former Foreign Secretary, Macmillan had strong views on all aspects of the Suez issue, economic, political, and military (despite the delicately worded disclaimers in his memoirs).[48] His initial contribution to the meeting on 27 July was concerned with financial and technical issues. Already the Chancellor, who had been present the night before when the news about the canal was received, had taken steps to block Egyptian access to sterling assets, instructing the Bank of England not to allow any immediate withdrawals from the £14m Egypt held on current account, and he planned to approach the French with a view to a joint agreement to block funds held by the Suez Canal Company. Although the President of the Board of Trade, **Peter Thorneycroft**, thought that blocking Egyptian access to their funds might damage the chance of bringing other powers into line, the Cabinet agreed to 'act in concert with the French Government in blocking Egyptian current financial balances held by the central banks of the two countries'.

Macmillan undertook to give further consideration to preventing Egypt from gaining access to Suez Canal Company funds. But as he told his ministerial colleagues, by nationalizing the canal the Egyptian government took on its liabilities as well as its profits. They would not be able to pay the necessary dues or compensation, nor run the canal properly, without access to funds held abroad, giving the British and French governments some leverage. Like Eden and Lloyd, however, he knew that in the longer term it would be difficult to maintain effective economic sanctions. Egypt could get both funds and raw materials from alternative sources. And any action taken by the government against Nasser risked his closing the canal to British shipping in retaliation, thereby damaging Britain more than Egypt. It was, as Macmillan admitted, a difficult balance.

On 27 July, however, Macmillan did not express much concern about the economic implications of any action taken against Egypt, even though the state of the country's finances was much on his mind. On becoming Chancellor in December 1955 he had professed himself shocked at the state of public finances, writing in his diary that his predecessor, Butler, had 'really let things slide for over a year, and never told his colleagues into what a mess they were slowly but steadily subsiding'. Although he was not yet sure how the problem should be tackled, it was clear that 'the surgeon's knife' would be necessary in the short run.[49] Britain was living beyond its means, he told his ministerial colleagues, its share of world trade declining while other countries like West Germany with fewer global obligations were moving ahead at Britain's expense. At the same time, the government was under pressure from the Organization for European Economic Cooperation to reduce trade tariffs, a pressure likely to increase if ongoing negotiations to create a European Common Market—negotiations the British had declined to join—were successful.[50]

Although during the first half of 1956 the Chancellor embarked on a programme of cuts in subsidies and benefits, raising prices in the nationalized industries and demanding what would now be called 'efficiencies' across Whitehall, by June he had only secured £72m of the £100m savings he sought. His Treasury officials were gloomy about economic prospects and the position of sterling, though in the Cabinet 'Everybody else (including the PM)' seemed 'quite unconscious of the danger' of financial collapse. On 4 May Macmillan confided to his diary that if he did not get the cuts he wanted he 'must in honour resign and the Govt is lost'; adding, rather characteristically, that this was 'Quite a good position, tactically!'[51] Perhaps the threat was not a serious one, and he did not, of course, resign: but he knew nevertheless that Britain's economic situation was bad and could only get worse if the Suez Canal were to be closed or costly military operations embarked on. Yet despite all this, at the meeting on 27 July Macmillan argued that 'whatever it may cost', the British government had no choice but to take firm action against Nasser, including, in the last resort, the use of armed force, alone if need be. There was clearly more at play here than either personal ambition or financial considerations.

Macmillan was knowledgeable about world affairs, read widely, and was well informed on the situation in the Middle East, having toured the region as Foreign Secretary in late 1955. He shared Selwyn Lloyd's anxieties about the challenges Britain faced, and saw Nasser's spearheading of an increasingly active Arab nationalist movement as a threat to British interests on a global scale. He was also concerned at both the political and economic implications of the Egyptian leader's potential interference with free passage on the canal. Most of all, he was worried about the government's ability to deal with all its problems at once. It seemed beset by difficulties on all sides, and losing the confidence of both the wider Conservative Party and public opinion. On 5 July, Macmillan had noted in his diary that at a three-hour Cabinet meeting that day discussion had darted about from home to abroad, with each question getting more difficult—'Cyprus, Ceylon, Middle East, then "hanging" [capital punishment] a steel strike, the motor car situation'. Two weeks later, he noted another catalogue of problems: Nasser, Nigeria, the Gold Coast,

Cyprus, Russia, inflation and the high level of defence spending. Eden, he thought, was not giving sufficiently strong leadership in Cabinet, in the party, or in Parliament.[52]

He was, nevertheless, loyal to the Prime Minister, and indeed shared many of Eden's views on Egypt and the Suez Canal. Macmillan's approach to foreign policy—indeed to all government policy—was informed by his considerable knowledge of history, as well as by his previous experience. In respect of Egypt, he was not the only person to see Nasser as a post-war Mussolini (Hitler was invoked by some, but Nasser seemed somehow more Italianate in style). It was an inevitable comparison for those who had lived through the 1930s. But Macmillan drew the comparison in a different way. A number of ministers, including Eden, referred in their memoirs to the need to stop Nasser, in the same way that Mussolini or Hitler 'should' have been stopped in the 1930s. Macmillan, however, was thinking in terms of offence, rather than defence. If the British took action against Nasser, he wrote later, they would appear 'not as reactionary powers returning to the old days of "colonialism" but as a progressive force trying to bring about permanent and constructive settlements...we should not resemble Louis XVIII returning in 1815 to a dull restoration, but rather Napoleon breaking through the Alps towards the reunification of Italy.'[53] This grandiose analogy gives some powerful clues to Macmillan's world view. It was that view, rather than narrower economic considerations, which seemed to motivate him at the Cabinet meeting.

In common with most senior British politicians in the 1950s, Macmillan held the conviction that Britain, while no longer a power of the first rank, remained a global power of considerable reach and influence. Anything that diminished that reach and influence must be resisted. Britain was an important player on the international scene, an atomic power, a founder member of NATO, and key ally of the United States and other Western states in the Cold War, and must be treated as such. Its political and economic interests must be respected and protected. But Macmillan was no diehard Tory: he was in the reformist and modernizing, rather than reactionary, camp in the Conservative ranks. He recognized the need for an orderly retreat from empire, was interested in the transition to independence being negotiated with such difficulty in Asia and Africa, and sympathetic in principle to the concept of self-determination, including in the Middle East.

At the end of 1955, after a lunch with the Egyptian Finance Minister, Macmillan wrote that the Egyptian government was 'young, inexperienced and without much background', but 'inspired with a genuine desire to improve their country and help their people. If it means having 60,000 people in prison camps and falling into Russian hands,' he commented, 'it can't be helped. They will win through in the end. It is the Young Turks, or even the early Fascist movement over again.'[54] This somewhat avuncular tolerance did not last long. By March 1956, Macmillan had begun to take a much less favourable view of Nasser, who seemed to be aiming at 'a sort of League of Arab Republics (the monarchies are to go) to include Libya, Tunisia, Algeria, Morocco as well as the Arab States in Asia Minor etc.' For Macmillan, as for Eden, the nationalization of the Canal Company showed just how dangerous Nasser had become.

The Chancellor made no reference at the Cabinet meeting to the possible attitude of the United States towards any action the British government might take in order to restore the Suez Canal to international control. He did not challenge Eden's assertion that if Britain led, the Americans were likely to follow. Yet Macmillan was well aware both of US views on the Middle East, and of the domestic restraints on American foreign policy. He knew President Eisenhower well from wartime days, and had close links with prominent figures in the US administration as well as family connections with America. As early as January 1956 he had noted in his diary that the Americans were thinking only about the presidential election, and doubted that Eden and Lloyd would achieve much on their visit to Washington. It is also clear, from the steps that Macmillan took in the few days immediately after the Cabinet meeting, that he knew the Americans were likely to be cautious about action against Egypt.

At dinner with Robert Murphy on 29 July, Macmillan left the US diplomat 'in no doubt that the British Government believed that Suez was a test which could be met only by the use of force' (a reaction that Murphy thought 'not unjustified'). He also told him that military operations could begin in August and might be 'all over in ten days'. Macmillan knew, of course, that this timetable was unrealistic, and admitted that the aim, followed up in talks on 30 July at which French Foreign Minister Pineau was also present, was to 'frighten Murphy all we could'. It was a successful tactic. Alarmed by Murphy's reports of the imminent prospect of military action, Eisenhower dispatched Dulles to London, where he arrived on 1 August. Macmillan told Dulles plainly that the British 'just could not afford to lose this game. It was a question not of honour only but of survival. We must either get Nasser out by diplomacy or by force.'

Dulles was alarmed, as Macmillan intended: 'We *must* keep the Americans really frightened... Then they will help us to get what we want, without the necessity for force.'[55]

This remark suggests that Macmillan appreciated the wisdom of avoiding military action over Suez. Yet at the Cabinet meeting on 27 July he, like Eden, agreed that Britain must use all means necessary, including armed force, if possible with but if necessary without support from the US, in order to secure international control of the Suez Canal and get rid of Nasser. Why, if he was so well informed both on the economic implications of the course of action proposed, and on the likely attitude of the Americans, was Macmillan so firm an advocate of action, an attitude he retained for much of the crisis? The rhetorical question posed by Anthony Sampson in respect of Macmillan's attitude to the later Anglo-French invasion of Egypt—'How was it that a man of such intelligence, such apparent detachment, such awareness of America, could have urged on so ill-judged and incompetent an adventure?'—might well be asked of Macmillan's approach to the Suez question in July 1956 as well.

Sampson's suggested answers to this question are worth considering, since they are based at least in part on interviews with those who had contact with Macmillan at the time, whether as younger colleagues or officials. According to these observers, Macmillan appeared to react emotionally to the nationalization of the canal, becoming 'closed to any reasonable argument' and retreating into an 'older, more Blimpish persona'. Some thought that with a politician's antenna he picked up the public mood, sensing the 'sound of sabre-rattling'. Sampson himself suggested that Macmillan's knowledge of Greek tragedy 'made him inclined to exaggerate disaster', but also that his attitude represented 'the swordsman, the aggressive man of action, longing to get out again after years of frustration'.[56] Perhaps all these factors were at play to some extent, but they do not remove the impression that there was a disconnect between Macmillan's knowledge and experience, and his insistence that action must be taken against Nasser at any cost.

This impression is reinforced if Macmillan's views on Britain's defence policy and military capabilities are brought into account. Was he really, as he told Murphy and Dulles, confident of a swift victory if Britain had to fight in Egypt, alone or with help? From the evidence of both formal and informal records of the Cabinet meeting on 27 July it is hard not to conclude that most ministers present seemed to think that sufficient forces were available to carry out a successful operation, preferably with international support but alone if necessary, and that this could be done reasonably swiftly. Eden, who envisaged naval action in the Mediterranean with the support of France and the US, paid tribute to the services 'for their readiness'; the Chiefs of Staff, tasked with preparing a plan, were asked to come up with a timetable by 31 July. In the light of subsequent criticism of the state of preparedness, speed of planning, and overall performance of the British armed forces in the Suez crisis, it is reasonable to ask what basis ministers had for their confidence, before turning to the views of the military chiefs themselves.

Most, if not all of the ministers present at the meeting knew that in terms of defence the situation faced in the summer of 1956 was complex, challenging, and presented irreconcilable demands. Defence is an area that absorbs huge amounts of resource and where planning and investment are necessarily on a long-term basis. In peacetime, it appears to offer the potential for big savings and the scaling back of programmes. In an unpredictable world, however, crises occur that may require the commitment of British armed forces, the ships, planes, and other transport to move them about, and the weapons for them to use. The tensions between long-term strategy, immediate requirements, and the need for deep spending cuts were (and remain) acute. British military resources were overstretched, and a radical rethinking of long-term defence arrangements was required.

The kind of resource commitment and defence production levels introduced for the Korean War in 1950–1 were unsustainable in the economic conditions of the mid-1950s. The Soviets now had not only a nuclear but a hydrogen bomb, and the global power game had changed; conventional forces could not defend Britain from a nuclear attack. Selwyn Lloyd, then Minister of Defence, had warned Eden in July 1955 that the British economy could not bear the long-term cost of the defence programme.[57] Macmillan shared this view. In his opinion, Britain's whole defence policy ought to be reconsidered rather than a piecemeal programme of cuts that were unlikely to achieve much in the way of savings.[58] What was needed was a new strategic concept.

The Policy Review process coordinated in 1956 by the Cabinet Secretary, Sir Norman Brook, gave the opportunity for developing such thinking. In March 1956 Macmillan and the Minister of Defence, **Sir Walter Monckton**, had presented a joint memorandum on defence policy arguing that Britain's vital interests should be identified, so that the question of how they could best be defended could be addressed. If the British nuclear deterrent was to be the defence of last resort, then there could be a complete shift in the size and disposition of conventional forces and weapons.[59] But the trouble with undertaking such reviews, particularly at a time of financial stringency, is that they are inevitably influenced by the need for spending cuts, and that while they are going on events in the wide world occur that derail even the best-developed strategies.

Monckton, three months into his new appointment, was sympathetic to the idea of a strategic shift, but anxious that any decisions should take account of the sort of wars Britain might be required to fight, and of her international obligations. Born in 1891, a former barrister who had drafted the Abdication statement for his lifelong friend the Duke of Windsor (formerly HM King Edward VIII) in 1936, Monckton had served in and around government since the Second World War while insisting that he was no politician, only taking a parliamentary seat in 1951. A skilled mediator and subtle thinker, he had been pleased to succeed Selwyn Lloyd in December 1955 after a testing four years as Minister of Labour, but approached his new portfolio with understandable caution.

In 1956 an integrated Ministry of Defence was still some years in the future, and the Admiralty, Air Ministry, War Office, Ministry of Aviation, and the Ministry of Defence itself all led a separate existence, with procurement handled by the Ministry of Supply. Monckton not only had to contend with powerful interests (and personalities) in all these bodies, but also with the Prime Minister and Chancellor of the Exchequer, both of whom took a proprietorial interest in defence matters. Despite their joint work on long-term strategy, Macmillan and his Treasury officials still pressed Monckton hard to produce economies in the shape of immediate cuts and decisions on medium-term reductions (in fighter command and warships, for example). Meanwhile, Eden sent Sir Norman Brook to talk to the Minister of Supply about postponement of procurement programmes. When Monckton spoke to Macmillan gloomily about the situation over dinner at the end of May 1956, the latter urged him to 'bring to an issue the question of his powers over the services', since he would never be able to achieve anything 'until the Minister of Defence is either abolished or really be made boss'. It seems unlikely, however, that Macmillan would have welcomed a more powerful and independent minister.[60]

Since the beginning of 1956 Monckton, while appreciating the need for economy measures, had argued in Cabinet that any agreement on defence cuts must be reached in the light of the sort of wars that Britain might be required to fight. Though in sympathy with proposals for multilateral nuclear disarmament, he worried that Britain might have to stop manufacturing nuclear weapons before it had built up an adequate stock to act as a deterrent. In particular, any alteration in Britain's strategic stance would have to be agreed with its allies in NATO, especially the US. On 9 March, in his Statement on Defence, Monckton stated that 'primary attention must now be given to preparations for cold war and for limited war'. It was not possible to prepare for global war as well: 'if global war occurred, our forces would have to fight with what they had.' The Chiefs of Staff and Joint Intelligence Committee were in agreement that the Soviet Union did not at that time desire a general and certainly not a nuclear conflict, and despite its desire for influence in the Middle East was unlikely to want to fight to secure it, though the supply of arms to Egypt and other Arab states was another matter.[61]

But if Britain were distracted by events in the Middle East the Soviet Union might well take the opportunity to increase its influence or even make an aggressive move elsewhere in the world (a point that was to be illustrated forcibly by the crushing of the Hungarian revolution in November 1956).[62] Radical defence cuts in this situation seemed risky. Limited war was a definite possibility: and Egypt had already been identified by the Chiefs of Staff as one of the most likely potential enemies, as Monckton told his colleagues on the Defence Committee on 10 July. At that meeting there had been considerable discussion about the kind of forces that would be required against Egypt, but also general agreement that in principle UK defence requirements in the Middle East should be reduced. There seemed little recognition that the two were incompatible.[63] The Committee did not discuss the ongoing military preparations for war against Israel if it were to attack Jordan or another Arab state, a prospect that seemed increasingly likely in the summer of 1956.

At the Cabinet meeting on 27 July, however, discussion was focused on the availability of forces for deployment against Egypt should that prove necessary. It was assumed that naval, air, and land forces would be required if a military operation were mounted, and ministers wanted to know what the Chiefs of Staff could provide. Summoned to Cabinet, the heads of the armed services naturally wanted to emphasize what they could do, rather than the difficulties, and there was the inevitable element of competition between them. Despite their positive responses, however, it was clear that nothing could happen quickly. **Earl Mountbatten** and **Sir Dermot Boyle**, Chiefs of the Naval and Air Staffs, were both keen to demonstrate the versatility and utility of their respective services.

The Royal Navy, said Mountbatten, would be needed to support land and air forces, and to operate the Suez Canal: they would want to present an 'impressive show of overwhelming force'. British naval forces currently in the Mediterranean could be augmented by ships from the Red Sea and Malta, while Egyptian ships in British ports might be 'delayed'. Boyle said that during the build-up of British land forces, the RAF could establish a ring of bombers round Egypt, stationed at various bases including Cyprus, to support the army with the credible threat of air strikes. But both men admitted it would take time to gather and transport (by sea) the necessary equipment, and to move ships into position. 'We can do it', was the message, 'but it will take time, and we need to know more about what we will be facing.'[64]

If anyone was well equipped to offer a realistic military perspective on the situation, it was the Chief of the Imperial General Staff, **General Sir Gerald Templer**. A wartime hero whose reputation had been much enhanced by his handling of the Malayan Emergency in 1952–4 (when he coined the phrase 'hearts and minds'), he became CIGS in 1955 at the age of 56 and in the same year produced an important report on the future of British colonial forces.[65] Born on 11 September 1898, he had considerable experience of the Middle East, serving in Palestine during the inter-war period, and more recently had spent much time in the region trying to soften opposition to the Baghdad Pact and to persuade Jordan to join it. As CIGS, he knew that Britain faced multiple threats worldwide that her armed forces were already hard-pressed to meet, and that a number of trouble spots were likely to flare up even more if British forces were diverted to a campaign in the Middle East. In this context he opposed both the prospect of defence cuts in the short term, and radical reform of military structures further down the line.

Templer told the Cabinet that Egypt's military forces consisted mainly of three infantry divisions and one armoured division, plus about 500 or 600 tanks; it was not clear whether the 600–800 Polish and Czech technicians with the Egyptian army would take part in operations. About three-quarters of Egyptian forces were at present in Sinai, facing Israel, but the armoured division was guarding the Suez Canal. Three British divisions would be needed for an operation against Egypt, one to win the fight and two to 'clean up'. This would mean bringing back at least one of the divisions currently serving in Germany, as well as bringing to readiness the Parachute Brigade in Cyprus; the 10th Armoured Division, currently in Libya, might be drawn upon. He warned, however, that it would take time both to collect these forces and to organize such an ambitious multiforce operation. In any case, Templer said, it would take 'some weeks' to complete a plan for an opposed landing of British forces at Port Said. He did not mention the plans that were already drawn up for a possible conflict with Israel, but he knew—and would emphasize to ministers in early October—that it would be impossible to mount both of these operations at once with the resources available, even if it were politically possible.

Templer was not in principle opposed to the idea of solving the Suez problem by force, and he admired and trusted Eden. But he was aware of the wider ramifications, on which his own intelligence authorities and the Joint Intelligence Committee provided information. If British forces were diverted to Egypt from other troubled areas, such as Cyprus, where a campaign against the British was being waged in favour of union (*Enosis*) with Greece, then the level of violence there would increase and cause greater problems for the British government. On the other hand, if it were perceived that Nasser's challenge to Western interests were successful, nationalist movements in other countries, such as Aden, Kenya, or Somaliland, would become bolder in their challenge to British power and influence. At the meeting on 27 July, none of these considerations was discussed, though they were raised in the planning stages that followed. The Cabinet meeting was, of course, a preliminary one: but it set the course that the government was to follow in the ensuing months, and the minutes give little indication that ministers understood how difficult it would be for their decisions to be implemented, especially if they did not get the international support for which they hoped.

The Cabinet meeting ended with a decision to appoint a small subcommittee—in effect, a War Cabinet—that would, from now on, take the lead in handling the Suez crisis. Its members were the Prime Minister, Lord President, Chancellor of the Exchequer, Foreign Secretary, Commonwealth Secretary, and Minister of Defence, and they went on to have their first meeting later that day.[66] These ministers, and others, met frequently to discuss all aspects of the crisis as it evolved, and their departmental officials were similarly preoccupied. A great deal of work was generated by the conference of canal users convened in London in August at the insistence of the Americans; by the referral of the question to the UN Security Council; and by dealing with plans for mediation drawn up by various interested parties. In military circles, much effort was put into preparing the plans for an attack on Egypt, an inevitably lengthy process (particularly since plans for a possible conflict with Israel remained on the table until October). British and American intelligence agencies discussed a series of clandestine schemes of varying practicability; contacts were made with potential successors to Nasser. There were consultations at all levels and with a variety of foreign representatives. In short, a great deal was going on: but very little of it fulfilled the desire for early and decisive action sought by Eden and agreed by the Cabinet on 27 July.

The Suez Canal remained in Egyptian hands and Nasser remained President of Egypt. Shipping passed through the canal more or less normally. Nasser made reasonable responses to representations from international envoys and organizations; and he continued, through his intelligence services, to stir up anti-British and anti-French unrest in the Middle East and more widely. Egypt remained a threat to Israel, which continued and indeed stepped up the tempo of its border clashes with Jordan and other Arab states. Instead of the hoped-for, indeed anticipated strong support from France and the United States, the British government met caution, equivocation, or, in the American case, downright opposition to the idea of using force to resolve the crisis. It seemed as if, despite all the dire predictions made as to the implications for British economic and political interests if the canal remained under Egyptian control, Nasser really was going to 'get away with it'.

It is not surprising that these circumstances produced a strong sense of frustration among British ministers, particularly on the part of Eden, who had come to view British foreign relations almost entirely through the prism of Suez. Other countries' interests and concerns seemed relevant to him only in that context. Even the broader Cold War issues—the extent, for example, to which the Soviet Union might be supporting Nasser—appeared of peripheral, rather than central importance to him. The Cabinet had agreed on 27 July that 'failure to hold the Suez Canal would lead inevitably to the loss one by one of all our interests in the Middle East', and that the canal must be returned to international control, with the added bonus of getting rid of Nasser. Ministers had assumed that Britain *should*—and therefore *could*—impose their will on Nasser, preferably with the cooperation of others, but if necessary alone.

The option of doing nothing, to see whether Nasser would keep the canal open with business as usual, was not considered. Yet none of the plans and proposals put forward in the next few months seemed likely to achieve what the Cabinet had decided upon. It is important to remember that sense of frustration, perhaps even desperation, when considering Eden's later ill-fated attempt to force the issue through secret negotiations with the French and Israelis; a sense of frustration that was shared by the French and Israeli governments too, though for different reasons. It is not the purpose of this chapter to explain 'collusion': but it is surely possible to see, in the decisions taken by the Cabinet on 27 July 1956 and the reasoning behind them, much of the logic of the development of the Suez crisis in the ensuing months.

Harold Macmillan and the Earl of Home, 1960

3

Challenging de Gaulle

Britain Applies to Join the EEC, July 1961

For better or worse the Common Market looks like being here to stay, at least
for the foreseeable future.*

Consider the following situation faced by the United Kingdom: a large
government deficit, slow economic growth and rising inflation, higher
taxes, and spending cuts; British businesses taken over by foreign ones,
while the concentration of news media in the hands of a few powerful
press barons threatens a monopoly; public disquiet at proposed changes
to the National Health Service, high levels of immigration, and the
decline of traditional industries. Overseas, a troubled international situation, particularly in the Middle East (Arab-Israeli relations, Iraq and
Iran) and Africa (where UN troops are engaged in the Congo and elsewhere); uncertainty about Britain's role in global affairs, particularly
when the memory of an unpopular and controversial military intervention is still vivid; and a European community, grouped round a strong
Franco-German nucleus, with which the British government and people
have an ambivalent relationship, especially in view of their strong ties to
the United States of America.

The date? Not 2011, but 1961, when Harold Macmillan's Conservative government decided to apply to the European Economic Community
in order to learn whether the terms of entry would enable Britain to
become a member. It was a momentous decision, whose significance is
not lessened by the fact that the UK did not actually join the EEC until
1 January 1973. It raised profound questions about Britain's national
interests and sovereignty, her economic, cultural, social, and political
identity, and her position in the world, questions that are still a matter of

* Harold Macmillan to Selwyn Lloyd, 22 October 1959.

debate and controversy more than fifty years later. Of course the situation was very different in 1961, when Europe and the wider world were dominated by the Cold War, decolonization was still far from complete, and 'globalization', as we now understand it, was in its infancy. But there are similarities: and it is worth drawing attention to them, because it helps to explain the complexity of the decision that Macmillan's government took in July 1961, and to understand what lay behind it.

The decision to apply for British membership of the EEC was taken at a meeting held in the Prime Minister's room in the House of Commons at 3 p.m. on Friday, 21 July 1961.[1] The Cabinet, summoned especially for the purpose by Macmillan, accepted that 'we should enter into negotiations with the EEC in order to find out on what terms they would agree to our joining the Community'. Though at the end of the meeting ministers agreed to resume their discussion the following week, the decision was not reopened. The next Cabinet, on the morning of Monday, 24 July, opened with confirmation that 'a formal application for accession to the Treaty of Rome should be made without delay'.[2] It is true that the 21 July meeting was just one in a long series, and represented merely the first step on the 'road to Europe'. Nevertheless, it marked an important change in policy, and provided the ministerial backing for carrying it forward to the Conservative Party, to Parliament, and to the British people; to the UK's traditional partners in the Commonwealth, and to their prospective partners in the EEC.[3]

A hot Friday afternoon is an unusual time to hold a Cabinet meeting except in times of crisis, particularly just before Parliament rises for the summer recess. Twenty ministers crowded into the Prime Minister's room on 21 July, plus the Cabinet Secretariat. (Since August 1960 the Macmillans had been living in Admiralty House, while 10 Downing Street underwent essential structural repair. But the Prime Minister found the new Cabinet room there 'intolerably big' and preferred to use his room in the House.[4]) It is hard to avoid the impression that the timing was a deliberate ploy on Macmillan's part: he knew his colleagues would want to go home, not engage in lengthy discussion. On the previous day, 20 July, he had announced in the House of Commons that he would be making a statement on the EEC on 31 July, and R. A. 'Rab' Butler (who was Leader of the Commons as well as Home Secretary) added that there would then be a debate before the House rose for the summer. This timing was certainly deliberate, to forestall any immediate counterattack from dissident Conservatives or the Labour Party. Such careful planning also suggests that the conclusions of the Cabinet meeting, and indeed of the debate, were to some extent regarded as a 'done deal'.[5]

Since 1945 British governments had taken a cautiously negative attitude towards the growing movement for economic and political integration in continental Europe. The experience of the Second World War, ending in victory but also in bankruptcy, and an increasingly threatening Cold War environment reinforced a deep-seated conviction that the United Kingdom's role should be that of an independent global power with ties to the United States of America, the Commonwealth, and Europe—in that order.[6] This conviction was not shaken by the increasing polarization of the post-war world between the American and Soviet superpowers. The Labour government took a major role in the development of a Western defence and security apparatus between 1945 and 1951, and in discussions on key European issues such as the future of a divided Germany. But Attlee and his colleagues, and their Conservative successors from 1951, had set their faces against any initiative towards institutional integration, whether the Schuman Plan that established the European Coal and Steel Community in 1950,[7] or the Messina talks in 1955 that led to the signature of the Treaty of Rome in 1957, creating the European Economic Community.[8]

Throughout the 1950s the UK's attitude towards 'Europe' remained both disengaged and sceptical, and few politicians of any persuasion, or government officials, showed much interest in it. Anthony Eden, as Foreign Secretary and Prime Minister, confessed himself bored by the issue, as did 'Rab' Butler; even Macmillan, though initially in favour of early post-war plans for a more united Europe, lost interest. The majority of Conservatives thought that 'the whole European "thing" was insubstantial', while the Labour Party was divided on the issue.[9] The 1956 Suez crisis, which gave a decided spur to the European movement in France and elsewhere on the Continent, had the opposite effect in the UK. In the context of increasing Cold War tension, not just in Europe but also in the Middle East, Africa, and elsewhere, European integration simply did not seem to British ministers the most pressing international issue. Forging ever closer ties with the US, particularly in the context of nuclear power, seemed much more important. Nor did there seem any urgency. Despite post-war weakness and the humiliation of Suez, there was a general assumption in Whitehall that no major European initiative could, or would, succeed if the British were not involved.

By the end of the decade, however, the EEC (or, as it was usually known in Britain, the Common Market) was up and running successfully and there was a growing realization that the UK might be losing out, both economically and politically, by its refusal to align itself with Europe more closely. The British economy, after a temporary upturn in 1958–9, was faltering, with a deteriorating balance of payments and growing industrial unrest in the face of higher taxes and spending cuts. There was much discussion in Treasury circles about why British growth lagged behind that of most advanced countries. Macmillan's famous (though usually misinterpreted) comment in July 1957 that the UK had 'never had it so good' was more likely to provoke a hollow laugh than agreement in 1960, though his government had been re-elected in October 1959 with the highest-ever Conservative majority.[10] The European Free Trade Association (EFTA), promoted by the UK as a counterweight to the Common Market, was turning out to be neither a viable alternative to, nor a meaningful associate for, the EEC, while the United States (which had its own balance of payments problems) was actively seeking a trade deal with the EEC that might damage further British prospects.[11]

Politically, Britain's position also seemed marginalized, on the edge of the increasingly cohesive grouping of the EEC with a strong Franco-German partnership forged by de Gaulle and Adenauer at its core.[12] As Soviet leader Nikita Khrushchev took an increasingly aggressive Cold War stance from 1958 onwards, focused on the future of Berlin, the idea of a strong and united Western Europe began to look both attractive and desirable in Whitehall. The Anglo-American relationship was still central to British policy and remained very close, particularly on security and intelligence matters (though recent British spy scandals had caused some embarrassment and loss of confidence).[13] But the Americans had encouraged closer European coordination since the Second World War, and a more cohesive Western European bloc appealed both as a political counterweight to Soviet pressure and for burden-sharing on defence and security. They preferred, however, a Western bloc in which their ally Britain was prominent to a European grouping over which their influence was limited. Both President Dwight D. Eisenhower and his successor John F. Kennedy, who took office in January 1961, were in favour of the UK's joining the EEC; a view that was influential, though not decisive, in the evolution of Macmillan's policy towards Europe.[14]

By the end of the 1950s a number of ministers and senior officials had come to accept that a closer relationship with Europe would be in British interests, and the Foreign Office and Treasury had begun to work seriously on the technical and practical issues involved. The idea acquired increasing momentum throughout 1960—despite a Cabinet decision on 13 July of that year that Britain could not accept full EEC membership on the terms of the Treaty of Rome—and was given further impetus by a government reshuffle that brought in several pro-European ministers.[15] The increasingly tense international situation, particularly over Berlin,[16] confirmed Macmillan's view that a unified Western Europe, with Britain at the heart of it rather than on the periphery, was an essential defence against Soviet encroachment. A meeting with General de Gaulle in January 1961 seemed to offer some encouragement, and the issues had been rehearsed thoroughly by the Cabinet at the end of April;[17] senior ministers had visited Commonwealth countries to sound out reactions to a British application to the EEC. A formal decision was now needed from the Cabinet.

There is an interesting discrepancy between the formal minutes of the meeting on 21 July and the record made by the Cabinet Secretary, Sir Norman Brook, in his notebook. According to the Cabinet minutes, the subject for discussion is listed as 'Commonwealth Consultation', and the meeting opens with reports from the Commonwealth Secretary, Duncan Sandys, and other ministers who had been sent to canvass Commonwealth views on a possible British application to the Common Market. This leads seamlessly into discussion of whether to announce an application to join the EEC, with Macmillan speaking about the need for a public statement before the summer recess just before the concluding summary recording that there was 'general agreement' that 'the right course was to enter into negotiations with the EEC and to announce at once that we intended to do so'.

The Cabinet Secretary's notebook records things rather differently. The subject is listed as 'European Economic Community', and the Prime Minister opens the proceedings with a bald statement that there must be an announcement before Parliament rises, either of a decision to apply to the EEC or postponement; meanwhile, 'let us hear results of C[ommon]wealth visits'. Having set the stage, Macmillan does not speak again, though all other ministers present do so. This apparently arcane detail of bureaucratic record-keeping is actually rather revealing, for it shows the Prime Minister opening the discussion with an imperative—a decision must be reached—and then letting his colleagues have their say without intervention, waiting for them to reach the decision he wanted. There is

no discrepancy of substance between the formal Prime Minister's summary and the remarks attributed to individual ministers in Brook's notes,
but the latter, shorthand, and informal version provides an insight into
the decision-making process.[18]

Whether he spoke first or last, it is to the Prime Minister that we must
turn first to get inside the decision taken on 21 July 1961. It is not hard
to summon a mental image of **Harold Macmillan**, a man of distinctive and much-caricatured appearance, surveying his colleagues that
Friday afternoon in his room at the House of Commons. As Prime Minister, he was responsible for the whole range of British domestic and
foreign policy, for the country's reputation and position in the world, for
its economic prosperity, and for its security, and it was a responsibility
that he took very seriously. His considerable intellect and long experience
equipped him well for this formidable task. Edward Heath, appointed
Lord Privy Seal in July 1960 with responsibility for European matters,
wrote later that Macmillan had 'by far the most constructive mind I have
encountered in a lifetime of politics', and that he 'took a fully informed
view of both domestic and world affairs, and would put the tiniest local
problem into a national context, and any national problem into its right-
ful position in his world strategy'.[19] This was a fulsome tribute indeed
from someone inclined to denigrate the intellectual abilities of friend and
enemy alike. But while awareness of the global context was vital to Macmillan's consideration of the European issue, it also increased the burden
of decision.

In the summer of 1961 Harold Macmillan, at 67 the oldest member
of the government and in his fifth year as Prime Minister, was feeling
rather out of sorts, complaining in his diary that he had 'no more *élan
vital*' and was 'beginning (at last) to feel old and depressed'. In mid-June
he had collapsed with exhaustion and was ordered to bed. Though far
too busy to obey the doctor's instructions for more than a day or so, he
was clearly under severe strain, facing an array of international and
domestic problems and finding it difficult to sleep; on 8 July Macmillan
admitted to his diary that it was 'quite an effort now to make an effort'.
But, he added, 'I cannot leave the ship now. I must try to get her into
calmer waters before I do so.'[20] Characteristically, he noted that reading
Arnold Toynbee's *A Study of History* was 'soothing, in a curious way', as
it described so many civilizations which had 'risen and fallen'. (In other
moods, Austen and Trollope did the trick.) In the opinion of John
Ramsden, historian of the Conservative Party, since the 1959 election

there had been 'something of the Donald Wolfits about the Prime Minister', meaning that he was playing the part of Prime Minister without thinking too hard about it.[21] Certainly Macmillan's health had never been robust, and he remained troubled by the after-effects of wounds received in the First World War. Although by 1961 his rather stormy marriage to Lady Dorothy Cavendish was settling into a mutually supportive partnership, the years of personal as well as political strain had undoubtedly taken their toll. A complex and private man, his somewhat studiedly languid and mannered exterior masked both anxiety and, at times, self-doubt.[22]

But like most Prime Ministers, Macmillan was remarkably resilient and adept at recharging his batteries. After the Cabinet reshuffle of July 1960 in which he had appointed both a new Chancellor of the Exchequer (Selwyn Lloyd) and Foreign Secretary (Lord Home), he had commented that both posts had been ripe for a change: 'unless one has the right temperament, the strain is too great for either a For[eign] Sec[retar]y or a Chancellor, year after year'; he did not include his own office, and indeed took a proprietorial interest in both foreign and economic policy himself. Of course both Home and Lloyd had considerable ministerial experience, and Macmillan himself had served as Minister of Defence, Chancellor of the Exchequer, and Foreign Secretary before becoming Prime Minister. He was a tough and wily operator with long experience in the family publishing business as well as politics. A past master at getting his own way, he was skilled at gathering round him people who were not only excellent at their jobs but provided essential intellectual input as well, and equally skilled at sidelining opponents. His press secretary, Harold Evans, noted in his diary on 16 July 1961, a few days before the Cabinet meeting, that he and other members of the No. 10 staff were worried that Macmillan was slowing down: 'He seems unable to sustain the same intensity of concentration and effort over prolonged periods.' Yet, Evans admitted, 'he still rises splendidly to the occasion, and his standard of effort remains far ahead of most of us'.[23] Certainly the Prime Minister was under severe strain in the summer of 1961, but his stamina should not be underestimated.

It would be an oversimplification to say that as he went into the meeting on 21 July the Prime Minister had decided that Britain should enter the Common Market, but true to say that his views had evolved to the point where he considered it was time to ask the question. Much scholarship has been devoted to analysing his motives. Some think they

were primarily commercial, others political; some assert that the decision was really taken by the Treasury, under the influence of its
Permanent Secretary Sir Frank Lee, or that Macmillan was strongly
influenced by the Cabinet Secretary, Sir Norman Brook, and close
advisers like 'Freddy' Bishop and Philip de Zulueta.[24] Certain of Macmillan's ministerial colleagues, in their memoirs, attribute the decision
to themselves. Yet another view is that Macmillan was in fact hopelessly
indecisive on Europe, overwhelmed by events and economic problems:
'agonizing for Britain', as the political commentator Hugo Young put
it; while the official historian of the UK's policy towards the European
Community was convinced that his real motive was 'to retain the level
of influence in Washington which exclusion from the Common Market
threatened to reduce'.[25]

   All these contain elements of truth: yet in understanding the decision
taken in July 1961 it is more instructive to be aware of all the considerations that lay behind Macmillan's views than to attribute relative
importance to them. Macmillan himself was well aware of the arguments both for and against British membership of the EEC, of likely
opposition from Commonwealth and agricultural interests, the Conservative Party, and the wider British public; to win through these difficulties,
he would need the support of his Cabinet.[26] He also knew that a British
application might not be successful, not just because of French opposition but because the terms of entry might be unacceptable. Certainly he
was equivocal towards the EEC: to his mind there was good reason to
equivocate. But he was sure that after many months of study, consultation, and discussion further postponement of a decision was a bad idea.

   A memorandum he wrote over the Christmas holidays of 1960–1 (his
so-called 'Grand Design'), partly to clear his own mind, partly to set out
his thinking for his colleagues and for the newly elected President Kennedy,
is a useful guide. The split between EEC and non-EEC states, Macmillan
wrote, could be 'dangerous and perhaps fatal' for the joint struggle against
communism, as well as having grave consequences for the British economy. 'However bold a face it may suit us to put on the situation, exclusion
from the strongest economic group in the civilised world *must* injure us. It
must also injure the world, because economic exclusion must in the long
run force us into military isolationism and political neutralism.' France,
Macmillan recognized, was the major stumbling block; de Gaulle wanted
'the recognition of France as a Great Power, at least equal to Britain', and
felt excluded from the Anglo-American partnership, particularly in NATO

and in respect of nuclear technology. Writing all this down enabled Macmillan to synthesize the problem: 'Britain wants to join the European concern. France wants to join the Anglo-American concern. Can terms be arranged?'[27]

Macmillan knew that American pressure, and if possible American concessions to the French desire for admission to the nuclear 'club' and reform of NATO, would be required for de Gaulle to take a positive view of a British application to the EEC. Visiting Kennedy in Washington in April 1961, he found the new President apparently sympathetic to his 'Grand Design', and according to economic adviser Robert Hall, present at their meeting, Macmillan argued eloquently that 'we would lose the cold war unless we acted more coherently in the West'. It was 'an American as well as a UK interest that the UK should be a full member in the political sense of the Treaty of Rome'.[28] In the next few months Macmillan's anxieties about the general state of the world worsened, with crises in Laos, Central Africa, and Berlin (to name but the most acute) and with increasing overstrain in the British economy. He hoped that Kennedy, due to visit Europe in June, would tackle de Gaulle on Britain's behalf. But when the President, shaken by the Bay of Pigs fiasco and in poor health, arrived in London bruised by a brutal encounter with Khrushchev in Vienna,[29] this hope was dashed. Kennedy had found de Gaulle 'very avuncular, very gracious, very oracular, and very unyielding' on all issues, of which Britain's relationship to Europe was just one—and by no means the most important.[30]

While this disappointment may have been one trigger for Macmillan's determination to force a decision on Europe, the economic situation provided another. As the Chancellor of the Exchequer, **Selwyn Lloyd**, did not attend the Cabinet meeting on 21 July, and the two Treasury representatives present did not speak, the minutes reveal little of what was in fact a major preoccupation of all those present. It is worth giving some detail here, since whatever ministers' views might be on the Common Market, the thought that Britain was struggling to reduce its deficit and being outperformed by Europe at a time when their own departmental budgets were also under threat concentrated minds more than any other argument that might be put forward. It was also an electoral issue. Ministers knew that the business community was worried: a few days earlier, the chairman of John Harvey & Sons, the Bristol wine group, had appealed publicly to the Chancellor to include a firm statement on the government's intentions towards Europe in the package of austerity measures he was due to announce in the House of Commons on 25 July. British firms, he said, were being hampered by uncertainty over the government's intentions and struggling to compete in Europe.[31]

Fifty years later, the Cabinet discussions on the economy in the period leading up to 21 July 1961 seem strikingly familiar. On 30 June, Lloyd told the Cabinet that 'the economic situation was more serious than at any time during the past ten years' and drastic remedial measures were necessary to reduce the deficit, including cuts in defence spending, a standstill on agricultural support, and a public sector wage freeze. The public would have to be told, he said, that they must bear an increased burden 'in order to enable us to fulfil our international aims, including the provision of reasonable help to under-developed countries, and the maintenance and protection of our national interests throughout the world'. On 20 July, the day before the meeting on the EEC, the Cabinet discussed further reductions in public spending: Lloyd warned that the proposed cuts might still not be enough, and more drastic steps might prove necessary.

Summing up, Macmillan warned that the Chancellor's measures 'must be sufficient to convince opinion, at home and abroad, that the excessive pressures on the economy would be brought under control. It would be of great importance to show that the difficulties were being dealt with on a national basis.' There was, he said, a widespread feeling among the public that 'profits from short-term investment should not be allowed to escape taxation. It was essential to secure a substantial degree of wage restraint, by whatever means, but this could best be achieved if people were convinced that the Government's policy was fair to all sections of the community.'[32] The stakes were, therefore, high for the government, both economically and electorally. As *The Times* put it, Macmillan was 'well aware from many sides that to prolong the period of indecision would be bathos. No one in fact seems to think that he means to end the session with a major anticlimax.'[33]

As the Cabinet meeting opened on 21 July 1961 Macmillan, having made his position clear, waited for his ministerial colleagues to state theirs. First to speak were three of the men who had been charged by the Cabinet on 30 May 1961 with consulting the independent Commonwealth governments to ascertain their views on British membership of the Common Market: Duncan Sandys, the Commonwealth Relations Secretary; Peter Thorneycroft, Minister of Aviation; and the Minister of Labour, John Hare. It had been Sandys's task to consult Britain's key Commonwealth partners, Australia, Canada, and New Zealand;

Thorneycroft went to Asia, and Hare to Africa.[34] Macmillan had insisted that the Commonwealth must be consulted before any decision was taken, and that 'only a Cabinet minister can develop the whole argument'. Those entrusted with the task must take care, when talking to Commonwealth leaders, to place the economic considerations 'in the context of the great political issues which were involved and the importance of reaching a settlement in the interests of Western unity'.[35]

Sandys, Thorneycroft, and Hare had all been appointed to their posts in the July 1960 reshuffle and were, in some respects, a somewhat ill-assorted trio, though each had relevant experience for the task. **Duncan Sandys**, at 53 a man of considerable ministerial experience but somewhat equivocal reputation, was known for toughness rather than subtlety: one colleague described him as 'a steam-roller' who 'would grind away in first gear and nothing could stand in his path'. Macmillan took a rather fastidious attitude towards Sandys's colourful private life, but nevertheless valued his toughness, coolness in adversity, and capacity for hard work.[36] He had entrusted him with the 1957 Defence Review, and with creating a new Ministry of Aviation in 1959, both difficult and controversial tasks that Sandys tackled effectively, proving his loyalty to Macmillan while making a good number of enemies. Sandys had European credentials too, dating back to the early post-war years, when he had been a forceful advocate of the European idea and had encouraged Winston Churchill (then his father-in-law) in the foundation of the United Europe Movement.[37] Though not Macmillan's first choice for the Commonwealth Relations Office (Butler turned the job down), Sandys seemed a good fit for a tough job that involved dealing with such intractable problems as the Congo, Rhodesia, and South Africa, as well as the possible fallout from a British application to the EEC.

Peter Thorneycroft, like Sandys, had been active in the European movement in the late 1940s and was an experienced parliamentarian who had held a number of previous ministerial posts. He had been President of the Board of Trade from 1951 before succeeding Macmillan as Chancellor of the Exchequer when the latter became Prime Minister in January 1957. A year later, however, Thorneycroft resigned, together with two junior Treasury ministers, in protest at proposals for increased government expenditure, an episode that some (like Heath) found hard to forgive.[38] Macmillan, however, took a more pragmatic view (later describing the resignations as 'a little local difficulty'), recognizing that Thorneycroft's experience, including his support for free trade, could prove useful in the European context, and brought him back into the Cabinet in 1960. The Ministry of Labour was **John Hare's** first Cabinet post, but he also had useful credentials for consultations on the Common Market, having served as a junior minister in the Colonial Office and as Minister for Agriculture, Fisheries, and Food (he was a particularly good fit for the latter job, as the owner of a 600-acre dairy farm in Suffolk and representing an agricultural constituency).

All three men had found the governments they consulted were generally more worried about the political implications of British membership of the EEC than about the effects on their trading relationships. Commonwealth leaders assumed, somewhat optimistically, that concessions could be obtained to protect individual exports such as New Zealand lamb or Canadian wheat, and that if necessary it would be possible to negotiate some separate arrangement with the EEC. As Sandys reported to the Cabinet on 21 July, there was 'no disguising the fact that if we did join the Community this would be an initial shock to the whole Commonwealth system', but equally, if Britain did not join, the decline in British economic and political strength would weaken the Commonwealth too. This was a view that he had found was generally understood in Australia, Canada, and New Zealand, all of whose leaders expected Britain to make an application to the Common Market and 'would be surprised if we did not do so'. Thorneycroft and Hare reported similar reactions.

The consultations showed that the chief concern of Commonwealth governments was the impact that British membership might have on international political dynamics. The Canadians, for example, were concerned at the prospect of being drawn increasingly into the economic and political orbit of the United States, though Sandys had reassured them that 'if a wider political association became necessary', the UK would favour 'the larger concept of an Atlantic union than any purely Continental system'. Hare and Thorneycroft, dealing with the 'new' rather than the 'old' Commonwealth, encountered rather different concerns. The Minister of Aviation reported that the Indian government feared that 'the emergence of a powerful economic and political union in Europe might retard the industrial advance of the under-developed countries' and risked creating a two-tier Commonwealth; any special arrangements made for trade should, India argued, be based on commodities rather than countries. This view found an echo in African countries such as Ghana, Nigeria, and Sierra Leone, where Hare encountered criticism of the 'allegedly neo-colonial character of the EEC' and the 'controlling influence which France was thought to be able to exercise over the former African dependencies'.[39]

Nevertheless, none of the consultations had revealed any serious Commonwealth opposition to the idea of Britain's joining the EEC. It would be a shock to the system, as Sandys put it on 21 July, but the Commonwealth was strong enough to bear it and independent governments accepted that the decision on whether to apply was the UK's business and not theirs. Of course when real negotiations opened on the terms of British entry, some years later, there were to be bitter struggles over the individual interests of countries such as New Zealand. But in July 1961 the reports made to the Cabinet by Sandys, Thorneycroft, and Hare on their travels could have been seen as an encouraging sign. The opposition of the Commonwealth had been rehearsed for years as a reason for *not* joining the EEC: perhaps these concerns had been exaggerated? As Macmillan and other ministers realized, however, it was in the UK itself, and particularly within the Conservative Party, that the government was likely to encounter strongest opposition to the idea of 'abandoning' traditional links with the Commonwealth in favour of Europe. The Foreign Secretary, Lord Home, had warned the Cabinet in April 1961 that it would be easy to arouse 'a great weight of sentiment' against any threat to the Commonwealth, provoking strong emotional reactions in the Conservative Party comparable to those over decolonization.[40]

The policy of encouraging former colonies towards self-government, driven forward since 1959 by Colonial Secretary Iain Macleod with Macmillan's approval, had already alienated traditional Tories who, as former Foreign Secretary Lord Halifax put it, did not yet realize that 'the days are past when we could assert our authority with a Maxim gun'.[41] And even forward-thinking Conservatives saw the Commonwealth as a continuing symbol of British greatness at a time when the Empire was shrinking, while many also had extensive business and property interests in Commonwealth countries; there was an innate contradiction between support for decolonization and the desire to defend property rights and special interests. As Macmillan noted in his diary on 19 May 1961, there were 'many very *anxious* Conservatives', commenting that 'It is getting terribly like 1846' (a reference to the split in the Party caused by Sir Robert Peel's repeal of the Corn Laws).[42]

At the meeting on 21 July, therefore, relief at the relatively positive reaction of Commonwealth governments was tempered by continuing anxiety about the political fallout at home and abroad. There was also a degree of sentimental attachment to Commonwealth ties amongst the Cabinet members themselves, as well as in the wider public, encouraged by the anti-European Beaverbrook press. Many ministers agreed with Sandys when he said that if he had to choose between Europe and the Commonwealth, he would choose the latter, although intellectually he realized that a closer relationship with the Common Market was necessary to check British decline. His sentiment was echoed in different words by the Home Secretary, Rab Butler, by the Lord Chancellor, Viscount Kilmuir, and by Colonial Secretary Iain Macleod, but they all voted in favour of an announcement that Britain would seek to join the Common Market. Even the Education Minister, **Sir David Eccles**, who (despite his own involvement in the European movement in the late 1940s) had warned in 1960 that 'Flirting with the Six might break the spirit of the Commonwealth', accepted that it was now essential to negotiate in order to find out what EEC entry terms would be.[43]

Government ministers, while recognizing the force of party and public opinion, had to put sentiment to one side. They knew that the Commonwealth was not the same organization in 1961 that it had been in 1949. Its internal dynamic had changed as more and more newly independent countries joined, and because of bitter political disputes over issues such as South Africa, which had left the Commonwealth earlier in 1961. Trade with the EEC was rapidly overtaking that with the Commonwealth, and the consultations conducted by British ministers had revealed that most governments would prefer as partner a prosperous Britain in Europe, rather than an isolated Britain in economic decline. There were also defence and security issues to be considered. Commonwealth countries like Australia were on the Cold War front line in South and South East Asia, important political and military partners for an overstretched Britain that still had global interests to defend. The attitudes of members of the 'newer' Commonwealth, such as India and Pakistan or the newly independent Nigeria, were also important: if they felt they had lost out commercially or politically by Britain's drawing nearer to Europe, there could be a backlash affecting British interests in Asia or Africa.

Such wider global and strategic considerations were very much in the mind of the Foreign Secretary, **Lord Home**,[44] though he said little at the meeting on 21 July, commenting only that there was no real alternative to an application to join the EEC, since without negotiations it would be impossible to discover what safeguards might be secured for the

Commonwealth. He considered the Commonwealth a foreign policy priority (though lower than NATO and maintaining a British global military presence), and had served as Commonwealth Relations Secretary from 1955 until his somewhat unexpected appointment as Foreign Secretary in July 1960 at the age of 58. This had aroused a great deal of controversy, both because Home was a peer and because he was seen as an 'old school' figure, tainted by his serving as private secretary to Prime Minister Neville Chamberlain 1937–40. In addition, his aristocratic and, some thought, effete manner alienated a number of people (Home was even better than Macmillan at looking languid). The press was almost unanimous in its criticism: the *Sunday Express* called him 'an unknown and faceless earl' and the *Daily Mirror*'s headline read simply 'No! No! No!' The Labour opposition moved a (heavily defeated) vote of no confidence. But Macmillan had been absolutely sure Home was the right man for the job, and was disinclined to take seriously the uproar that resulted from the appointment; he wanted a knowledgeable and experienced Foreign Secretary with whom he could share the direction of overseas policy.[45] In crude terms, Macmillan needed someone to handle relations with the Soviet bloc while he 'organized' a cohesive Western bloc to counter it.

The Prime Minister was not disappointed in his choice: Home's languor belied a tough core. In his view a strong Common Market under French leadership and without Britain would have a disruptive effect on the Western Alliance and was a threat to the political position of the UK as a world power.[46] But in July 1961 Home's concern was less with the EEC than with countering aggressive Soviet tactics that threatened the stability of Europe and, therefore, the security of the UK. Since the failure of the four-power Paris summit in May 1960 relations between the Western powers and the Soviets had been tense, with the threat of a crisis looming over the status of Berlin and the linked issue of recognition of the existence of the communist regime in East Germany (the GDR). In January 1961 Khrushchev announced his intention to 'settle' the Berlin question that year, leading to much discussion amongst the Western allies as to what they would do if the Soviets took unilateral action that infringed their rights in the divided city; the danger increased with a dramatic upsurge in the flow of refugees from East to West.

Home agreed with his Foreign Office advisers that it was important not to 'hot things up', and favoured a Western initiative to open negotiations with the Soviets over Berlin. 'The whole question', he wrote to

Macmillan on 27 May, 'really turns on whether the West is prepared to risk nuclear war for the defence of its position.' Macmillan was worried that the Americans were more inclined to a show of military strength than negotiations, and did not take kindly to British criticism of their ideas; tense relations had a bad effect on sterling that could exacerbate an already critical situation. On 24 June he drafted a gloomy minute to his Foreign Secretary saying that 'If nuclear war takes place over Berlin, we shall all be dead.' Home's strategy was to lower the temperature while standing firm against Khrushchev, no easy task; a British note of 17 July reaffirmed the legal basis of the Allied position in Berlin and warned the Russians of the dangers of interfering with it. Three weeks later, on 13 August 1961, the East German government announced strict controls on movement to the West and began to erect barricades sealing off the Soviet sector: the Berlin Wall was being built.[47] At the meeting on 21 July, though no enthusiast for European integration, Home had no intention of arguing against a proposal that could contribute to the strengthening of Western defence. The Lord President of the Council, **Lord Hailsham**, supported this view: the Berlin crisis, he said, was 'not a moment to divide ourselves'.

Meanwhile, British forces had been mobilized to protect the newly independent state of Kuwait, following an Iraqi statement of 25 June 1961 asserting that Kuwait was an 'integral part of Iraq'. On 29 June Home told the Cabinet that he hoped a declaration of support for Kuwait might deter Iraq from launching an attack, but if military action should prove necessary it was essential to get the 'clear and public support' of the US, and to explain the situation to President Nasser of Egypt in advance to avoid uniting Arab countries in opposing British action.[48] In a speech to a Conservative Party rally the day after the Cabinet meeting of 21 July, Home linked Berlin and Kuwait in his references to the challenge of communism: 'What are we doing while the Communists plot to bring us down? The first necessity is to awake to the nature of the challenge.' The answer, he said, was to 'use the resources of diplomacy to see where a way can be found'.[49] Later, in his memoirs, Home noted that there were two errors commonly made about British foreign policy: the failure to recognize that its role in the world had changed; and the assumption that because Britain's power had diminished it had no influence. Britain was, he wrote, 'a medium-sized power, but it is useless to cry over spilt milk, particularly when in the creation of a Commonwealth of nations, totally independent of us, we did much of the spilling ourselves'.[50]

A more adversarial contribution to the discussion on 21 July might have been expected from **Reginald Maudling**, President of the Board of Trade, who was convinced that there was no possibility that the EEC would meet Britain's conditions for entry. A brilliant and ambitious, if somewhat unpredictable, politician, Maudling was 44 in 1961 and, like his rival Iain Macleod, was regarded by some as a rising star in the Conservative firmament. As Paymaster-General between 1957 and 1959 Maudling had been given the job of heading the British team in discussions about a free trade area in Western Europe, leading to the establishment of the European Free Trade Association (EFTA) in 1958, an organization in which he had invested considerable political capital.

Maudling's experiences in negotiating with the six members of the EEC, particularly the French and Germans, had led him to believe that for Britain to try and join the Common Market would be both fruitless and a mistake; he had argued to that effect successfully in July 1960. Nor was Maudling surprised at the failure of discussions on a closer association or 'near-identification' between the EFTA and the EEC. He refused to take part in the Commonwealth consultations, and on 15 June 1961, when it was clear that momentum in favour of British application was increasing, tried in vain to get the whole idea re-examined in the light of a note from Olivier Wormser, head of the Economic Affairs Division of the Quai d'Orsay, pointing out the obstacles to British membership.[51]

Despite this, on 21 July Maudling supported the Cabinet's decision that a British application to join the EEC should be made, while warning that there would be 'a row' about it. As President of the Board of Trade, he knew that opinion on the Common Market in the British business community, and indeed within the trade union movement, was increasingly divided. At the end of 1958 he had been visited by the presidents of both the Federation of British Industries (FBI, predecessor of the CBI) and the National Farmers' Union (NFU), both of whom were then hopeful of the EFTA and fearful of the EEC, and to whom he promised full consultations before the British government entered any commitments towards Europe. Since then, however, a division had emerged between smaller companies and farming interests, who feared that they would lose out to European competition, and larger enterprises, including leading merchant banks, who saw opportunities in the Common Market for Britain to take a leading role, with London the focus of an enlarged community. By September 1960 *The Director* was warning that 'industry had decided to plump for Europe even if it means leaving Harold Macmillan and his ministers waving goodbye from the dock'.[52] Although Maudling still considered that the Six would not offer Britain terms that it could accept, he recognized the political and commercial necessity to find this out by experience.

Some of Maudling's concerns were undoubtedly shared by one very senior minister, **R. A. (Rab) Butler**. Though still disappointed, if not bitter, at losing out to Macmillan as successor to Eden, he remained an important figure in the Cabinet as Home Secretary, and a happy second marriage in 1959 had transformed his personal life. Macmillan (despite referring in his diary to Butler's increasing 'weakness and oddness') was mindful of the need to keep his rival onside.[53] Butler had, after all, been a prime architect of the reconstruction of the Conservative Party after the war, and the electoral successes of the past ten years owed much to his efforts. His reservations about the EEC were partly a matter of temperament: Butler was a cautious politician who is said to have 'had "Doubts" very much as Victorian undergraduates had religious "Doubts" about everything'.[54] Like many other Conservatives, he also felt deeply about the prospect of abandoning traditional links with the Commonwealth based on imperial preference in favour of European arrangements. Nevertheless, his contribution to the discussion on 21 July was a measured one, accepting that 'we must find out what terms we can get' from the EEC, though stressing that the course proposed was very dangerous both in respect of the Commonwealth and of agriculture.

Butler was particularly sensitive to the farming lobby, as MP for an agricultural constituency, Saffron Walden: in January 1961 he had persuaded Macmillan that the NFU must be part of any discussions between the EEC and the EFTA.[55] In Cabinet on 26 April he had warned that the government would be 'in very grave difficulties if they could be represented as having broken their pledges to the farmers'. Minister of Labour John Hare pointed out that even the farmers realized that 'in the long run British agriculture was likely to suffer more severely if we stood outside the Common Market than if we joined it', while **Christopher Soames**, Minister of Agriculture (and another of Churchill's sons-in-law), insisted that government policy was to ensure that farmers did not lose out.[56] At the meeting on 21 July, however, Soames admitted that though the NFU might take an extreme line in opposing EEC membership 'unless Europe adopts our system of agric[ultural] support', their intransigence was losing support in Parliament and more widely with the growing realization that the current level of agricultural subsidy was unsustainable inside or outside the EEC. Butler understood this, but was convinced of the need to protect rural interests, for electoral as well as economic reasons.

Between 1959 and October 1961 Butler held three jobs, as Chairman of the Conservative Party and Leader of the House of Commons as well as Home Secretary—these were, as his biographer Anthony Howard put it, the 'years of Pooh Bah'.[57] Butler was, therefore, well qualified to identify the potential pitfalls of EEC membership electorally as well as politically and economically. Faced with a course of action he did not like but accepted as the best, perhaps only, option in the interests of the country, he tried to take an objective view and assess the dangers of the government's position. Butler knew that the government faced in July 1961 a formidable array of problems, many of which were connected with the Commonwealth-versus-Europe question. On immigration, for example, there was increasing concern about the impact of non-white migrants, 60,000 of whom had entered the UK in 1960. On the one hand the government wished to be seen to be aware of public concerns about pressure on housing, or matters of public health; on the other, any attempt to legislate in a way discriminatory to non-white immigrants would be very difficult at a time when the government was trying to secure, in ongoing constitutional talks, safeguards against such discrimination in Southern Rhodesia (a subject arousing strong sentiment in the Commonwealth).

As Home Secretary, Butler was also concerned about public reaction to plans for the provision of defence facilities in the UK for West Germany, as part of the Federal Republic's integration into NATO; there was still a good deal of anti-German sentiment in Britain. Again, this was an issue with far wider ramifications, in the light of strong US views in favour of a German contribution to Western defence and an equally strong French suspicion both of NATO and of German rearmament. On the domestic front, Butler, together with Maudling and Hare, also had to deal with the effect of a number of serious industrial disputes in the summer of 1961 that impacted on the public, such as a dock strike, while trying to introduce much-needed reform in the nationalized industries. Similarly, in the face of a gloomy economic outlook, he was trying to retain the traditional support of the business sector for the Conservatives while at the same time introducing curbs on restrictive practices. All these difficulties were made worse by developments in the newspaper industry. A proposed merger between the magazine publishers Odhams, the Thomson Group (owners of the *Sunday Times*), and/or the *Daily Mirror* group was provoking calls for an inquiry, producing a situation where the government faced a potentially hostile press whether it tried to intervene or, in modern parlance, 'let the market decide'.[58]

Meanwhile, as Leader of the House, Butler would have to manage in the Commons the outcome of a Cabinet decision in favour of applying to the Common Market, and the ensuing debate that had already been announced. Despite the overwhelming electoral victory in October 1959, he was worried about votes and marginal seats. A number of Tories, younger members as well as older diehards, were restless and testing party discipline: as Home Secretary Butler faced battles over such divisive issues as capital punishment, decriminalizing homosexuality, and Tony Benn's attempts to renounce his peerage.[59] Europe was then, as now, a red rag to some Conservative bulls.

All these factors must have been in Butler's mind on 21 July when he told his colleagues that, while his political inclinations were strongly against going into Europe, he favoured an announcement that the government would apply to join the EEC in order to 'find out what terms we can get'. He added that it would be wise to try and make it plain that *applying to join* was not the same as actually *joining* the Common Market. **Charles Hill**, the former 'Radio Doctor' now serving as Chancellor of the Duchy of Lancaster, agreed on the importance of this distinction, as did Iain Macleod; but the Minister of Housing and Local Government, **Henry Brooke**, warned that for the government to be seen 'trying the temperature in order to run away' might alienate the Conservative Party: 'Let it be an act of courage.'

It may have been an act of courage for the Cabinet to take a unanimous decision in favour of a British application to the EEC on the afternoon of 21 July 1961, but the mood was not one of self-congratulation; it might better be described as gloomy resignation, even on the part of pro-European ministers like Soames. Only **Edward Heath**, Lord Privy Seal with responsibility for foreign affairs in the Commons, spoke in positive terms, expressing the view that a British application to join the Common Market would not only surprise the French, possibly bringing about a change (for the better) in their attitude, but would also release other influences in Europe to Britain's advantage. The Cabinet minutes expressed this rather forcefully, stressing the importance of creating the right impression in Europe, and of entering negotiations in good faith: 'If the decision were represented as a purposive one and not as an unwilling surrender to circumstances it might be expected to bring powerful forces in Europe into play in our favour.' Yet unwilling surrender to circumstances was a good description of how most ministers regarded the decision taken that afternoon, its negative aspects softened only by the expectation that negotiations with the EEC were most likely to fail. Heath was in a minority in looking on the bright side.

One of the few outright pro-Europeans in the Cabinet, Heath had, like other ministers present on 21 July, embraced the European idea in the early post-war period, and had used his maiden speech as an MP in 1950 to argue in favour of the Schuman Plan. Unlike most of his colleagues, however, he had remained convinced that Britain's future, and its continued power and influence, lay inside and not outside Europe.[60] Clever, focused, and ambitious, Heath had shown early political talent and had honed formidable political and organizational skills in the Whips' office, as Deputy then Chief Whip between 1951 and 1958. Though disappointed when Maudling, rather than he, got the job of negotiating the EFTA in 1958, he threw himself into the Ministry of Labour before he was offered the welcome opportunity in July 1960, at the age of 44, to carry European policy forward.

During the second half of 1960 and 1961 Heath played an important part in bringing the government to the point of decision in regard to the EEC. He understood the issues, and travelled widely to talk to European leaders and gauge the temperature of opinion towards Britain. Heath was, as Macmillan told Alistair Horne, 'brilliant on Europe . . . he had an infinite capacity for details and was very patient and very good with the continental mind', although the Prime Minister added that he considered Heath a 'first class staff officer' rather than a commander.[61] Macmillan relied increasingly on him in developing policy towards Europe, and Heath was to play a key role in the negotiations that followed the decision to proceed with a British application to the EEC.

Despite his pro-European views, Heath understood the reservations of some of his Cabinet colleagues, and in some cases shared them. On 13 July 1960, when still Minister of Labour, he had supported the Cabinet decision to reject the Treaty of Rome unless Britain could join on 'special terms'. But as the prospects of an agreement between the 'Six and the Seven' had diminished, he had reached the view by early 1961 that Britain must either abandon all hope of a close relationship with Europe for some years, or take a bold step and go for membership even if it meant painful concessions. Heath favoured the latter course, considering that on political and economic grounds joining the EEC was the best way to preserve British global influence and prosperity, as well as reducing the danger of international conflict. He also took the view that difficulties with members of the Six would be manageable if British entry could be negotiated successfully.

Heath was dismissive of the idea that membership of the Common Market would lead necessarily to the growth of federalism in Europe, arguing that, on the contrary, British membership of the EEC would dilute federalist tendencies among the Six, and strengthen, rather than weaken, ties with the Commonwealth. In such arguments he was on tricky ground, as he was on the related issue of sovereignty—one of several points of particular sensitivity to the Conservative government barely mentioned at the meeting on 21 July, though it was certainly a matter of great concern to some ministers present. The idea that membership of a European organization would affect Britain's ability to take independent decisions had been used as an argument against engagement with the European movement since 1945. 'Sovereignty' can be employed as an emotive concept as well as a question of legal definition, and is open to a range of interpretations in the political context.

Heath had had a significant exchange of correspondence on the subject at the end of 1960 with Lord Kilmuir. Anticipating that it was 'probable that a solution of our relations cannot be achieved without some political act which continental opinion can take as an earnest of our determination to play a full part in and with Europe', he sought the Lord Chancellor's opinion on the constitutional position. Heath thought the idea of supranationality had been overemphasized: 'in the modern world, if from other points of view, political and economic, it should prove desirable to accept such further limitations of sovereignty as would follow from the Treaty of Rome, we could do so without danger to the essential character of our independence and without prejudice to our vital interests.' The 'strict legal interpretation' of the provisions of the treaty could, he believed, be 'off-set to some extent by the consequences of our accession', and the system of qualified majority voting would enable Britain to exercise a veto over questions that threatened to impinge on sovereignty, particularly if Norway and Denmark offered their support.[62]

Lord Kilmuir[63] was not anti-European. He had been a member of the Parliamentary Assembly of the Council of Europe 1949–52 and *rapporteur* of the committee that had drafted the European Convention on Human Rights. However, in his reply to Heath he emphasized that the surrenders of sovereignty involved in membership of the EEC were serious, and that 'as a matter of practical politics, it will not be easy to persuade Parliament or the public to accept them'. There were three areas in which membership would affect British sovereignty: Parliament would have to surrender some of its functions to the Community, and the Crown transfer part of its treaty-making powers; the British courts would sacrifice some degree of independence by becoming subordinate in some respects to the European Court of Justice. It was no good glossing over the difficulties: they should, he considered, be brought out into the open, otherwise opponents of British membership would 'certainly seize on them with more damaging effect later on'. Nevertheless, Kilmuir stressed, these objections were not in themselves decisive: 'In the long run we shall have to decide whether economic factors require us to make some sacrifice of sovereignty: my concern is that we should see exactly what it is that we are being called upon to sacrifice, and how serious our loss would be.'[64]

The issue of sovereignty had been raised during the long Cabinet discussion on 26 April 1961, when Butler had argued that membership of the Common Market would diminish the powers of Parliament, and subordinate the British legal system to the European Court. Heath had argued that these were not insuperable problems, and on that occasion Home had supported him.[65] At the Cabinet meeting on 21 July, however, the only person to mention sovereignty was Scottish Secretary **John Maclay**, who said that in general opinion was more favourable towards the Common Market in Scotland than it was in the south, and that the Scottish trade unions and farmers realized the potential advantages of membership. The main worry for Scotland, Maclay told his colleagues, was the possible sacrifice of sovereignty: nevertheless, he favoured an application to join the EEC. He supported the Minister of Defence, **Harold Watkinson**, when the latter said that if Britain did apply, it must be a step towards a 'larger concept': the unification of the free world.[66]

The failure to discuss difficult issues like sovereignty on 21 July was not accidental. It was in the interests of those in favour of a decision to apply for membership of the EEC to steer away from possible deal-breakers. Heath, for example, despite Kilmuir's advice, took the view that 'it might be undesirable to let this sleeping dog lie altogether, but there was no need to wake it too energetically'. Macmillan, too, was probably glad that sovereignty was not discussed further. In public, he took the line that any loss of sovereignty would be minimal and outweighed by the political and economic benefits of membership. In his speech to the House of Commons on 2 August he observed that in the years since the establishment of the EEC he did 'not see any signs of the members of the Community losing their national identity because they have delegated a measure of their sovereignty'; it was, he suggested 'a matter of degree'.[67] All this was part of a deliberate strategy to downplay the significance of a British application, and indeed of British membership of the EEC if things got that far. It was partly for electoral reasons—to avoid alarming the party, Parliament, or the public—and partly to avoid raising unrealistic hopes of the forthcoming negotiations or of the response that would be encountered to a British application from the existing members of the Community. It was also, in Hugo Young's view, a very British way of doing things: 'On those occasions when an agreement finally becomes expeditious, or impossible to avoid, let the world be informed of its banality, its minimal implications for the constitution, the utter impossibility of its changing reality in ways that anyone would notice.'[68]

While Macmillan might be thought to have been glossing over a difficult area to get the decision he wanted, the reluctance to face uncomfortable facts or unpleasant possibilities was shared by many of his colleagues present on 21 July. Ministers might have taken the decision to apply to the Common Market reluctantly, or in the expectation that such an application would not succeed: but there was also an underlying assumption that if negotiations were in fact to succeed, with acceptable terms agreed, Britain would then be a leading partner in the Community and would be able to shape it to fit in with British interests. Macmillan and his Cabinet colleagues belonged to a political generation whose experience, assumptions, and prejudices had been shaped indelibly (even for those who had not seen active service) by the world war that had ended only fifteen years earlier. The early Cold War period had brought both the promise of peace and reconstruction and the threat of a new global conflict.

But neither threat nor promise eradicated a common set of underlying attitudes inherited from the wartime experience: fear of Germany, distrust of France, dependence on but resentment of American power; and, above all, the belief that Britain, despite the trauma of the Suez crisis in 1956, remained an important global power—a world power of the second rank, admittedly, since it could not match the US and Soviet superpowers, but still more important than any other power—certainly more important than any *European* power. In 1961 these attitudes underpinned the thinking of even the most forward-thinking and European-minded British politicians, and they had a profound effect on British policy. Some argued that such attitudes were outdated and even self-deluding, but there is no doubt that they have proved remarkably durable.

After the Cabinet meeting Macmillan retired to Chequers, while other ministers went to their constituencies or, like Home, fulfilled party duties. Recording the meeting in his diary on 22 July, the Prime Minister wrote: 'Whether or not, having taken this momentous decision and communicated it to the Governments of the Six, we shall reach agreement on the vital points of (a) Commonwealth (b) British agriculture, I cannot tell. I sh[oul]d judge that the chances are *against* an agreement, unless—on political grounds—de Gaulle changes his mind.'[69] Future events were to show this as a realistic appraisal. For the moment, however, Macmillan felt a sense of relief and purpose, and any anxieties about political or public reactions to the decision were unfounded.

The next Cabinet meeting, on Monday 24 July, was dominated by discussion of the economic situation and the contents of the statement that the Chancellor was to make on 25 July, announcing measures including raising the bank rate, increasing customs duties and purchase tax, calling for an increase in the banks' special deposits scheme, and making an application to the International Monetary Fund.[70] These measures, rather than Europe, dominated the news for the next few days. During the parliamentary debate on 31 July a succession of speakers rose to 'laud the Commonwealth connection, yearning for the vanished, English-speaking world'. Such emotional appeals did not, however, translate into any concerted opposition when it came to the vote.[71] The government's motion was carried by 313 votes to 5; a formal application to the EEC was made on 10 August. There was little press comment, nor, at this stage, much public interest.

It was a very low key beginning to what was to be a long and increasingly difficult journey for successive British governments. Detailed negotiations on the terms of Britain's entry, in which Heath played a prominent part, ended after many disappointments and difficulties in General de Gaulle's veto and announcement at a press conference on 14 January 1963 that the United Kingdom was not yet ready to accept the conditions of membership of the EEC. A further abortive attempt to join would be made by Harold Wilson's Labour government in 1967, and it was only when Heath himself was Prime Minister that British membership was finally achieved in 1973. But the decision taken on 21 July 1961 was, nevertheless, an important turning point. In Heath's memoirs, he wrote that it 'represented an historic moment in post-war politics', determining the direction 'not just of British policy, but also that of Europe and the Atlantic alliance'. At first glance this might seem a somewhat grandiose judgement of hindsight: but a figurative glance round the Cabinet table on that hot Friday afternoon, combined with an awareness of the problems faced by the ministers present, makes one think that Heath was not so far off the mark. After all, he was there.

Harold Wilson and George Brown, 1967

4

Challenging Britain's World Role

The Decision to Withdraw from East of Suez, January 1968

For God's sake act like Britain[*]

The decisions discussed in the earlier chapters of this book have indicated that there were three constants in British foreign policy after 1945. First, successive governments, both Labour and Conservative, continued to take decisions in the belief that Britain remained a significant world power with a global role and global responsibilities, despite its economic and military weakness and the dominance of the superpowers. Second, because Britain's prosperity and security depended on US financing and support, the Anglo-American relationship was seen as paramount and governments were reluctant to go against American wishes. And finally, successive governments had been willing, if they considered it in the British national interest, to use military force overseas.

The decision taken by Harold Wilson's Labour government in January 1968, to withdraw British forces from East of Suez and the Persian Gulf by the end of 1971, challenged all these three assumptions. It accepted that Britain's world role had changed and that it was no longer either possible or desirable to maintain a permanent military presence in the Far East or Middle East. The decision was taken despite strongly expressed disapproval by Britain's partners, and in particular by the United States government. And it reinforced the government's determination since 1964 to avoid using military force if possible, and

---

[*] Reaction of Dean Rusk, US Secretary of State, to the news that Britain was to withdraw its forces from East of Suez in 1971, as reported to the Cabinet by George Brown on 12 January 1968.

specifically not to commit British forces to the war in Vietnam. This triple challenge, and the political, economic, and global context that produced it, make the decision a good example of the complexities of foreign policy-making.

The East of Suez decision was signed off finally at a Cabinet meeting on the morning of Monday, 15 January 1968. This was the penultimate session of a gruelling marathon: eight Cabinet meetings in eleven days, more than thirty-two hours of discussion on what were called 'post-devaluation measures', the package of public expenditure cuts made necessary by the devaluation of sterling on 18 November 1967, in order to meet obligations to the International Monetary Fund (IMF) and to reduce the balance of payments deficit. The exhausting and often acrimonious discussions exposed deep divisions within a government already plagued by rivalry and mistrust. The newly appointed Chancellor of the Exchequer, Roy Jenkins, had spent the Christmas holidays preparing a tough package, and, supported by the Prime Minister, was determined not to water down his recommendations. Other ministers, while appreciating the seriousness of the economic situation, sought to protect their departmental budgets and projects. Those responsible for domestic and overseas spending sought to shift the burden on to each other. (Everyone agreed on cutting local authority spending, 'for the obvious reason that other people's spending looks easier to cut than one's own'.[1])

Some issues, however, aroused strong feelings in the Cabinet as a whole. In particular, ministers were divided over what Jenkins called in his memoirs the 'controversial quadrilateral': the postponement of a plan to raise the school-leaving age from 15 to 16; the reintroduction of prescription charges; the cancellation of the contract to buy F-111 strike aircraft from the United States; and the date of the withdrawal of British forces from East of Suez and the Persian Gulf.[2] Each of these four must be seen in the context of the others. But the emphasis here will be on the last of the four, the withdrawal from East of Suez. Although that possibility had been long debated, so had the date of its implementation, and when the decision was finally taken many saw it as the end of an era, a 'major change in British foreign policy comparable in some respects with the decision to give India independence'.[3]

Although the decisions on the two foreign policy elements of the quadrilateral, East of Suez and the related issue of the F-111 contract, were agreed in principle during the very first of the Cabinet meetings on 4

January 1968, they were not finalized until the end. For this reason it is less helpful in this case to focus on one particular meeting, but rather to look at the whole series, with particular attention to the first meeting, and to those on Friday, 12 January and the morning of Monday, 15 January.[4] On 12 January, Foreign Secretary George Brown reported to the Cabinet on a visit to the United States; and on the 15th Commonwealth Relations Secretary George Thomson reported on his trip to Malaysia, Singapore, Australia, and New Zealand. In between these two meetings, the Prime Minister of Singapore, Lee Kuan Yew, came to London, to lobby both the Prime Minister and the Chancellor. The Chiefs of Staff also made representations. It was the decisive weekend for the post-devaluation package.

The idea of cutting down or withdrawing completely British forces stationed in the Far East and Middle East was not new. The Treasury, in particular, had identified Britain's role East of Suez as a key target for defence savings as early as 1960, and the 1968 decision was the culmination of a long process.[5] In the post-war world, when former colonial territories were gaining independence and the demands of European security were increasing, maintaining a permanent British military presence outside Europe had begun to seem both unnecessary and prohibitively expensive. Britain spent a higher proportion of its national income on defence than any other Western European country, yet was finding it increasingly hard to meet the growing military and financial demands made of NATO and Western European Union (WEU) members. Yet in 1964, the year that a Labour government was elected for the first time since Attlee left office in 1951, there were more British troops in the Far East than there were in Germany, the front line of the Cold War. Apart from a large presence at Singapore, other bases or staging posts included those in Borneo and in the Indian Ocean, as well as the garrison in the Crown Colony of Hong Kong.

This extensive and expensive military capability served a number of purposes. In the context of the Cold War, it was intended to safeguard British commercial and political interests against a perceived communist threat from the Soviet Union and/or China. Apart from a general deterrent effect and the safeguarding of vital British trading routes, this included protecting colonial dependencies in the Indian and Pacific Oceans, such as Mauritius and Fiji, whose defence and internal security were a British responsibility. Britain also had multilateral obligations in the region, under SEATO and other agreements,[6] that involved supporting newly independent territories such as the Malaysian Federation and Singapore against communist subversion. Indeed, between 1963 and 1966 British forces were engaged in Confrontation with Indonesia over its incursions into Malaysia. Commonwealth partners such as Australia were also involved in these struggles, and considered a British military presence important to their own security.

The availability of forces East of Suez also provided the essential military back-up for British responsibilities in the Middle East, including the security of Aden and commitments to Kuwait and Gulf sheikdoms. A withdrawal from East of Suez meant, therefore, withdrawal from the Middle East. This made the idea doubly unpalatable to the United States. President Lyndon B. Johnson, who had taken over from the murdered John F. Kennedy in November 1963, considered that the overarching purpose of the British presence East of Suez was to enable Britain to share the job of 'world policeman' and to keep unstable areas stable in times of conflict—such as the war the Americans were waging in Vietnam.[7] While they were preoccupied with South East Asia, the US government also welcomed a British military presence to act as a deterrent to any Soviet aggression in the Middle East, as well as protecting Western oil and other commercial interests.

Nor did the Americans want Britain to reduce its military contribution in Europe. At a time of increased spending on the Vietnam War, the US was trying to get its European partners to accept greater responsibility for their own defence, and was alarmed by British attempts to reduce the cost of maintaining their forces in Germany. President Johnson and his advisers left Harold Wilson and his colleagues in no doubt that continuing American financial support, and cooperation in nuclear and intelligence matters—all of vital national importance for Britain—depended upon their agreeing to remain East of Suez and maintain defence commitments. As McGeorge Bundy, Johnson's National Security Advisor, told the President on 28 July 1965: 'We want to make very sure that the British get it into their heads that it makes no sense for us to rescue the pound in a situation in which there is no British flag in Vietnam, and a threatened British thin-out in both east of Suez and in Germany.'[8]

By the mid-1960s, Britain could no longer afford to maintain a large military presence in the Far East and Middle East without substantial financial support from the Americans, whether in the form of loans, buying British military equipment, or propping up the value of sterling. For the first few years of the Labour government, maintaining Britain's global commitments and receiving in return American bailouts during recurring financial crises had seemed a reasonable bargain. Harold Wilson and his colleagues, just as much as their Conservative predecessors, believed that Britain's worldwide interests and influence needed to be backed up by a military capability, and that it was important to keep closely in step with the Americans.[9] The Prime Minister (a self-confessed 'East of Suez man') told the House of Commons in December 1964 that Britain could not afford to give up its world role, and similar statements were made by ministers at regular intervals.[10] It is true that these were paralleled by serious discussions about the reduction of East of Suez commitments, encouraged by Cabinet Secretary Sir Burke Trend. But dates for a final pull-out and the question of whether there would be any residual capability left in the region were left deliberately vague, and there was little indication that the government was ready for any fundamental reassessment of Britain's world role.[11] Even ministers who thought this role anachronistic and unsustainable were reluctant to accept the diminution in global influence and prestige that renouncing it would bring.

However, Britain's worsening economic situation, including a severe balance of payments crisis in the summer of 1966, and a combination of domestic and international pressures meant that by 1967 there was no alternative to major cuts in government expenditure. At home, a solid Labour majority emboldened trade union militancy and backbench restlessness, and everything the government tried to do was undermined by economic weakness. Slow to modernize and suffering labour shortages, Britain was being overtaken by expanding European economies, while buffeted by a cycle of inflation and deflation (what would later be called boom and bust) and recurrent sterling crises. At the same time, the Six-Day Arab-Israeli War of June 1967, in addition to adding to Cold War tension, exacerbated Britain's balance of payments problems and the weakness of sterling when the Suez Canal was closed, threatening oil supplies. Relations with China were stormy, after the sacking of the British Embassy in Peking by Red Guards on 22 August 1967 during the Cultural Revolution. The struggle to bring Ian Smith's rebel Rhodesian regime to heel through economic sanctions was proving both expensive and ineffective, while there were ongoing obligations to help former colonial territories (such as Nigeria, in the throes of a bitter civil war) to deal with internal and external threats.

There was no avoiding the conclusion that Britain's global responsibilities were unsustainable. For three years the Labour government had relied on financial help from the United States, hoping that things would improve. Instead, they got worse. The Americans realized this, though they continued to argue against any reduction in British defence commitments. A brief for President Johnson dated 1 June 1967, prepared for the forthcoming visit to Washington of the British Prime Minister and Foreign Secretary, acknowledged that

> In a siege environment—with economic stagnation at home and no progress towards Europe—it would be exceedingly difficult for any elected politician to do all the things we would like Harold Wilson to do: stay in the Far East, back us on Vietnam; avoid balance of payments trouble and any risk of devaluation (whatever the costs in domestic deflation); maintain a constructive stance vis-à-vis Europe (no further cut-backs in the B[ritish] A[rmy] O[f the] R[hine], no giving up on entry to Europe etc). Taken together, all this simply does not add up to a workable platform for Wilson's 1969–70 elections.[12]

This realistic assessment of the Wilson government's position did not incline the US Administration to continue providing support for sterling. In the autumn of 1967, just as growing disorder in Aden led the government to pull British forces out earlier than planned,[13] a series of damaging industrial disputes, particularly a seamen's strike in September, proved the final straw. On 18 November 1967 the pound was devalued from $2.80 to $2.40. This decision, long resisted by the Prime Minister but long considered inevitable by many economists, led to the resignation of the Chancellor of the Exchequer, James Callaghan.[14] As Callaghan admitted, devaluation, if unavoidable, was seen as hard evidence of the government's failure. Nor did it provide any quick fix for the British economy. There was a huge outflow of sterling reserves, the financial markets lost confidence, and there was talk of the need for a second devaluation.

The first task of the new Chancellor, Roy Jenkins, was to produce a post-devaluation package of expenditure cuts in order to reassure the markets, satisfy the IMF, and reduce the deficit. A memorandum circulated to the Cabinet on 20 December 1967 described the economic situation as 'extremely menacing' (a phrase Jenkins later said was intended to 'create a suitable mood of malleable apprehension'). That day the Chancellor also had a meeting with ministers and officials from departments responsible for overseas spending, warning them that the government had 'come to the point of defeat on the economic road'. Cuts were no use by themselves: commitments must be given up as well. The stage was set for a battle royal in Cabinet. It was also set for the decision to withdraw from East of Suez. As Patrick Gordon Walker, Wilson's first choice of Foreign Secretary in 1964, later wrote, economic emergency 'made articulate a decision that had subconsciously been reached; but which the Cabinet as a whole and the Prime Minister had flinched from recognizing'.[15]

In order to restore Britain's balance of payments position over the next two financial years, the Chancellor was looking for savings of £800–850m, with a view to reducing aggregate demand (that is, all consumer spending, as well as public and private expenditure and investment) overall by £1,000m with the aid of taxation. Jenkins anticipated a struggle with his colleagues, criticism from the Conservatives, protests from Labour backbenchers (who suspected the government of agreeing to unacceptable terms from the IMF), and opposition from the Trades Union Congress (who warned of public outcry if cuts were made in health and education). Yet reductions in every departmental budget were unavoidable. The country was in for a period of austerity. Politically, therefore, it was important that the pain should appear to be distributed fairly. If hard measures had to be taken to cut or cancel domestic programmes, defence and overseas budgets had to be seen to take their share of cuts as well.

This was the situation at the beginning of 1968. Jenkins later described his own mood as one of 'excitement, indeed exhilaration. At least we were out of the trenches and into a war of movement.'[16] But the New Year began with more depressing news. The United States was also experiencing balance of payments difficulties. On 1 January President Johnson announced a five-point plan to 'keep the dollar strong'. It imposed restrictions on US investment in Europe and other developed nations, and on foreign lending by US banks. US citizens were urged to limit non-essential travel overseas, and $500m was cut from the cost of maintaining American troops in Europe. All this was bad news for the British economy. *The Times* thought the announcement as significant as the announcement of the Marshall Plan, the prospect in 1968 as gloomy as it had been optimistic in 1947.[17] It made the post-devaluation package, and the Cabinet meetings that debated it, even more important.

The first three weeks of January 1968 were an intense experience for everyone involved. Apart from the frequency and length of the Cabinet meetings, the second week in January saw heavy snow in Britain and a big freeze that cancelled most sporting events. The bad weather affected all of Europe and even parts of the Middle East, and was followed by gale force winds and flooding. As always in Britain, snow made travelling difficult. The Lord President of the Council, Richard Crossman, recorded in his diary for 9 January a 'tremendously heavy fall of snow—nearly a foot at Prestcote—which cut the children off from school'. Harold Wilson, he noted, was 'snowed up in Manchester'.[18] But while Cabinet meetings might be delayed, they were not postponed or cancelled. The government was committed to reaching agreement so that a statement could be made when the House of Commons returned from the Christmas recess in mid-January.[19] So ministers trudged through the snow, postponed other engagements, dragged themselves from their sick beds, and forgot about getting a good night's sleep.

A number of those present at the Cabinet meetings recorded them, either at the time or later. The contemporary accounts are more atmospheric, those with hindsight inevitably more exculpatory. But even allowing for personal bias, exaggeration, and hindsight, adjectives such as 'grim', 'icy', 'traumatic', and 'sulphurous' give a pretty good idea of what the meetings must have been like. At the same time, however, the formal Cabinet minutes record balanced, well-informed, and generally sensible discussion of the issues, even if it became heated at times. Transport Minister Barbara Castle, suffering from pneumonia but attending nonetheless, noted in her diary the 'high level of debate and conscientiousness'. Perhaps, she thought, 'we really only function as a Cabinet when we have failed and further retrenchment is necessary. If we only spent a quarter of this energy and time and cohesiveness in working out a strategy for success we should be in a very different position now.'[20]

Richard Crossman noted another positive aspect: an 'astonishing improvement in public opinion'. The general public, aware from the press and now widely available television sets of the severity of the economic problems facing the country, were impressed by the fact that the government was meeting almost daily to thrash out a solution. Reports of disagreements in Cabinet actually increased this favourable opinion: people felt they were part of the debate. The atmosphere of crisis had brought about a change in the prevailing atmosphere of public disengagement in politics, even producing the short-lived but extremely successful 'I'm Backing Britain' campaign (complete with theme tune recorded by Bruce Forsyth) that encouraged people to work extra time without pay to boost productivity.[21] As Crossman put it, instead of government policy being decided first and communicated later, 'we are doing things in series and in full sight of the public . . . We thought it was a tremendous disadvantage but at least in terms of public opinion it has some real advantages.'[22]

Roy Jenkins, in his memoirs, said that the series of crisis Cabinet meetings in January 1968 were the Prime Minister's 'chosen tactics'.[23] From what is known of **Harold Wilson**, it was certainly very much in character to have calculated the political advantages, both in terms of bringing recalcitrant ministers into line and in improving the government's public image. In many ways this complex man and remarkable politician was in his political prime. An economist by training, Wilson was intellectually curious and easily bored. He enjoyed the minutiae of government and relished political gossip. At the same time, he liked to project a public image of the ordinary man, smoking a pipe, wearing a mackintosh, and liking brown sauce on his food: competent, sensible, and in control. Still only 51 in January 1968, he had served as a Cabinet minister under Attlee, and worked closely with men like Cripps and Bevan, giants of the Labour movement, before succeeding Gaitskell as Labour leader. He had led his party to electoral victory in 1964 after thirteen years of Conservative rule, and converted a majority of four into one of ninety-seven in March 1966. He dominated the Opposition in the House of Commons, and handled a Cabinet full of difficult personalities and competing ideologies with deftness. Some accused him of being interested only in power, and lacking principle. This is said of most successful Prime Ministers. Even those who opposed or disliked Harold Wilson admired his political mastery.[24]

On the face of it, however, 1967 had been a very difficult year for Wilson as well as for the British government as a whole. His efforts at mediation with the Soviet Union over Vietnam had not only been unsuccessful but had exposed the extent to which the US President, whom Wilson had been careful to cultivate, disregarded both Britain and its Prime Minister. A second British application to the EEC had been rejected, and the Middle East was in crisis following the Six-Day War. The devaluation of sterling had been a bitter pill to swallow for a man who recalled the problems this had brought to the Labour Party not just in 1949 (when he himself had been involved in the decision to devalue), but in 1931 when the refusal of Ramsay MacDonald's ministers to agree to expenditure cuts had led to the formation of the much-reviled National Government. In 1951 he had resigned from the Attlee government, together with Health Minister Nye Bevan, over the imposition of health service charges at a time when money was being spent on rearmament. Now he had to contemplate the reintroduction of prescription charges by his own government. And the 'East of Suez man' was now pledged to support a decision to withdraw from both the Far East and the Gulf by 1971, against the wishes of both the Americans and Commonwealth partners like Australia.

Wilson also faced problems within his own government. From 1966, with a bigger majority and no imminent election, an element of relaxation and even complacency allowed space for speculation about the leadership and rivalries between leading figures. The Cabinet contained some big personalities, like George Brown, Jim Callaghan, Denis Healey, and Roy Jenkins, inclined to flex their political muscles if things did not go their way. Wilson felt compelled to spend an increasing amount of time second-guessing his colleagues and protecting his own position. To make things worse, in 1967 he seemed to lose his touch with many of those who had so far admired his performance as Prime Minister. He had managed to alienate many in the trade union movement, the press, the senior civil service, and a sizeable section of the Parliamentary Labour Party by his handling of industrial disputes and the D-Notice affair (when he reacted strongly to a press story that breached national security).[25] The diaries of interested—and on the whole sympathetic—observers such as Crossman, Castle, and Technology Minister Tony Benn record frequent ministerial outbursts and resignation threats. Wilson's handling of a major row in December 1967 about whether the government should maintain its embargo on arms sales to South Africa, though successful in rallying the Cabinet to him, showed the depth of feeling in some quarters.[26]

All this fuelled Wilson's suspicions, encouraged by advisers such as George Wigg, that there were plots afoot against him, whether by communist elements in the trade unions, by the security and intelligence services, or by his own ministerial colleagues.[27] The Prime Minister was said to trust no one except a small group of advisers that included his influential personal and political secretary Marcia Williams, Labour MP Gerald Kaufman, and the two economists, Tommy Balogh and Nicholas Kaldor (known in Whitehall and media circles as 'Buda' and 'Pest').[28] But though these suspicions were later to become an obsession, they should not be overemphasized during the mid-1960s. Wilson still had good working relations with the security services, and dismissed a plot to replace him as Prime Minister as 'idle tea-room gossip', though he remained vigilant against possible threats.

Despite all this, Harold Wilson began 1968 in calm and confident mood. He had just returned from Australia, where he attended a memorial service for Premier Harold Holt and took the opportunity for private discussions with the US President. Johnson's request to sound out the Russians, during Wilson's forthcoming visit to Moscow, about North Vietnamese views on a possible ceasefire had reinforced his belief in the importance of Britain as an intermediary, and that it was important to continue cultivating the Soviet leadership in the interests of global as well as European security.[29] Although the situation in the Middle East continued to give cause for concern, here again the Prime Minister was proud of British efforts at mediation, including the drafting of Security Council Resolution 242 under which Israel was to withdraw from the territories it had taken during the Six-Day War, while the Arab states recognized Israel's right to exist.[30] British efforts in these two major areas of international tension convinced Wilson that Britain still had an important role to play.

Wilson had also been surprisingly upbeat in the aftermath of devaluation, saying that he regarded it as an opportunity for a new start. He had agreed in advance the drastic proposals his new Chancellor drew up over Christmas, even though the domestic measures were bound to be unpopular and the defence cuts likely to upset Britain's global partners. Getting the package through was, he wrote later, 'the most formidable task I had attempted in over three years of government'. His appointment of Jenkins as Chancellor, instead of Anthony Crosland whom Callaghan had recommended, was a sign of that determination. As Jenkins said, Wilson had decided that 'the best hope for safety and stability was that he and I should be bound together, if not by hoops of steel, at least by bonds of mutual self-interest'. Though the two men were not natural allies, they got on well on a personal level (sharing a passion for railway timetables).[31] The Prime Minister, who had an exceptional grasp of policy issues as well as acute political antennae, had clearly decided that it was best to put a good face on unpleasant realities and try to turn them to the government's advantage. That was very much his style. As his rival, Jim Callaghan, admitted, 'Harold Wilson was a fighter who never lacked courage when his back was to the wall'.[32] The Cabinet meetings of January 1968 provided a useful opportunity to re-stamp his authority and show that he and the government were on top of the situation both economically and politically.

As far as the decision on East of Suez was concerned, Wilson knew that it would play well with many in the wider Parliamentary Labour

Party who believed that Britain should be prioritizing European defence, not supporting neo-colonial conflicts in the East. This was a strand of opinion represented by Christopher (later Lord) Mayhew, who published a book about 'Britain's role tomorrow' after resigning his junior ministerial post in 1966. Mayhew wrote that maintaining a worldwide military presence placed an unbearable strain on Britain: 'Instead of bestriding all parts of the globe, we found ourselves falling between all stools, spending huge sums abroad yet increasingly ineffective and isolated.' And a continued British presence East of Suez smacked of colonialism. Echoing sentiments expressed by Attlee in 1950, Mayhew argued that 'Asians, Africans and Arabs increasingly prefer to see the peace kept by people from their own region and race'. Organizations like SEATO, Mayhew said, were 'far too white and far too Western', a sentiment also expressed by Foreign Secretary George Brown in Washington at a SEATO meeting in April 1967.[33] Though this view was neither understood nor shared by the Americans, it had considerable resonance in Britain.

Pro-Europeans of all parties also supported a withdrawal from East of Suez on the grounds that continuing support for US policies in the Far East might prejudice British chances of ever joining the EEC. There had been hints from members of the Six that policies pursued by the British government in response to American pressure were an obstacle to closer linkage with Europe. French President Charles de Gaulle, delivering his second 'non' after Britain reapplied to join the EEC in May 1967, employed this argument. In his case, this may have been little more than a useful excuse, but it is certainly true that the EEC's final rejection of the application in December 1967 was accompanied by disparaging European comments about Britain's economic credibility.[34] As Cabinet Secretary Sir Burke Trend, a valued adviser to the Prime Minister, wrote in a memorandum of 22 December 1967, objections to British membership of the EEC would be reduced greatly if Britain were stronger economically. This was a powerful argument for 'pressing ahead as quickly as possible' with disengagement from the Far East and Middle East 'so as to ensure the early restoration of our economic strength'.[35]

These arguments also fed into the growing groundswell in Britain against the Vietnam War, both among politicians and in the general public. Opposition deepened as the conflict escalated, and increasingly mobile news media transmitted disturbing stories and pictures. There was widespread public protest in the form of marches, sit-ins, plays, and songs. While popular demonstrations do not tend to have much effect on government policy, particularly in respect of foreign affairs, some government ministers were also uneasy about Britain's association with the war through its close relationship with the US. Wilson was forced to employ all his considerable skill and tenacity in treading a delicate line between US pressure and domestic opinion, supporting the Americans over Vietnam by all means short of committing British forces to fight.[36] But as the US devoted more and more men and money to a conflict that made many British people deeply uneasy, opposition continued to grow, and with it opposition to the idea of a permanent British presence in the Far East.

All this was undoubtedly in Harold Wilson's mind as the first of the Cabinet meetings began on 4 January 1968. The government had to be seen to be acting decisively and effectively, not just to rescue the economy but also to boost Labour's domestic reputation—and his own. His handling of the series of meetings was masterly. He wrote later that he had been trained in Cabinet management by Clement Attlee and, like him, was 'rarely disappointed' in getting the result he wanted. Attlee himself, writing after Labour's election victory in 1964, commended Wilson's early performance as a Cabinet minister, saying that he knew what he was talking about, stuck to it, and 'didn't talk too much', a key Attlee virtue. The role of a Prime Minister, Attlee said, was to cultivate the 'group personality' of the Cabinet 'if it is efficient and right-minded; to do his best to modify it, if it is not'.[37]

Wilson's tactics during the January 1968 meetings showed how well he had learned these lessons. His contributions were usually short, low key, but pointed. Roy Jenkins commented that Wilson, although supportive, left the advocacy of the post-devaluation measures to him, showing 'no panache of leadership' and allowing the Cabinet 'to bore itself into exhaustion'.[38] In fact, the minutes show the Prime Minister time and again bringing the discussion back to first principles and summing up in such a way that ensured the desired outcome. Aware that many of the issues in the post-devaluation package would be closely contested, he would 'count the voices' at the end of a discussion (a practice of which some, like Callaghan, disapproved). Votes are not, traditionally, taken in Cabinet. But, said Wilson, 'in this review so much was at stake, and views were so evenly divided, that any attempt to express a consensus, or indeed a majority view, would have been challenged.'[39]

Wilson had picked the right man in **Roy Jenkins** to drive the post-devaluation package through. Even if his choice of Chancellor was based on a desire to keep a close eye on a rival and secure his own position, there is no doubt that Wilson also recognized Jenkins's strength of intellect, parliamentary skills, and determination, already displayed at the Ministry of Aviation and the Home Office.[40] Jenkins came from a Welsh family that had 'Labour Party' running through it like a stick of seaside rock. His father, a miner, had become a Labour MP and Attlee's Parliamentary Private Secretary. As Anthony Howard wrote, 'Insofar as a member of "the people's party" can be born to the purple, Roy Jenkins could plausibly claim that something very like it had happened to him.'[41] Able, ambitious, restless, urbane, and well connected in social as well as Labour circles, Jenkins had been a successful, reforming Home Secretary and now, at 47, saw the Exchequer as his big opportunity. As far as foreign policy was concerned, he saw Britain's future in Europe and had little patience with those who sought to perpetuate what he considered to be outdated and unaffordable global commitments.

Jenkins made it clear from the first of the Cabinet meetings on 4 January that there must be substantial reductions in defence and overseas budgets. But spending in those areas can take a long time to implement and involve extra costs initially. This meant, he said, that it was very important to take firm, long-term decisions 'of such a character as to demonstrate clearly that we were now prepared . . . to cut our coat according to our cloth'. Accordingly, the government should announce that it would withdraw from East of Suez and the Persian Gulf by the end of the financial year 1970/1, together with consequent reductions in defence equipment and personnel and 'a significant reduction in our very substantial purchases of foreign aircraft'. He was not prepared to accept Foreign Office and Commonwealth Relations Office arguments that 1972 was the earliest possible date for withdrawal, not least because that would push the implementation date into the next Parliament. Nor did he accept the arguments of the Ministry of Defence that the F-111 aircraft was essential to British security. The contract, which would cost £400m over the period up to April 1976, offered an opportunity for real savings, and without the East of Suez commitment the aircraft were not needed anyway.[42]

With this, battle was joined. In one corner were the Prime Minister and Chancellor of the Exchequer. In the other were the Secretaries of State for the Commonwealth, for Defence, and for Foreign Affairs. Each side had a roughly equal number of Cabinet supporters. Foreign Secretary **George Brown**, by early 1968, was in self-destructive mode, his drinking barely controlled, and was to resign from the government two months later. In January, however, he was still capable of impassioned and incisive contributions in Cabinet. Brown, who had begun his career as a union official and served on the fringes of the Attlee government, was a talented and energetic politician of strong principle but unpredictable temperament. After a somewhat turbulent stint at the Department of Economic Affairs, he had been delighted by his appointment to the Foreign Office in August 1966 at the age of 53, commenting later that it had brought home to him more than any other government department the 'exciting but also the frightening responsibility of power'. Denis Greenhill, then a Deputy Under-Secretary for Defence and Intelligence, wrote that those who worked closely with him in the Foreign Office 'found they could sometimes forgive his instability, intolerance and cruelty in face of his undoubted brilliance and the rightness of many of his policy aims'.[43]

George Brown's socialism was rooted in his working-class background and he was largely self-educated. As his personal life became increasingly troubled and his drinking more problematic, so his resentment of his more privileged and university-educated colleagues seemed to grow, particularly since Brown rated his own intelligence and abilities highly. All this made him a difficult colleague. Indeed, by January 1968 the tolerance of fellow ministers was stretched almost to breaking point by his increasingly frequent outbursts, and his relations with the Prime Minister—who was extremely tolerant of Brown—were particularly strained. Nonetheless, the Foreign Secretary remained a considerable figure in the Cabinet. As Denis Healey put it in his memoirs, Brown was 'like the immortal Jemima: when he was good he was very, very good, but when he was bad he was horrid'.[44]

Although Brown had a particular interest in Europe—his appointment was seen as an indication that Wilson was serious about another application to the EEC[45]—he made it his business to review British foreign policy as a whole. In his memoirs he recalled how he had been 'not only impressed, but almost oppressed, with the sense of how many issues we were faced with and had to handle at the same time'. He was particularly concerned with Britain's relationship with NATO, which he considered was not really an alliance of fourteen powers, but 'thirteen little chaps who couldn't say "boo" to a goose, the goose being, of course, America'.[46] He accepted, however, the key importance of the US to British and European security, and the need to keep the Americans onside.

He had recognized early in the government the need for a withdrawal from East of Suez and the Middle East, and as Foreign Secretary had played his part in trying to explain the decision taken in the summer of 1967 to the US and Britain's Commonwealth partners. But he also accepted the arguments of his Foreign Office advisers that it would be dangerous to withdraw too quickly. On 4 January 1968 he and the Commonwealth Relations Secretary, George Thomson, argued that 'the earliest date that would be tolerable' for the completion of the rundown of British forces was 31 March 1972.

Brown warned his Cabinet colleagues that a 1971 withdrawal would entail 'serious risks for the stability of the area', possibly even leading to the fall of Lee Kuan Yew's government in Singapore and its replacement by a communist regime. As for the Persian Gulf, he opposed announcing any date for withdrawal, to avoid intervention by other interested powers (such as the Soviet Union) and disruption of oil supplies through disorder in the Gulf States. Even if Britain were to give up being a world power, the Foreign Secretary argued, it would still have global interests and would need friends and allies to defend them. 'We could not afford to flout international opinion in the way the French did.' There was little sign in all this that the Foreign Office had taken on board the full magnitude of the government's problems, or had appreciated fully the determination of Wilson and Jenkins to stick to their post-devaluation guns.

In normal circumstances, Brown and Jenkins got on fairly well, and in preliminary discussions the Chancellor had found the Foreign Secretary open to reason. However, he found Commonwealth Relations Secretary **George Thomson** less amenable. Thomson, who had begun his working life as editor of *The Dandy* and *The Rover*, was a Scottish Fabian Socialist who became a committed European. But he was always closely concerned with Commonwealth issues, and held strong views on the government's responsibilities towards former colonial territories. As Minister of State in the Foreign Office from 1964 to 1966 and then unofficial 'Minister for Europe' as Chancellor of the Duchy of Lancaster from 1966 he had been involved in a range of difficult issues including Aden, the Congo, the Nigerian civil war, and Vietnam.

Denis Healey, an old friend, described Thomson's calm and reasonable approach to difficult problems as having 'a core of steel, which made him an ideal diplomatist during the prolonged and painful renegotiations of our policy outside Europe'. Thomson was leaving for the Far East on 5 January to explain the government's decisions on East of Suez, and at the Cabinet meeting on 4 January demanded to know how to 'explain to our Commonwealth allies why we had been obliged to change our minds about the rate of our withdrawal only a few months after we had assured them that the Defence Review of July 1967 would be the last in the life of this Parliament'. He was particularly concerned about the impact on Singapore, where, he said, British withdrawal would create widespread unemployment and possible instability. The threat would be reduced if withdrawal were spread over a longer period.[47]

While the difference between withdrawal in 1971 and 1972 might seem small enough to be negotiable (and the final decision did include an element of compromise), its significance was as a symbol of the underlying reluctance of many ministers—not only Brown and Thomson—to accept a fundamental change in Britain's world role. (Crossman called it a 'status barrier': like the sound barrier, breaking it 'splits your ears and it's terribly painful when it happens'.) Brown, Thomson, Denis Healey, and Michael Stewart (First Secretary of State, and a former, and future Foreign Secretary) all made long speeches on 4 January arguing for withdrawal to take place by 1972 rather than 1971. Home Secretary **James Callaghan**, now freed from the obligation to represent Treasury views and seeking to position himself as a possible future Prime Minister, supported that view. On the other side Jenkins, Crossman, Castle, and others urged 'that it was essential to have fully withdrawn from the Far East before we went to the country so that we could take full credit for a big decision and for a positive and constructive new policy'.[48] The last bridge, between agreeing that withdrawal was inevitable and setting a definite date for its completion, was still proving very difficult for the Wilson government to cross.

Defence Secretary **Denis Healey**, another dominant figure in the Wilson Cabinet, had his own reasons for supporting the later date for the withdrawal from the Far East. For one thing, it was in line with the views of the armed services, who, as Healey later put it, 'saw our East of Suez role as an opportunity to get a greater share of the defence cake'. 'Besides', he added, perhaps somewhat unfairly, 'they much preferred fighting in the glamorous orient to patrolling the North German plain or the East Atlantic'. Healey, a man of impressive intellect and considerable energy, had spent most of his career in the areas of defence and foreign affairs, but unlike many of his colleagues had not served as a minister until he was appointed Defence Secretary in 1964 at the age of 47. His distinguished military service in the Second World War smoothed his way with senior military figures, although he found the continuous inter-service rivalry and competition for funds particularly trying at a time of severe financial constraint. 'I sometimes felt', he wrote later, 'that I had learned nothing about politics until I met the Chiefs of Staff.'[49]

On becoming Minister of Defence, Healey found himself responsible for very big budgets, and for a very large number of military and civilian staff. He also found that there is a wide a range of departments and individuals who have a vested interest in defence, including the Treasury (which has to find the huge sums required) and the Foreign Office, which relies on defence capability to back up its policies. Every Prime Minister is keenly concerned with defence, and Harold Wilson was no exception: his scientific adviser, Sir Solly Zuckerman, also expected to be kept well informed. And on top of all this, the Minister of Defence has important relationships with overseas analogues, within alliances and partnerships as well as in less formal groupings. Healey was a dominant figure within NATO, and an important interlocutor of the US Chiefs of Staff.

All these people and organizations held views on the direction that British defence should take. Managing expectations and ensuring that obligations are met takes time, just as defence contracts have long lead times and are difficult to alter or terminate quickly. Like most of his colleagues, Healey accepted the need for British forces to withdraw from East of Suez, and understood the necessity for cuts in defence spending. But he also believed that it was important for Britain to maintain the capacity to protect its global interests, and those of its friends and allies, by force if necessary. Healey considered the way British forces had been used in the Indonesian Confrontation, for example, as a 'textbook demonstration of how to apply economy of force, under political guidance for political ends'.[50] The ability to take this kind of action required some residual capability, or having agreements in place with local partners—which also took time to negotiate.

The problem, the Defence Secretary argued, was how to manage a contraction of Britain's global commitments without loss of influence or regional stability. For Healey, that meant retaining a high level of independent military capability, including strike fighter aircraft like the fifty F-111s he planned to buy from the Americans.[51] Cancellation of that contract was, he told the Cabinet on 4 January, 'the last step which the Government should contemplate if they were to pay proper regard to defence needs'. Without a British presence East of Suez, the F-111s would be even more important than before. Without them, Britain would be entirely dependent for air cover on American or French aircraft, which was unacceptable. The Chancellor replied that on the contrary, it was only sensible. The F-111 aircraft had always been intended for use East of Suez, rather than in Europe, and in any case fifty fighter aircraft would not enable Britain to act independently. 'None of our European partners', said Jenkins, 'had thought it necessary to provide such aircraft themselves; and it was unacceptable for us, in a weaker economic position, to do so.' Britain's partners in NATO were content to rely on the United States' capability: 'we should do likewise.' It would be indefensible to press ahead with drastic cuts in civil spending while spending £400m on fighter aircraft.

Technology Minister **Tony Benn** supported this argument. On the left wing of the Labour Party, he was disposed to agree with those who argued that a major change in defence policy was not only necessary but desirable, although he was prepared to fight hard to protect projects such as *Concorde* in which his department had a major stake in respect of investment in technology. As far as East of Suez was concerned, Benn wrote that he 'could see little credibility in a lame duck military presence on borrowed money and the best thing to do was to speed up the withdrawal'. The F-111 contract was more difficult. Its cancellation might prejudice orders for British equipment, such as Rolls-Royce engines for the American Airbus project. But if the F-111 contract were not cancelled, then something else, such as British-made Harrier aircraft or the Polaris nuclear deterrent, would have to be given up. The decisive argument, however, was that Benn found it 'inconceivable that we could change our defence role and maintain the same hardware purchases'. Although Healey dismissed Benn's argument as fallacious, the decision was obviously finely balanced.[52]

In the end, Wilson, Jenkins, and their supporters insisted that the 1971 date must stand, and the minutes record that the Cabinet so agreed. But in view of the strength of feeling displayed during the long meeting (it began at 3 p.m. and finished at 7.30), it was agreed that if Brown returned from Washington and Thomson from the Far East reporting a 'strong reaction' to their notification of the 'accelerated' withdrawal, they might 'invite' the Cabinet to reconsider. This meant, effectively, that the decision was deferred. Transport Minister **Barbara Castle**, who had written approvingly in her diary that 'the defence package would give the much-needed psychological impetus, not only to the Party, but to many others who had been urging for years that Britain should find a realistic role,' noted that she, Tony Benn, and Peter Shore (Secretary of State for Economic Affairs) looked at each other grimly when the delay was agreed: 'We don't intend to let the slippery eels get away with it.' Similarly, the Cabinet agreed that Healey could, if he wished, 'propose alternative economies with a view to securing defence savings no less than would be secured by cancelling the order for F-111 aircraft'.[53]

The Chancellor, naturally, was keen to achieve the full range of savings he considered essential, with the Prime Minister's support. In response, it was predictable that ministers such as Healey would fight to protect their own projects. It was also understandable that the Foreign Secretary and Commonwealth Secretary, about to set off for what they anticipated would be difficult conversations in Washington and the Far East, should wish to leave some wriggle room in order to make their talks more meaningful. But two aspects of the discussion on 4 January were notable, one for its presence and one for its absence. First, the political and public impact of the expenditure cuts was clearly in ministers' minds: it was emphasized again and again, in this and later meetings, that the package had to be credible and fair. Second, although ministers were well aware that the US government opposed both the early withdrawal from East of Suez and the cancellation of the F-111 contract, potential American reactions to the decisions were hardly mentioned.

Between 4 and 12 January there were heated discussions in Cabinet on all elements of the post-devaluation package. On 5 January the contentious issue of postponing the raising of the school-leaving age produced a passionate outburst from George Brown, who accused the Chancellor and the Education Secretary, **Patrick Gordon Walker**, of perpetuating class distinctions by cutting secondary rather than university education. According to Barbara Castle, Brown maintained that the lack of a proper education 'rankled all one's life', provoking the comment from Harold Wilson that 'no one would notice any deprivation in you, Foreign Secretary'. But as Gordon Walker noted in his diary, it was preferable to put off raising the school-leaving age than to bring a 'most powerful interest' down upon the government by cutting universities, which would also mean cutting spending on science. Jenkins agreed, though he later wrote that he had been very uneasy about postponing raising the school-leaving age, particularly because in what he called an 'almost ludicrously Oxonian Cabinet' it was those without a university education, Brown, Callaghan, and Minister of Labour Ray Gunter, who protested most strongly. However, he felt that 'the measures had to be driven through in four columns abreast, and that if I weakened on one because of my personal predilections the exercise would be dead'. The raising of the school-leaving age from 15 to 16 was postponed by two years.[54]

The final element of the 'controversial quadrilateral', the reintroduction of prescription charges, also provoked heated argument before it was finally decided on 11 January that a charge of 2*s*. 6*d*. would be imposed, but with special exemptions for the elderly and other vulnerable people. Both the school-leaving age and prescription charges were only settled by a very narrow majority. Other issues, including Britain's participation in the Anglo-French *Concorde* project, the scrapping of a road-building scheme, cuts in the Ministry of Technology's defence research budget, and the costs of maintaining and possibly improving Polaris warheads, also aroused strong feelings. By Friday, 12 January, therefore, when the East of Suez decision was to be revisited, some were disappointed, some were angry, and all were tired. Tony Benn noted that after being up working until 2.30 a.m. for four nights in a row, he had to have a nap at lunchtime.[55]

Two Cabinet meetings were held on 12 January, one beginning at 11 a.m. and one at 2.30 p.m. In the morning, ministers agreed on reductions in the overseas aid budget, accepted reluctantly by **Reginald Prentice**, Minister for Overseas Development. He pointed out that the costs of aid had been increased by the devaluation of sterling, and that it would be difficult to meet Britain's obligations even without the cuts. Again, the credibility of the post-devaluation package was raised: Britain should not be seen to adopt a more generous attitude to overseas aid than other developed countries, particularly the US which was also restricting its aid budget. Even with the cuts, however, the Chief Secretary to the Treasury, **John Diamond**, explained that certain obligations were unavoidable. Government expenditure overseas would rise from £338m in 1967/8 to £381m in 1968/9, including £21m of military aid, principally to Southern Yemen. Ministers found these figures worrying, and the Prime Minister wondered whether, in the light of 'our changed position in the world', British overseas representation should be cut back. (Resentment at the supposed extravagance of diplomatic missions usually crops up when governments are looking for savings.) **Fred Mulley**, the FO Minister of State, pointed out that British missions abroad were vital to promote exports, and would be even more important in areas from which the military were being withdrawn.[56]

Towards the end of the morning meeting **Anthony Crosland**, the President of the Board of Trade, mounted an attack on the whole approach the Chancellor of the Exchequer was taking in the post-devaluation measures. Crosland had hoped, and indeed expected to become Chancellor on Callaghan's resignation in November 1967. In her biography of him, Crosland's wife gives a vivid account of the period while waiting to hear who would succeed Callaghan, describing herself, like the wives of Callaghan and Healey (another Treasury contender) as feeling worried and sick. Crosland was a former economics don (like Wilson), a creative thinker and Labour modernizer of considerable style, though somewhat abrasive and impatient. He was 'dismayed and depressed' when his old friend Roy Jenkins—whom he regarded as junior to himself—got the job that Callaghan had as good as promised to him. Jenkins, in his memoirs, expressed the view that although Crosland was 'cleverer than I was and substantially more skilled in economics', Wilson found him difficult to get on with, and thought Jenkins the more skilled parliamentarian. It also solved the problem of what to do with Callaghan. Crosland, then aged 49, was appointed as President of the Board of Trade, but his relations with Jenkins remained strained.[57]

On 12 January Crosland argued that it was unrealistic to aim at reducing aggregate demand by £1,000m; £750m would be a wiser target. He also thought that only £400m should be found through cuts in public expenditure. Higher taxes on consumer spending would, he said, be 'politically acceptable in the present climate of opinion'. Crosland particularly opposed cuts in the education budget, and regarded the postponement of raising the school-leaving age as the decision that 'stood out among all the others as the only one which ran counter to the Government's basic personal principles'. Finally, he challenged Jenkins's assertion that it was necessary for the government to decide now on an overall figure for savings that would govern future economic policy. It would, Crosland said, 'be necessary over the next 12 months to be flexible in managing demand to match the situation as it developed'.

Jenkins replied that the way the situation was developing at present, it would be necessary to reduce demand more, rather than less. Even with cuts of £800m he would still need to raise taxes in order to reduce demand sufficiently, and some of the measures agreed, such as changes in family allowances and NHS charges, would reduce the capacity of people to pay tax. Although Crosland received some support for his views (including from George Brown, who had just arrived straight from the airport), before breaking for lunch the Cabinet agreed that the level of cuts should be upheld. 'Public opinion at all levels was now expecting strong action, and it would be disastrous if the Government's measures were thought to be too timid either in their total effect or in respect of particular measures.' However, they also agreed to resume discussions on the balance of the package, and Tony Benn noted in his diary that Jenkins, 'having been challenged in this way', agreed to justify the measures he had drawn up.[58]

The Cabinet reconvened after lunch. George Brown, who had had a nap but was still tired and emotional, gave the Cabinet a report of a 'bloody unpleasant' interview the previous day with the US Secretary of State, Dean Rusk. Barbara Castle called it a 'masterly piece of dramatic rendering' to which his colleagues listened in silence 'as he thundered on for half an hour, merely raising an eyebrow at his more purple passages'. Brown said that Rusk had professed himself 'shocked and dismayed' by the announcement that the British government proposed to withdraw from the Far East and the Persian Gulf by the end of March 1971, and to cancel its order for F-111 aircraft.

Britain was, Rusk said, opting out of its world responsibilities. The only way to avoid 'irreparable damage' to Anglo-American relations, according to Rusk, was for the British government to reverse the decision to cancel the aircraft order and extend the time limit for withdrawal to 1972. He admitted that the US government was more worried about withdrawal from the Gulf than from the Far East, where 'they were hopeful of bringing the Viet-Nam war to a fairly early conclusion and thereafter of being able to exercise sufficient influence in the area from their island bases in the Pacific'. Rusk's views had been endorsed in a further interview with a State Department official, who according to Brown, said: 'You're not going to be in the Far East. You're not going to be in the Middle East. You're not even going to be in Europe in strength. Where are you going to be?'[59]

The Foreign Secretary thought there was no good answer to this question. He was clearly shaken by his experience, and even those who disagreed with him were impressed by the force of his presentation. Brown urged his Cabinet colleagues to postpone withdrawal from the Far East, to give no date for Middle East withdrawal, and to proceed with the F-111 order. In this he received support from Jim Callaghan, who argued that it would be disastrous for Britain if the US 'gave up on them'. Denis Healey agreed, arguing that if Britain withdrew *outside* Europe, the US would tend to withdraw *from* Europe—thus making British military capability (such as the F-111s) even more important. **Lord Longford**, Lord Privy Seal, worried that if the government ignored Brown's warnings the future would be grim.

The warnings were reinforced by a report from FO Minister of State, **Goronwy Roberts**, who reported on a visit to the Persian Gulf. Reactions to his announcement that Britain intended to withdraw its forces by March 1971 had, he said, ranged from a readiness to make alternative arrangements to 'downright panic'. All agreed, however, that three years was too short a period to allow for the resolution of border disputes so that stability could be maintained when the British had gone. (The Minister of Labour, **Ray Gunter**, expressed doubts that these disputes would be settled however many years the British remained there.) Roberts, like Brown, told the Cabinet that withdrawal from the Persian Gulf should be delayed and no date for it announced.

As in previous discussions, a number of ministers were very worried about the consequences of going against the wishes of the United States (although some, like Crosland and Gordon Walker, said they felt Britain had already paid a heavy price for American friendship). But the Prime Minister was unimpressed by these anxieties, and by the apocalyptic warnings of his Foreign Secretary. His statements on the afternoon of 12 January are particularly interesting, as they give a clear indication of the broader considerations that underlay his approach to the whole post-devaluation package. In particular, they show the extent to which his handling of the issue was influenced by domestic political considerations. The US Administration was, he thought, doing exactly the same thing. His understanding of this no doubt emboldened him to take a strong line against American attempts to bully the British government into changing course.

Wilson told the Cabinet that it was unwise to underestimate the extent to which the US Administration was affected by domestic politics. 1968 was a presidential election year, and Johnson's government was worried about a swing towards isolationism. The Americans had been told in July 1967 that Britain was pulling out from East of Suez; only the date had changed. They had not thought to consult the British before announcing their damaging economic measures on 1 January. Rusk could not now complain that the decision to withdraw from East of Suez or cancel the F-111 order was a fait accompli. The time had come, Wilson said, to look after British interests first, whether the Americans liked it or not.

'Our common interests', Wilson said, 'were frequently frustrated by the United States Administration's regard for their public opinion. He recognized that they had their domestic difficulties; they should also recognize that we had ours.' If the US tried to punish the British economically, the latter could reply in kind. He had already told the Americans that Britain could not continue to tolerate an arrangement whereby all West Germany's foreign exchange was used to pay for the cost of maintaining US forces there, while the British had to find the money to pay for theirs. It was a tough speech from a Prime Minister who had worked so hard on the Anglo-American relationship since 1964. As Barbara Castle put it, 'he's certainly travelled a long way since those early days of bonhomie with Johnson!' But it was based on cold political calculation, and the belief that the government's credibility rested on how it handled the economic crisis.[60]

A final decision on East of Suez could not be taken until the following Monday, when George Thomson would report back on his visit to Malaysia, Singapore, Australia, and New Zealand. Meanwhile, the Cabinet turned to a discussion of defence cuts and the F-111 contract. Again, Healey presented his arguments powerfully, putting forward suggestions for alternative savings and warning that drastic cuts could endanger the lives of British servicemen and damage their morale, as well as making nuclear war more likely. The Prime Minister also admitted that the Chiefs of Staff had made 'legitimate and reasonable' representations to him. However, neither he nor Jenkins was willing to give way. Tony Benn, summing up in his diary what he described as 'an intensely interesting policy discussion...a thing we never normally have', commented that Healey had behaved with 'enormous courage and dignity in the face of a shattering blow, quite as great for him as devaluation was for Jim Callaghan'.[61]

In many ways the meetings on 12 January proved to be the climax of the series of Cabinet meetings insofar as defence and overseas spending were concerned. The battle lines were drawn, and each side had made its arguments clear. Above all, the Prime Minister had not wavered in his support for the Chancellor's adamant refusal to change his measures in any material way. The arguments made over the weekend by the Prime Minister of Singapore, Lee Kuan Yew, who was 'in a very excitable state', had no effect other than to convince Wilson and Jenkins that Lee wanted the presence of British forces to remain more for his own political and economic ends than out of any real military need. When the Cabinet reassembled at 10 a.m. on Monday 15 January, it seemed at first as if the Prime Minister was still undecided. He had circulated to the Cabinet two telegrams he had received from President Johnson, expressing outrage at the decision to withdraw British forces in 1971, and threatening retaliation for cancellation of the F-111 contract. (George Brown also produced a document: a letter from the Governor of the Bank of England to Sir William Armstrong at the Treasury, apparently warning of the consequences for sterling of withdrawing from Singapore and Malaysia, though this turned out to be a red herring.[62])

The Commonwealth Secretary, back from the Far East, now reiterated the arguments against withdrawal from East of Suez and the Gulf by 1971. He stressed how much the governments of Malaysia, Singapore, Australia, and New Zealand felt the British government was letting them down, and considered the F-111 aircraft essential to the credibility of the British defence effort. He had also been lobbied (as had Goronwy Roberts in the Gulf) by local British representatives unhappy about the decision to pull out. On 15 January Thomson urged that the date for withdrawal should be fixed at 1972, in the interests of peace and stability in the Far East, and of continued friendly relations with the Commonwealth countries concerned. The strength of his presentation, together with the barely veiled threats in the American telegrams, had an effect on the Cabinet. Even Barbara Castle confessed herself 'a bit shaken'. But the Prime Minister 'cheerfully dismissed' the US threats, assuring the Cabinet that when he saw President Johnson in Australia he could not have been friendlier, and understood the British position. 'After all, America was very good at looking after number one and would respect us for doing the same.'[63]

Wilson now tipped the balance of the argument conclusively in his and the Chancellor's favour by suggesting a compromise: withdrawal from the Far East and from the Gulf would be completed by the end of 1971, rather than in March. This concession would, he said, demonstrate that the British government had taken account of the views of its friends and allies. With that, the battle was won. The Cabinet agreed that 'the withdrawal of our forces from Singapore and Malaysia and from the Persian Gulf should be completed by the end of the calendar year 1971'. And after a last ditch attempt by the Defence Secretary, who warned that cancellation of the F-111 contract would lead to the loss of orders by British defence contractors, the Cabinet agreed that the decision to cancel should not be reviewed.[64] With a statement due in the

House of Commons the following day, and a parliamentary debate, there was no possibility of leaving either decision open any longer. Final decisions on the domestic cuts were taken at the last Cabinet meeting on the Monday afternoon. By this time, as Barbara Castle put it, the Cabinet felt the whole package was 'so precariously linked together that we dare not disturb any single part of it'. There seems little doubt that this had, throughout the meetings, been the Prime Minister's intention. Some ministers were bitterly disappointed. But others, like Castle, felt that the package was 'a sophisticated combination of principle and expediency'. That, she said was 'what politics is about'.[65]

No government, whatever its political complexion, likes having to implement large reductions in public expenditure. Cuts are always difficult and unpopular, not just with the public whose jobs, services, and standard of living may be affected, but with ministers whose departmental budgets are hit. Every decision has a knock-on effect, and the pressure is increased by the knowledge that the financial markets are waiting to see what happens and are only too ready to react negatively if they disapprove of or distrust the result. Cuts in domestic spending force changes in government policy, risk industrial unrest, and threaten economic slowdown. To governments looking for big savings, overseas budgets may seem a logical and even attractive target. The sums involved are large and the impact on public opinion perceived as less negative. But cuts in those areas are very difficult to implement, have a long lead time, and have far-reaching implications for international obligations and national security.

All this was as true in 1968 as it is more than forty years later and it underlay each of those long and difficult Cabinet meetings. In hindsight, the decisions taken in 1968 on foreign policy issues may seem to some extent almost a foregone conclusion, and the dire consequences predicted by those on both sides of the argument unnecessarily alarmist. Britain continued to see itself as an important player on the global stage, if one with reduced responsibilities. Relations with the United States continued to be of prime importance. The economic situation improved, but was still precarious. But the Cabinet meetings held that January did represent a significant milestone in the evolution of British foreign policy. Britain still had a world role, but it had changed.

Edward Heath (*right*) and Sir Alec Douglas-Home (*left*), 1970

5

Challenging the KGB

Operation FOOT, September 1971

*The expulsion of 105 spies was the most important security action
ever taken by any Western government.**

On a cool but sunny Tuesday afternoon, 21 September 1971, Conservative Prime Minister Edward Heath held a secret meeting of ministers
and senior officials in 10 Downing Street, to decide whether and when to
tell the Soviet government that a large number of its representatives in
the United Kingdom, employed in their embassy, trade delegation, and
other organizations, were to be expelled for 'inadmissible activities'—in
other words, spying. The codename for the proposed operation, whose
details were classified top secret, was FOOT.[1] Three days later, Sir Denis
Greenhill, the Permanent Under-Secretary of State at the Foreign and
Commonwealth Office (FCO), gave a shocked Ivan Ippolitov, the Soviet
Chargé d'Affaires, a list of 105 officials who had to go. Those in the
country must leave within two weeks; those currently overseas would not
be allowed to return. What is more, the Soviets would not be permitted
to replace the expelled officials. 'We have', said Greenhill, 'been patient
long enough.'[2]

Operation FOOT remains the single largest expulsion of intelligence
officials by any country.[3] London had often engaged with Moscow in tit-
for-tat expulsions of a few diplomats at a time, the most recent episode
only a few months earlier in 1971. It was part of the Cold War game.
A move on the scale of Operation FOOT was, however, unprecedented,
and sent shock waves through not just the Kremlin, but through the
international community as a whole (not least because such a dramatic

---

* Edward Heath, *The Course of My Life* (London, 1998).

stroke seemed distinctly un-British). Espionage may be a fact of life, but governments rarely talk of it openly nor bring it willingly to public notice. We now know, from sources such as the material smuggled out of the USSR by KGB archivist Vasili Mitrokhin,[4] that Soviet espionage in the 1960s and 1970s was massive both in scope and in numbers. Most Western governments had taken steps in the 1960s to try and cut down the number of Soviet representatives (or at least to demand similar increases for their own Moscow staffs). But a mass expulsion of spies, instead of quietly asking them to leave individually, would undoubtedly attract widespread publicity, and no one knew how the Soviet government, under Party leader Leonid Brezhnev, might react. How did the Conservative government elected in June 1970 and led by Edward Heath come to such a bold—some thought foolhardy—decision?

Full details of Operation FOOT and the events that led up to it were not made public officially by the British government until 1998, though the expulsion of the Soviet officials was widely reported in the media at the time, with photographs of queues of disconsolate Russians waiting to board aeroplanes at Heathrow.[5] A few of those involved have mentioned the episode in their memoirs, with varying degrees of discretion but with a universal tendency to claim credit for the decision—understandably, since in hindsight Operation FOOT was a Cold War coup for the British government both in intelligence and foreign policy terms. But on that September afternoon in 1971, the decision seemed extremely risky.

The Foreign and Commonwealth Office had drawn up a list of possible consequences, worst case being a complete rupture of Anglo-Soviet relations for the first time since 1927.[6] At the very least, FOOT seemed likely to produce a period of increased East–West tension, trade disruption, and stalled negotiations, not to mention reprisals against Britons working or doing business in the Soviet Union or Warsaw Pact countries. Even at the height of the Cold War, East and West shared many global policy concerns, and were involved in a wide range of negotiations and treaty obligations. Everyone present at the meeting on 21 September was concerned about the potentially damaging consequences of a decision to go ahead with an operation that could disrupt the uneasy political and economic Cold War balance.

Yet clearly something had to be done. The numbers employed in Soviet missions in the UK had by the mid-1960s reached record levels, and though a ceiling was imposed on the size of the embassy in 1968 the Russians had sidestepped it by filling the Soviet Trade Delegation with intelligence officers and by making use of 'working wives'. By the spring of 1971 there were nearly as many working in the Trade Delegation as in the embassy, and the total of Soviet officials in the UK (plus wives) was not far short of 1,000, higher than in any other Western country.[7] The Security Service, or MI5, the UK's domestic intelligence agency, believed that possibly a quarter of these were engaged in 'undiplomatic activities', including running secret agents, and warned ministers in May that government departments (including the Ministry of Defence), all three armed services, and the Labour Party had been penetrated. Flagship projects like the Anglo-French supersonic aircraft *Concorde* (which had just made its first transatlantic flight) and the Bristol Olympus 593 aero engine were known targets, together with British computer companies and nuclear energy plants.[8] MI5, preoccupied with internal investigations and hampered by scarce resources and the difficulty of bringing successful prosecutions, could not cope with this enormous growth of the KGB (Soviet security service) and GRU (military intelligence) residencies in London.[9]

During the spring and summer of 1971, schemes for tackling the problem, whether by negotiation, expulsion, or insistence on parity between the British and Soviet embassies in Moscow and London, had been worked out by the Foreign and Commonwealth Office and intelligence agencies, though no action was envisaged before the end of the year. Then a series of events in late summer made a decision imperative. On 30 August a British naval officer, David Bingham, confessed he had been passing information to the Russians. On the same day Oleg Lyalin, a KGB double agent who had been supplying information to MI5, was arrested for drink-driving in Tottenham Court Road (protesting that the police could do nothing as 'I am a KGB officer!').[10] He decided to defect rather than obey a summons to Moscow.

Lyalin had been providing MI5 with details of the London activities of the KGB's Department V, specializing in sabotage and covert action, and though some of his revelations appeared a little far-fetched (such as plans for a naval attack on the Yorkshire coast), the intelligence agencies thought his defection might provoke a reaction.[11] There was a risk that the Russians might have got wind of the plans to curb their activities in the UK and might try a pre-emptive strike: a virulent press campaign against British ministers was a clear sign the Soviet government was rattled. The Foreign Secretary, Sir Alec Douglas-Home, was about to leave for United Nations meetings in New York, where he would meet his

Soviet counterpart. If Operation FOOT were to go ahead, it would be best to do it before they met.

The meeting held on 21 September 1971 was not a formal Cabinet meeting and no record was circulated. The decisions taken were recorded in a letter from the Private Secretary at No. 10 to those who had been present.[12] Round the table in Downing Street were the Prime Minister, Edward Heath; the Foreign Secretary, Sir Alec Douglas-Home, with his Permanent Under-Secretary Sir Denis Greenhill; the Home Secretary, Reginald Maudling, with his Permanent Secretary Sir Philip Allen; the Secretary of State for Trade and Industry, John Davies; the Defence Secretary, Lord Carrington; the Lord President of the Council, William Whitelaw; and the Cabinet Secretary, Sir Burke Trend, with Peter Moon of the No. 10 staff taking the note. Though the decision to be taken was based on secret intelligence, no member of the UK's intelligence agencies was present. They had presented their evidence and advice, and it was now for ministers to decide. Indeed, not all ministers present were privy to the details of the evidence, but each had a vested interest in the outcome.

Anything that could have potentially drastic consequences for Britain's relations with the Eastern bloc was the business of the Foreign Secretary, just as anything that threatened the security of the realm was the business of the Home Secretary. Those consequences included the disruption of commerce, the concern of the Secretary for Trade and Industry, as well as the possibility of a hostile military response, the Defence Secretary's business. The Lord President was there to advise on party and parliamentary angles, for it was clear that if FOOT went ahead it might impact on other government plans. The two permanent secretaries had not only been involved in preparatory discussions but were also their ministers' links with the intelligence agencies—Greenhill with the foreign intelligence agency, the Secret Intelligence Service (SIS, or MI6) and with the signals intelligence agency, Government Communications Headquarters (GCHQ); Allen with the Security Service or MI5. Trend, as Cabinet Secretary, was closely involved with intelligence matters insofar as they affected the business of government.

Edward Heath, chairing the meeting, may well have felt impatient at having to devote Tuesday afternoon to dealing with Russian spies. As a man, his twin personal passions were music and sailing; as Prime Minister, they were to secure Britain's admission to the European Economic Community, and to restore her global reputation. Anglo-Soviet relations were not high on his list of priorities (in fact, he distrusted everything about the Soviet Union except its musicians). Nor had he any particular interest in secret intelligence, unless it could warn him about industrial troublemakers. Heath later told Peter Hennessy that he felt it was a 'very real problem' that the Prime Minister could not always know what was going on in the intelligence agencies, although he was 'fortunate in having colleagues who were first of all able to judge the things which went beyond themselves and secondly only too ready to come and talk to me about it'. He had not been impressed by his early meetings with intelligence chiefs, particularly the Director-General of MI5, Sir Martin Furnival Jones.[13]

Nevertheless, Heath recognized the force of warnings of Soviet penetration, which not only threatened national security but also damaged the government's reputation both internationally and in the country, where press reports about Soviet spies roaming the shires unchecked stimulated discontent among Conservative backbenchers. Not long after taking office, he had been disturbed by an article in the *Daily Express* by Chapman Pincher, alleging that British intelligence had been 'downgraded below the safe limit', and criticizing the appointment of ex-diplomat Sir John Rennie as Chief of MI6: 'the accent is on diplomacy rather than defence'.[14] Though reassured by the Cabinet Secretary, Heath felt that firm action to restore the reputation of the UK's intelligence establishment was overdue.

As well as impatience, the Prime Minister felt resentment towards his predecessor, Harold Wilson. Soviet espionage was, in Heath's view, only one of many issues the Labour government had handled badly between 1964 and 1970. Wilson and his colleagues, though well aware of the problem caused by increasing numbers of Soviet spies, had done little to tackle it, principally to avoid disrupting Anglo-Soviet relations. The Foreign Office, despite their concern over Soviet activities, had supported this strategy, including the decision in 1969 to exchange Soviet spies Helen and Peter Kroger for Gerald Brooke, a British citizen imprisoned in Russia.[15] Early in 1970, however, Greenhill warned that the British government had 'slipped into a position where we appeared to regard the present (high) level of Soviet intelligence activity here as reasonable. This was not good enough.' Members of Parliament, if they knew what was going on, would, the Permanent Under-Secretary said, demand to know why nothing had been done to stop it. He urged ministers to tackle the Russians on the subject.[16]

Despite Greenhill's advice, this did not happen. Every Labour government since 1924 had had an uncomfortable and ambivalent relationship with the Soviet Union. Greenhill wrote in his memoirs that senior members of the Labour Party often seemed ill at ease with Soviet leaders, 'as if they were nonconformists meeting the Pope'.[17] Some sections of the Labour movement were also very hostile towards the British security services, and unwilling to accept MI5's word that a large number of Soviet spies were operating in the UK. Harold Wilson had his own suspicions of the security services,[18] though as Prime Minister he maintained a good professional relationship with the intelligence agencies. But he and his colleagues had in any case to consider wider international ramifications.

Concern about Soviet espionage was tempered by the desire not to lose out either diplomatically or commercially to other European countries like France, only too ready to mop up lucrative contracts if the British and Russians fell out. Close Anglo-Soviet links were also encouraged by US President Lyndon Johnson, as a back channel to Hanoi in his attempts to secure an end to the war in Vietnam; this was one reason for Wilson's visit to Moscow in 1968.[19] What is more, following the tension produced by the Soviet invasion of Czechoslovakia in August 1968, the Russians showed signs of being more accommodating towards the West on a range of issues, such as trade and European security. They began to play a useful part in arms limitation and Middle East peace talks, and even agreed to a treaty with West Germany as a result of Chancellor Willy Brandt's *Ostpolitik*. For the Labour government, the potential advantages of harmonious Anglo-Soviet relations and wider *détente* trumped the concerns of the intelligence community and departmental officials. Britain did not want to be left behind its NATO allies in reaping the benefits of a lessening of East–West tension. The problem of the Soviet spies was accordingly bequeathed to their successors: the meeting called by Prime Minister Edward Heath on 21 September 1971 had to try and solve it.

It is a pity that Edward Heath is now often remembered as he was in later years, a disappointed, isolated, and rather bitter old man, heavy and slow-moving. In 1971, he was 55, vigorous and at the height of his powers a year after scoring a notable election victory to oust Harold Wilson from Downing Street. A tough, formidable and highly motivated politician, he had prepared himself and the Conservative Party thoroughly for office while in opposition.[20] He had moved into Downing Street with strong views on how the government and the country should be run, and was, as Lord Carrington later put it, more interested in 'results and realities' than in party politics (despite the years he had spent in the Whips' office). His Cabinet, as Peter Hennessy says, was 'a businesslike affair, run as a tight ship'.[21] By nature solitary, with no partner or close family, impatient of social niceties, Heath could appear autocratic and abrasive, but inspired respect and often loyalty from his colleagues, even if they found him hard to know well. Always on top of his brief, he was generally decisive, but on an issue like Operation FOOT he was naturally cautious, willing to listen to advice but anxious to be clear as to the potential impact of any decision on other areas of government policy. And in September 1971, the Heath government faced a formidable array of serious difficulties.

Most pressing was Northern Ireland, where a breakdown in law and order had led to the introduction of internment on 9 August, and to the early recall of Parliament. Since then there had been hundreds of arrests, some deaths and an escalating spiral of violence, as well as strikes and accusations of brutality by the security forces. The Queen, Heath wrote later, was 'horrified' by the violence, but he had accepted the necessity for internment reluctantly, aware that British policy might alienate both the Americans and the EEC. Although the Anglo-American relationship was, as always, central to British policy, Heath was not as close to President Richard Nixon as Wilson had been to Johnson, and some strain was caused in August 1971 when the US government had suddenly imposed a freeze on wages and prices, suspended the convertibility of the dollar, and imposed a tax on imports, all of which had a damaging effect on the already struggling British economy. Meanwhile, relations with the trade unions were deteriorating and widespread strikes were threatened in protest at the government's industrial relations policy, while state intervention to bail out Rolls-Royce and other key companies was causing considerable unrest in the Conservative Party.

The Prime Minister, a committed pro-European, was also anxious about the forthcoming parliamentary debate, scheduled for October 1971, on the conditions under which Britain might enter the EEC. After the rejection of British applications in 1963 and 1967, the prospect of success—Heath's long-held ambition—at last seemed within reach after his successful meeting with French President Pompidou in May. Both sides of the House were divided on Europe, however, and Heath also worried about his future European partners' reaction if Britain caused a major row with the Russians. His instincts were for firm action to remedy a situation he regarded as unacceptable, and he had announced in the House of Commons on 17 June that the Foreign Secretary would 'soon' be making a statement on reducing the number of foreign spies. Nevertheless, he desired reassurance on the possible fallout.

The man responsible for providing that reassurance was Foreign Secretary **Sir Alec Douglas-Home**, at 67 the oldest member of the Cabinet, whose role at the meeting on 21 September was to persuade his colleagues that FOOT should go ahead immediately and was worth the risk. He had, of course, held several ministerial posts in the Foreign Office during his long career, including serving as Macmillan's Foreign Secretary from 1960,[22] until he relinquished his peerage to succeed him as Prime Minister in 1963. A man of little personal vanity, Douglas-Home found the Foreign Office both congenial and stimulating. He had agreed readily to return there in 1970 under Heath, who relied on him and his judgement in all areas of foreign policy, while retaining personal control of the EEC negotiations. It was, according to one analysis of the Heath government, 'immensely helpful' for the Prime Minister to have 'an experienced, respected elder statesman holding together the traditional strands of British diplomacy (and reassuring conservative opinion both at home and abroad) while he pushed on with the transformational initiative of Europe'.[23]

Pragmatic and tough, though deceptively languid in style—Macmillan described him as 'iron painted to look like wood'—Douglas-Home was an old hand at dealing with the Russians and in particular with the veteran Soviet Foreign Minister Andrei Gromyko, who had been in the job since 1957. To some officials Douglas-Home's approach seemed simplistic. It was an image it suited him to foster, writing in his memoirs, for example, that the individual Russian was 'a naturally friendly and gay person, but the Communist system is like a wet blanket and stifles fun'.[24] Foreign Office files for the period, however, reveal his close and penetrating interest in policy detail, his distinctive handwriting much in evidence. As Foreign Secretary, Douglas-Home had ministerial responsibility for MI6 and GCHQ, and in contrast to the Prime Minister had a natural feel for intelligence matters and an understanding for the importance of deception and surprise: factors that were central to the success of any move against the Soviet Union.

Douglas-Home understood that from the Soviet point of view Britain's post-war influence was much diminished, and that as the perceived junior partner to the United States, and physically outside continental Europe where the Cold War frontline lay, it did not deserve any special consideration. It was notable that Brezhnev's 1971 report to the Communist Party Congress, often an important indicator of Soviet thinking, barely mentioned Britain. Nevertheless, Douglas-Home knew that less influence did not mean no influence. The Soviets were well aware Britain still had plenty of weight in the world, though doubting its willingness to throw it about. Like his Labour predecessors George Brown and Michael Stewart, Douglas-Home also understood the importance of keeping on good terms with the Russians and encouraging *détente*, at a time when Britain faced serious problems on the foreign as well as the domestic front. There was fighting on the Indo-Pakistan border, a Commonwealth row over the British export of arms to South Africa, a worrying naval build-up in the Indian Ocean, trouble in Ceylon (Sri Lanka), Malta, Rhodesia, the Middle East, and in South East Asia, where the Vietnam War dragged on. On most of these questions Britain was either openly at odds with the Soviet bloc or suspected their involvement in inciting trouble in order to increase their sphere of influence.

A Foreign Office planning paper of May 1971 listed Soviet aims: to undermine Western influence in the Persian Gulf and the Arab world, to gain greater influence over India and check Chinese influence in Africa, to encourage the formation of Soviet-friendly governments in countries like Somalia and Mauritius, to acquire naval and air facilities in the Indian Ocean area, and to undermine the credibility of Western defence arrangements in South East Asia.[25] Yet when the Soviet Ambassador in London, M. Smirnovsky, announced in May 1971 that the main aims of Soviet foreign policy were the elimination of conflict in South East Asia and the Middle East, renunciation of the use of force, and the promotion of peace and *détente* in Europe, Douglas-Home could not afford to be too openly sceptical. Of particular importance was Soviet participation in multilateral talks on disarmament and the Middle East, and issues of European security, including the future of divided Germany and of Berlin.

Berlin, situated in Soviet-controlled East Germany but divided into East and West zones and administered by America, Britain, France, and the Soviet Union, was in many ways a microcosm of the Cold War, as the confrontations during the Berlin crises of 1948–9 and 1961 had shown. As one of the controlling powers, Britain had a key interest in the negotiations proceeding during 1971 on access arrangements, inner-Berlin communications, and the political status of the East and West zones. The Soviets, superb negotiators as always, were obdurate and demanding. In June, however, they began to show signs of moving towards agreement more swiftly than anticipated—whether they lost patience or interest, or felt they had secured all the concessions they were going to get, is not clear. In discussions with his officials on plans for Operation FOOT, Douglas-Home made it clear that he was anxious not to derail the Berlin negotiations: 'If these talks are going well', he told Julian Bullard, head of the Eastern European and Soviet Department, at the end of June 1971, 'it seems a pity to have a major row at this point of time.' He greeted the signature of the Quadripartite Agreement on Berlin on 3 September as an acceptable compromise, though the Prime Minister thought 'the most that we can say is that we have made the best of a bad bargain, not that we have got a fair deal'.[26]

The agreement did, however, clear the way for action to counter Soviet espionage. As he set out the proposals for Operation FOOT on the afternoon of 21 September 1971, Douglas-Home knew that the Foreign Office was not united on how to deal with the problem of Soviet espionage. The outgoing British Ambassador in Moscow, Sir Duncan Wilson, had until his departure in August 1971 recommended a 'more *nuancé* public attitude towards the Soviet threat' (which meant not raising unpleasant subjects). But other officials with long experience of the Russians were clear that only plain speaking and firm action could improve Anglo-Soviet relations. As Deputy Under-Secretary Sir Thomas Brimelow remarked grimly at a meeting in May 1971, 'The Russians often spoke of European security, but paid no regard to the security of this country.' George Walden, on the Soviet desk, put it more bluntly: 'the game was based on the premise that the Russians were the cat and that we were the mouse.'[27]

Douglas-Home's own instinct was to tackle the issue through diplomatic channels, as part of a broader dialogue. By midsummer, however, when neither letters nor personal representations had produced any satisfactory Soviet response (a visit to Moscow by Greenhill in June was clouded by a request to withdraw two British diplomats), he admitted this tactic was not working. In June, with agreement on Berlin in prospect, Douglas-Home drafted a memorandum for the Prime Minister setting out options for action. Before sending it, however, he consulted the Home Secretary, who was responsible for the internal security of the UK and therefore was directly concerned with the issue.

Reginald Maudling, who had been beaten by Heath to the leadership of the Conservative Party in 1965, had held ministerial office since 1952, including serving as Chancellor of the Exchequer between 1962 and 1964. He regarded himself as the Prime Minister's deputy in the government as well as in the party. Yet he was not one of Heath's inner circle of close advisers (though they got on better than the media suggested). In Opposition, according to Maudling's private secretary, Heath had been 'very dependent on Reggie' who was 'often reassuring Ted, saying not to worry about things'.[28] In government, however, relations between them were cordial rather than close. If Heath required reassurance, it was not to Maudling that he looked, perhaps because he valued opinions expressed more frankly and forcefully by people like Carrington or Whitelaw.[29]

Clever and capable, Maudling was famous for his 'bedside manner' and gave the impression of indolence. Some of his colleagues, perhaps unfairly, thought that when push came to shove he could not be relied on to defend government policies forcefully. Maudling's own view was that Cabinet membership was hard work that required putting in long hours, but that any minister who felt overburdened by work 'does not know how to organize his life sensibly'.[30] Heath wrote of him in retrospect that Maudling had 'a brilliant brain and a complete grasp of the complexities', but was 'not at his most effective in dealing with people less intrinsically reasonable than himself' (a judgement levelled by some at the Prime Minister, too). At the age of 53, Maudling had accepted the post of Home Secretary in 1970 with somewhat rueful grace, commenting in his memoirs that 'one sometimes thinks that anything that no one else wants lands up with the Home Office' (a sentiment shared by many Home Secretaries since then).[31]

Maudling was responsible for government policy on immigration and race relations, law and order, and Northern Ireland—all thorny problems for the Heath government. In general the Home Secretary was inclined to a more cautious approach than the Prime Minister, though the difference was more apparent than real. Heath, while favouring more radical action in principle, was also willing to accept advice that it was impractical. On immigration, for example, though he had distanced himself from the extreme views voiced by Enoch Powell in his 'rivers of blood' speech in 1968, Heath knew that a majority of Conservatives and many of the general public wanted stricter controls on immigration, particularly from the 'new' (that is, black) Commonwealth. The problem became more urgent when it looked as if both the Kenyan and Ugandan governments might expel their Indian populations, many of whom held British passports. Maudling thought it better not to be too prescriptive about who should be allowed into the country, other than those with a legal entitlement, and Heath reluctantly agreed.

Maudling's belief that it was usually better to wait and see how things worked out extended to Northern Ireland. He and the Prime Minister were at one, however, in deploring the violence fed by passionate hatred on both sides of the conflict, and in their reluctance both to visit Northern Ireland (Maudling apparently referring to it as a 'bloody awful country') and to introduce internment until there was no alternative. But the increasingly violent tactics of the IRA, including a bombing campaign on the mainland in 1971, meant that there was no question that Ulster could be out of sight and out of mind for Maudling—nor for MI5, for which he had ministerial responsibility as Home Secretary. In fact, MI5 had only begun to engage seriously with Northern Ireland in the past few years. Maudling's predecessor as Home Secretary, Jim Callaghan, had been taken aback to learn in November 1968 that MI5 relied on the Royal Ulster Constabulary for information and had no independent sources there. According to the foremost historian of Irish security, in 1969 Northern Ireland 'might as well have been North Korea, so sparse was the reliable information available'. The priority might have been higher if they had known that the IRA and other groups were seeking to buy arms from the KGB.[32]

Maudling considered that the Home Secretary should keep in close touch with MI5, but let them get on with their job. In his memoirs, he asserted that there was 'a widespread failure to appreciate the importance of Intelligence, military and political', and that 'an efficient Intelligence service is just as fundamental to the defence of the West as guns, tanks or warships'.[33] In 1971, however, he found it hard to take entirely seriously what he was told by his Permanent Secretary, Sir Philip Allen, and by MI5 about the activities of Soviet spies in the UK. At the end of May he had expressed surprise that it was possible to identify positively so many Russian intelligence officers, and at the level of resource required to keep them under observation. MI5 assured him that they had ample evidence of Soviet espionage, and argued against the idea of imposing parity between the numbers of British and Soviet representatives without specifying which ones had to leave Britain. As Director-General Martin Furnival Jones pointed out, 'The aim should be to get rid of the people we knew to be spies. However we went about reducing the Soviet establishment, the Russians would react badly.'[34]

Maudling, however, remained unconvinced, considering that any kind of grand gesture against the Russians would be likely to do more harm than good. His relations with MI5 had not been helped by his rather clumsy (and unsuccessful) attempts, at Heath's request, to extend MI5's intelligence collection on industrial subversion.[35] What Maudling was not aware of at the time (nor was any minister, though the Cabinet Secretary knew), was the amount of resource being absorbed by internal investigations into possible Soviet penetration of the Security Service, following on from the defections of the 'Cambridge Five' in the 1950s and 60s. And what MI5 was not aware of was the fact that the KGB had in fact no 'moles' in the Service, despite the conspiracy theories of Peter Wright and others. When Lyalin told MI5 the KGB regarded it as 'virtually impossible' to crack, they simply did not believe him, given the detail he provided about the London residency's activities.[36] Both the Home Secretary and his Security Service, however, could only proceed on the knowledge they had at the time. MI5 considered that drastic action was needed to remedy a security situation they could not cope with. Maudling considered the whole thing rather overblown, and thought, according to Greenhill, that 'after a mass expulsion the Government would be the laughing stock of the British public and that we should all look very foolish'.[37]

Despite his reservations, however, Maudling was determined that any recommendations to the Prime Minister on Soviet espionage should come from him, as Home Secretary, and not just from Douglas-Home, 'having regard to the domestic and political problems which this issue raises'. The Foreign Secretary did not dissent, but the need for discussion and persuasion meant that it was not until the end of July 1971 that a joint memorandum went to Heath, setting out two options: a mass expulsion, or the imposition of parity between British and Soviet embassies while asking the Russians to remove, without publicity, 100 'specified intelligence officers'. The first option would, as MI5 argued, be more effective from a security viewpoint; but the Home Secretary felt 'that there could be difficulty with public opinion in this country when we had to say that spying had been going on for a long time on this scale—and that some of the intelligence officers had been allowed in since we took office'.[38]

Both Maudling and Douglas-Home agreed, however, on the importance of not disturbing Anglo-Soviet relations during the 'delicate and important negotiations' on Berlin. In response, the Prime Minister expressed doubts whether any British move would affect the Berlin talks (though the Russians might use the argument 'as a cover'), but agreed that since 'when we take action we must do everything required at one blow', Douglas-Home should write again to Gromyko and the position be reviewed at the end of October. By then, the Prime Minister commented grimly, 'they will have got away with it all for a year'. Douglas-Home wrote to Gromyko, who as usual did not reply. Then a combination of factors prompted the Foreign Secretary to decide the timetable should be brought forward: the conclusion of the Berlin agreement, the defection of Lyalin and confession of Bingham, the suspicion that the Russians thought something was in the wind; and, on a more practical level, the fact that the difficulty of obtaining visas for British citizens travelling to the Soviet Union was impeding both diplomacy and trade. In a minute to Maudling of 11 September, Douglas-Home argued that Heath's preference for doing everything 'at one blow' meant that the option for mass expulsion—Operation FOOT—should now be put into effect 'as soon as the necessary preparations can be made'.[39] On his return from a trip to North Africa from 12 to 19 September for talks on Middle East peace negotiations, Douglas-Home suggested the Prime Minister might call a meeting to discuss the tactics and timing of FOOT and deal with any remaining objections, including the possible adverse effect on British trade.

It was, indeed, the potential damage to British trade with Russia and the Soviet bloc that concerned **John Davies**, the Minister for Trade and Industry, also summoned to the meeting on 21 September 1971. Davies found the whole issue of Soviet espionage in the UK puzzling and slightly grotesque, and was reluctant to accept the necessity for taking a course of action that might damage British commercial prospects. At 55, he was a successful businessman with a background in the oil industry, who had served as Director of the CBI from 1965 to 1969. Elected to Parliament for the first time in 1970, he was immediately given the job of Minister of Technology in Heath's government, achieving even more rapid promotion a few months later when his department became in October part of the newly configured Department of Trade and Industry (DTI) in the reshuffle caused by the death of Iain Macleod. Unfortunately, business expertise does not always translate well into the machinery of government, and Davies was out of his depth both in the DTI and in politics. There was general agreement that his appointment, which Heath had hoped would bring 'a vigorous fresh approach to the atrophied corridors of Whitehall', was not a success.[40]

Neither Davies nor his officials were party to the secret intelligence received by the Home and Foreign Offices on the Soviet threat, and were both dismayed and amazed by what they were told about the extent of Soviet penetration. At an interdepartmental meeting held on 25 May 1971 and attended by the heads of both MI5 and MI6, Davies's Permanent Secretary, Sir Antony Part, asked the question 'How much damage did the Russian intelligence effort do?' 'Many millions of pounds', he said, were involved in British exports to the Soviet Union, and the security threat 'would have to be shown to be severe to justify the possible damage to our trade'. The FCO, however, took the view that the level of Anglo-Soviet trade was not high enough to be seriously threatened. British exports to the Soviet Union had stood still since 1968, amounting to only 1.2 per cent of British exports as a whole, and were not likely to change much in the near future. The Soviets claimed this was the fault of British firms, not politics. After the meeting Julian Bullard expressed surprise at the level of ignorance displayed, commenting to Sir Thomas Brimelow that 'If we are to overcome the resistance of the Department of Trade and Industry to FOOT it is important that Sir Antony Part should have clear evidence of the scale and nature of the Soviet intelligence attack.' A letter was sent to the DTI on 1 June setting out details of Soviet penetration of British government and industry, and a message on comparative trade figures was passed on to DTI representatives in trade talks in early July 1971.[41]

Davies remained unhappy about the potential damage to trade, but there was never any question that he would not defer to Maudling and Douglas-Home on the need for action. The DTI continued to make representations to the FCO on the desirability for minimum publicity, and of not setting a rigid ceiling for numbers in the Soviet Trade Delegation in case the Russians might in future have a genuine case for increase in connection with particular trade developments. Neither Douglas-Home nor his officials, however, were disposed to take much notice of either of these points. They wanted to exploit the inevitable publicity when Soviet officials were expelled. Greenhill advised on 17 September that it was right to 'take command of the situation *at the start*... with an operation on this scale it is, in my view, impossible to avoid publicity'. He reiterated the point at the meeting on 21 September: 'Only by taking the initiative could we keep control.'[42]

Against this background, the FCO took the view that although the Soviet Foreign Ministry would undoubtedly claim that trade would suffer if the British government took steps to limit Soviet intelligence-gathering operations, it was unlikely to make any real difference. As Bullard commented to Brimelow on 12 July 1971, 'What chiefly stands in the way of increased trade at the moment are the humdrum facts that the Russians are short of foreign currency, that at the moment they seem to be giving some preference to French and West German suppliers, and that in the field of manufactured goods they have little to offer that British firms feel inclined to buy.'[43] At the meeting on 21 September Davies was not ignored—there was some discussion of the extent of the real threat represented by Soviet espionage—but he was effectively outvoted. He signed up to the general agreement that in addition to the risks involved in the Russians acquiring secret information through their activities, there were also strong political grounds for putting an end to a situation that in itself prevented any fundamental improvement in Anglo-Soviet relations.

Neither of the other two ministers present on 21 September, Carrington and Whitelaw, saw it as their duty to argue against Operation FOOT. **Lord (Peter) Carrington**, surprised and pleased to be offered at the age of 51 a portfolio (Defence) not usually held by a minister sitting in the House of Lords, recorded in his memoirs that his priority on taking office had been to calm down the armed services, in some turmoil after the Defence Review undertaken by his predecessor Denis Healey. And although the Labour government's decision in 1968 to withdraw from East of Suez had been opposed by many Conservatives, the ensuing reorganization of defence commitments and cost savings were by no means unwelcome. Naval rivalry between East and West in the Indian Ocean, together with ongoing conflicts in South East Asia, the Middle East, and southern Africa, led the Heath government to row back on the decision to the extent of announcing in February 1971 that an extra British frigate would be deployed East of Suez the following year, but there was little attempt to expand the British military presence more generally. Carrington's view was that British influence outside NATO, while important, should be exercised in a manner that was more self-financing and pragmatic than adventurous.[44] A row with the Russians that might result in improved Anglo-Soviet relations when it blew over could be a positive development, particularly since none of the possible Soviet reprisals envisaged by the FCO involved the use of force.

As Lord President of the Council, **William Whitelaw** enjoyed Cabinet membership without departmental responsibilities, his role at once archaic (as chair of the Privy Council, a body that predates the Cabinet itself) and contemporary, advising on ministerial appointments and on parliamentary matters. Aged 52 when he took office in June 1970, Whitelaw, like Heath, had long experience in the Whips' office, dating back to 1959. Unlike the Prime Minister, he thought it important to keep taking the temperature of the Conservative Party and tune in to its various factions. He had already assumed the persona for which he was to become famous in Margaret Thatcher's government after 1979: a reliable and reassuring yet wily and ruthless presence, a solid source of both encouragement and criticism who always had his ear to the Whitehall ground. In his memoirs, he described Heath's election victory and his own appointment as Lord President as 'the most exciting day in my life', and summarized in a powerful passage the experience of serving as a Cabinet minister:

> It is not just the feeling of history which pervades the Cabinet room, where so many momentous decisions have been taken, nor is it simply the realization that you are at the centre of events and sometimes at moments of historic importance. There is also the valuable feeling of comradeship, strangely combined with the inevitable clash of powerful personalities. Then there is the challenge of deciding on the right tactics to be employed, both when to speak and when to be silent. A wise Cabinet Minister thinks carefully about all these matters and discusses his plans with those of his colleagues closest to him. But of course there are times when emotions take over and well-laid plans are abandoned. All this adds up to the simple fact that the Cabinet is essentially a human institution, which should be studied and enjoyed, but never treated lightly by any Cabinet Minister.[45]

Although the meeting held in Downing Street on 21 September was not a formal Cabinet meeting, it is certain that Whitelaw was, nevertheless, studying 'when to speak and when to be silent', and keeping an eye on the powerful personalities round the table. His priority that afternoon was to ensure that any decision taken caused as little difficulty as possible for the government in the wider Conservative Party and in Parliament. He had no special interest in Operation FOOT on its own account, nor did he enjoy regular exposure to secret intelligence. He was, however, keenly aware of the presentational and parliamentary problems facing the government as a result of the policies it was pursuing. The Conservative Party was deeply divided about entry into Europe, to which the

Prime Minister was committed, and the Chief Whip, Francis Pym, had advised that despite the success of the Heath–Pompidou meeting it would not be wise to seek a vote before the summer recess. Whitelaw was also worried about industrial relations, anxious to avoid a repeat of anything like the parliamentary crisis in January 1971 when forty Labour members had stood in front of the mace and defied the Speaker when the government had introduced a guillotine motion on the second reading of the Industrial Relations bill. The recall of Parliament in September to discuss the crisis in Northern Ireland added to the government's difficulties.

Whitelaw, like Douglas-Home, had doubts about the wisdom of a parliamentary statement on Operation FOOT. Since the Prime Minister had promised on 17 June that a statement would be made on Soviet espionage, it would be hard to avoid making one at all. In one way, it was fortuitous that the House had been reconvened to consider the situation in Northern Ireland; on the other hand, some Members might disapprove of this extra parliamentary time being diverted onto another subject, or might even seek to prolong the emergency session to discuss FOOT. Either way, a statement would add to the publicity for FOOT, which the Secretary of State for Trade and Industry was anxious to play down. Whitelaw thought that there were difficulties however the matter was handled, but that on balance it might be better to delay the statement until the House had risen. There would undoubtedly be left-wing criticism, from the Labour and Liberal parties and possibly even from some on the left of the Conservatives, and it might be helpful to gauge reactions to FOOT before a statement was made. Whitelaw was disposed to agree with Douglas-Home that public opinion might well be favourable, even if there were surprise at the large number of expulsions. All those present on 21 September agreed that 'on the whole the public expected the Russians to spy and was not unduly shocked when spies were caught'.[46]

At the meeting on 21 September 1971, therefore, ministerial interests and concerns about the proposed expulsion of Soviet intelligence officers were both pressing and varied. But there were other factors, too, that had to be taken into account when making a decision. Some of these concerns were unspoken and indeed unwritten (particularly since the decision at hand was intelligence led), barely hinted at in the documentation but still important. The best way of identifying these is by looking at the man present at the meeting who was perhaps most aware of the wider implications of Operation FOOT: **Sir Burke Trend**, Treasury man and quintessential mandarin who held the post of Cabinet Secretary from 1963 to 1973. Aged 57 in 1971, he had served in key policy advice roles since 1937 and was immensely experienced. The Cabinet Secretary does not necessarily change when the government does; he knows the history of the policy issues and how different governments have handled them; he is intimately concerned with intelligence matters to which ministers are not privy; he polices the way ministers and the civil service work, and has a keen eye for consistency, propriety, and precedent. It is his job to worry about how the government looks, works, and acts. In recent years the role of Cabinet Secretary has evolved, and the Cabinet Office is a large department rather than a small unit, but in 1971 Trend was, by virtue of his office, a close adviser of Edward Heath, just as he had been of Harold Wilson.

Trend had formed a very close relationship with Wilson (Richard Crossman famously calling him 'Harold's grand vizier'). They thought a great deal of each other, even if they had their ups and downs when Trend tried to pit civil service influence against political power. The Cabinet Secretary also worked well with Heath, though the relationship was less intimate. (Trend is barely mentioned in Heath's memoirs, apart from a rather sour reference to his arranging the date of the Commonwealth Heads of Government meeting in 1973 in such a way that Heath was prevented from competing in the Admiral's Cup in his yacht *Morning Cloud*.[47]) Heath later confided that he had found Trend's approach to government business 'academic', imbued with 'caution, thoughtfulness and a sense of history'. Trend, for his part, considered that these were virtues rather than vices and found the Prime Minister's 'propensity to want action and to supply it himself if it was not forthcoming from his Ministers' somewhat unsettling.[48] Nevertheless, Heath relied on Trend to tell him what no one else was in a position to know or say. The Cabinet Secretary's was a weighty step in the corridors of power, a fact of which he was well (sometimes rather too well) aware.

Although the available evidence does not allow for certainty as to the full range of Trend's concerns and advice, much can be deduced with confidence. As Cabinet Secretary, he was copied in on interdepartmental correspondence about FOOT, and understood the concerns and reservations of both ministers and officials. Unlike Conservative ministers, however, he had also been privy to the Wilson government's deliberations about Soviet espionage, and knew that if it were decided to make public the extent of Soviet penetration by implementing Operation FOOT there might well be questions in Parliament, in the media, and from the public as to why nothing had been done about the problem earlier. Officials would have to prepare answers to this question: although ministers are always keen to blame their predecessors, a perceived failure to identify and rectify a serious problem reflected badly on the whole government machine, something the Cabinet Secretary and his senior Whitehall colleagues wished to avoid. It was also, Trend knew from experience, undesirable to reveal information that might cause wide-spread public alarm, as well as giving too much away about British intel-ligence's sources and methods. This was an argument for not disclosing Lyalin's revelations in any detail.

Unlike ministers, Trend was well briefed on all the intelligence involved in the decision. He was in regular contact with the intelligence agencies as well as with Sir Dick White, who after serving as both Direc-tor-General of MI5 and then Chief of SIS (MI6), the only person ever to hold both posts, had 'retired' in 1968 to become chairman of the Cabinet Office's new coordinating committee on intelligence. Trend's level of access gave him an overview of the intelligence scene that enabled him to identify pitfalls and possible consequences that others might overlook or dismiss. He knew (as ministers did not at this stage) that MI5 was investigating its own former Director-General, Roger Hollis; he knew, too, about the 1964 confession by Anthony Blunt that he had been working for the Soviet Union.[49]

Trend was fully briefed on the revelations of Lyalin, and the details of the Bingham case. He was in constant and close touch with the Foreign Office, and understood the difficulties that the ongoing 'visa war' posed to British diplomats (and to MI6 officers operating under diplomatic cover). Trend also appreciated FCO and MI6 concerns that Britons working in the Soviet Union were prime recruiting targets for Soviet intelligence. In that respect, Trend considered, it would be no bad thing if some of them were expelled from Russia in reprisal for FOOT. On the other hand, those reprisals might also mean that SIS lost valuable intelligence-collecting facilities through arrangements that relied on Anglo-Soviet cooperation (such as those that operated in Germany, for example).[50]

Trend had been present at the interdepartmental meeting on Soviet espionage on 25 May 1971, when he asked whether, if the Russians were told to cut down the numbers in their legal residency, they would not just increase their illegal presence and create greater problems. Furnival Jones had replied that this would be difficult as illegals were more difficult to run. Trend expressed the view that 'if we were going to have a row anyway, it was better to get what we wanted out of it', but warned that 'we still had to consider whether the game was worth the candle…the commercial stakes involved appeared very high and he was not sure which way Ministers would jump'.[51] He had also attended a meeting held at the end of June between the Foreign and Home Secretaries, when the two men had decided to present a joint memorandum to the Prime Minister, but to go slowly because of the risk of upsetting negotiations on Berlin. The Cabinet Secretary's own instincts were towards caution and a slower pace, but on the other hand he had to anticipate what ministers might do and how to handle things if that pace were accelerated—as it was at the beginning of September.

Trend also had in mind a factor that hardly appears in the official documentation about FOOT. What were other countries doing about the problem, and how much should the British government consult or tell allies about their plans? Although secrecy and the avoidance of leaks were of primary importance (a point stressed frequently by Douglas-Home), it seems odd that there is so little mention in the recorded deliberations about other countries, particularly the United States, with whom the British intelligence relationship was, and remains, umbilically close. There had been some reference to other countries at the meeting of 25 May, when the Chief of MI6 ('C') said that 'our allies in Western Europe' would probably welcome forceful action by the British, and might even follow suit. Nevertheless, Trend's recommendation that the Prime Minister should be told that 'the Americans were more firm in these matters than we are' was the only reference made to the United States on that occasion.

The Cabinet Secretary had his own contacts in Washington, and may have known, therefore, that President Nixon and his Assistant for National Security Affairs, Henry Kissinger, had expressed considerable (and public) dissatisfaction in 1971 with the American intelligence community and were too preoccupied with its reorganization to pay much attention to British problems.[52] Even so, Trend thought, the Americans would hardly be indifferent if Operation FOOT caused a major crisis with the Russians. He would undoubtedly have been happier if the proposed move against the Soviet Union had been endorsed by allies. It seemed risky to go out ahead of the pack in this way. In a minute of 20 September to No. 10, Trend argued that 'our proposed action, although clearly right and necessary in itself, would carry even more conviction if we were seen to be acting in concert with other countries whom we know to be as concerned as ourselves about this problem'.

Trend accepted that it was not possible to warn allies in advance, as 'this would have promptly leaked back to Moscow'. But there was, he thought, 'something to be said for letting them know what we are doing, at the moment when we do it, and suggesting to them that if they, too, have a similar problem they might go and do likewise'. Even a limited response, Trend thought, would 'add considerably to the conviction with which our own action should be received'.[53] Neither Heath nor Douglas-Home, however, saw any necessity to seek such endorsement, and even Maudling, who thought FOOT might make Britain a laughing stock, does not appear to have suggested it. On 21 September, it was decided to go ahead and implement FOOT three days later, and despite Trend's advice Douglas-Home decided to wait and inform the American, Australian, Canadian, and New Zealand representatives, 'as soon as action has been taken with the Soviet Chargé d'Affaires'.[54]

The meeting on 21 September was not quite the last word on the decision to implement Operation FOOT. On the following day, Heath asked Douglas-Home to reassure him that 'our case is fully prepared to defend the steps we are taking against those who will criticize them on political grounds and to show that there was no satisfactory alternative way of handling the situation'. The Foreign Secretary, about to fly off to New York, had no hesitation in assuring the Prime Minister that he was 'completely satisfied that we shall be able to show that the problem is very serious and that it could not have been solved in any other way'. He provided a detailed assessment of possible reprisals and responses, prepared by his Foreign Office advisers. The most likely Soviet response would be for the Russians to restrict or stop travel by British diplomatic staff, and to harass them in other ways. Such tactics might also be applied to British businessmen travelling to the Soviet Union. At the bottom of the list was 'Arrest one or more British subjects…on a trumped up charge'. On the list of further measures that the British government might take, the least severe was to initiate publicity and release the names of those expelled; at the top of the scale, to break off diplomatic relations.[55]

Very few of these contingency measures were employed by either side. The bold stroke of Operation FOOT delighted Britain's friends and dismayed her adversaries. As Sir Dick White told his biographer Tom

Bower: 'After that, it was downwards for them and upwards for us.' Oleg Gordievsky, who worked as a British agent inside the KGB from 1974 to 1985 before escaping to Britain, described Moscow centre as 'stunned' by FOOT: 'the golden age of KGB operations came to an end.'[56] The Soviet reaction was predictably outraged, but milder than feared. When Sir Alec Douglas-Home met the Soviet Foreign Minister in New York at the end of September, Gromyko was almost inarticulate with rage, mixing his metaphors wildly as he accused the British government of using outrageous tactics 'to distract attention from the bottle necks, the rents and tatters of their own policies'. The Soviet Union would not, he said, 'descend to such depths but would certainly retaliate'.

On 8 October the British Ambassador, Sir John Killick, was summoned to the Soviet Foreign Ministry to receive a statement of Soviet reprisals. Some joint ventures were cancelled, and there were a few expulsions; but on the whole, there was more noise than action. Killick, musing on the aftermath of FOOT at the end of November 1971, asked rhetorically 'whether the KGB, for all their resources and efficiency, are out of their minds'.[57] In the end, closer contacts suited both the British and the Russians, and were gradually resumed. Indeed, it is possible that renewed Soviet suggestions for a European security conference—what was to become the Conference on Security and Cooperation in Europe— owed their origin in part to the Soviet desire to redress the balance that, with Operation FOOT, they felt had been tilted against them. For a while the Soviet government kept the British at arms length, although the latter took care to indicate that they, at least, were ready and willing to resume business (more or less) as usual. The coolness persisted for some time, while Brezhnev made a great show of improving ties with France. The Anglo-Soviet relationship may have been dented for a while, but it was certainly not broken.

Of course, Operation FOOT did not stop Soviet intelligence officers operating in the UK altogether. No one in the British government or the intelligence agencies expected that it would, although they were determined not to let the problem escalate again in the way that it had been allowed to do up to 1971. As Sir Thomas Brimelow put it in a letter of 23 December 1971 to Sir John Killick in Moscow, 'We are not aiming at absolute security, or "whiter than white". We have achieved a paler shade of grey; and we wish to obstruct darkening with age.' But, he stressed, 'We do not feel contrite about FOOT.'[58] Operation FOOT had been well prepared, the options considered, the arguments well reasoned.

As always, luck played a part, but as a case study in decision-making on a sensitive issue it is instructive. The last word might perhaps be given to the prime mover of FOOT, Sir Alec Douglas-Home, referring in his memoirs to the Soviet intelligence officials expelled in September 1971: 'Our knowledge of the gentlemen concerned was confirmed by defectors, and I decided Mr Gromyko's time was up.'[59]

Margaret Thatcher and Lord Carrington (*left*), 1979

6

Challenging the Argentines

The Decision to Send a Task Force to the Falklands, April 1982

We knew what we had to do and we went about it and did it.*

Even among her detractors, the image of Conservative Prime Minister Margaret Thatcher as an 'iron lady', leading the country in a successful military campaign to repel the Argentine invasion of the Falkland Islands, remains pervasive thirty years later. Yet when the Cabinet met at 7.30 p.m. on the evening of Friday, 2 April 1982 to take a decision on sending a naval task force to the Falklands, both she and her ministers knew it was a tremendous gamble, both militarily and politically. The idea of a foreign power seizing British territory, however remote and sparsely inhabited, seemed extraordinary. But the decision to send British forces to the South Atlantic—possibly to fight and be killed—seemed fantastic, too. There was, however, near unanimity on that mild April evening, only Trade Secretary John Biffen expressing doubts. In an atmosphere of what the Chancellor of the Exchequer, Sir Geoffrey Howe, later called 'shocked disbelief', the Cabinet invited the Defence Secretary, John Nott, to arrange for the task force to sail as soon as it was ready.[1]

To a large extent the decision taken by the Cabinet that night rubber-stamped a course of action already set in train. Since the Chief of the Naval Staff, Sir Henry Leach, had told the Prime Minister at a meeting held on the evening of 31 March that a task force could be ready to sail early the following week, its dispatch had seemed inevitable unless there

* Margaret Thatcher, 26 June 1982.

was a last-minute change of heart by the Argentine junta. After a late-night meeting on 1 April between the Prime Minister, Foreign Secretary, and Defence Secretary, Leach had been authorized to put the fleet on alert. But the final order to sail had to await a Cabinet decision. Peter Hennessy has written that according to one of Mrs Thatcher's 'most astringent critics' in the Cabinet 'the task force would never have sailed without Cabinet approval. There is no question of that.'[2]

Of course, the Prime Minister already knew the views of key ministerial colleagues and did not expect opposition. But a decision to commit British forces to military action is a matter for the Cabinet, and it was important that each minister should assume his or her share of collective responsibility and commitment to whatever the future might hold. That future was very uncertain, both because the crisis was taking place 8,000 miles away; and because the government was likely to get a rough ride in Parliament and the press over the Falklands crisis, whatever happened. As George Walden puts it, 'When it comes to foreign policy every back-bench MP and the editor of every newspaper...becomes a little Lord Palmerston.'[3] At the same time, the spectre of Suez, when a military expedition had ended in humiliating failure, floated uneasily over the Cabinet table.[4] Failure could destroy the government, but so could failure to act. Success, however difficult or expensive, could not only redeem Britain's honour but also deflect political opposition.

The story of the events leading up to the Argentine invasion and how it came to catch the British government largely by surprise has been told in detail elsewhere, including in the two-volume history of the conflict by Sir Lawrence Freedman, based on full access to official papers and interviews with key participants, as well as in the 1983 report of the committee of six Privy Counsellors set up under Lord Franks to review the way the government had carried out its responsibilities in the Falklands crisis.[5] There is no need to rehearse here the evidence given in these and other accounts. For present purposes, the interest in the decision taken on 2 April to send a task force to recapture the Falklands lies in its wider context. For it supplies clear proof of two golden rules of foreign policy-making: that it is ministers who take decisions; and that those ministers always think about more than one thing at a time.

A little bit of background is required. Britain and Argentina had disputed the ownership of the Falkland Islands (or the Malvinas, as they are called in Argentina) for over 200 years. Though the islands had been under continuous British occupation since 1832 (1982 marked the 150th anniversary), the arguments about sovereignty were, and remain, contentious.[6] Negotiations on the terms on which a settlement might be reached, including the idea of transferring sovereignty of the Falkland Islands to Argentina and then leasing them back, had been going on intermittently for years. It had always foundered on the determination of the islanders to remain British, for which they were able to muster some influential parliamentary support. Like most long-running disputes, the Falklands question had raised its head more persistently at some times than others. Generally, however, it had not been high on the agenda of either Britain or Argentina, although the latter was more inclined to nurse a sense of grievance. In 1980 the failure of a leaseback deal brokered by Nicholas Ridley, then a Foreign Office minister, increased the tension. By the summer of 1981, the Foreign Secretary, Lord Carrington, was aware that Argentine impatience was mounting and 'we had a certain sense of sands running out'.[7]

We now know that the ruling military junta in Argentina, led since December 1981 by General Leopoldo Galtieri, had decided to make settling the dispute with Britain over the Falkland Islands a priority for 1982, largely for domestic reasons. It was not satisfied with the results of Anglo-Argentine talks on sovereignty held in New York in February. The junta had an invasion plan in its pocket when a dispute over the landing on South Georgia by an Argentine salvage crew in mid-March escalated (possibly deliberately) into confrontation. But at the time no one in Whitehall knew this, despite reports of mounting tension. Everyone, including the Joint Intelligence Committee, assumed that if the Argentines wanted to force the issue over the Falklands they would do so in stages, breaking off diplomatic relations or cutting the islands' communications links. That assumption was false, just like the Argentine assumption that Britain would not seek to take back the Falklands by force.[8]

In fact, the junta did not take a final decision to invade until Friday 26 March, and even then was 'apparently not so much intending to present the British with a *fait accompli* in the Falklands but to force a serious negotiation in circumstances favourable to Argentina, so that they would agree to the transfer of sovereignty legitimized through the UN'.[9] In London, the general view in the next few days was that the situation was 'serious but not necessarily moving to a head'. The Prime Minister and those of her colleagues most closely concerned became increasingly anxious as reports were received indicating the possibility of an escalation of the dispute over the landing on South Georgia, but it was only on

31 March that firm intelligence arrived that an Argentine fleet was expected to arrive at the Falkland Islands on 2 April. Before that, as Mrs Thatcher wrote in her memoirs, 'I do not think any of us expected an immediate invasion of the Falklands themselves.'[10] Indeed, even as arrangements were being made for the assembly of the task force and other naval dispositions, it was difficult to be sure—and hard to believe— that the Argentines were really going to do it.[11]

For most of the Cabinet ministers present at the meeting on the evening of 2 April, the Falkland Islands had barely registered on their radar until the last few days. They had had plenty of other things to worry about. For the Thatcher government, 1981 had been a bruising year of hard economic choices, high unemployment, strikes, and riots, not to mention problems in Northern Ireland, with the government under attack not just from Labour but from the new Social Democrat/ Liberal grouping whose platform was 'A Fresh Start for Britain'.[12] Relations within the Cabinet itself had been strained by policy disagreements over the direction of the government's economic policy and the Treasury's rigid control of departmental spending. By the spring of 1982, however, the ministerial team seemed more cohesive and there were some promising signs that an economic corner was being turned. For the first time in eight months, the government had regained its lead in the opinion polls. No one had envisaged fighting a war.

The meeting at 7.30 p.m. on 2 April was the second convened that day to discuss the Falklands. Some ministers had been caught by surprise when they received an early call to assemble at 9.45 a.m. It was a Friday so a few had already gone back to their constituencies. Norman Fowler, the Secretary of State for Social Services, noted that he and his colleagues 'used whatever means of transport were available': he arrived in the family car, while Lord Hailsham, the Lord Chancellor, arrived on his bicycle.[13] But the Prime Minister had not yet received confirmation of an Argentine landing, and apart from reporting the unsatisfactory results of an attempt to get the Americans to intercede with Galtieri, there was not much to say.[14] When the Cabinet met again that evening, she began by announcing that it now appeared that Argentina had, in fact, invaded the Falkland Islands, although there was no direct information on what had happened or whether there had been any casualties. Though by now the news was not unexpected, it was still a shock. William Whitelaw, the Home Secretary, who had been summoned back from a visit to the Hampshire Fire Brigade, wrote later that 'there was no doubt then about the feelings of shame and disgrace at the humiliation of our country'.[15]

Everyone at the meeting that evening was, naturally, focused on the matter at hand. As the Chancellor of the Exchequer, Sir Geoffrey Howe, wrote in his memoirs, 'All the normal features of government seemed for the moment to have been suspended.'[16] But that does not mean that those present could ignore entirely the other issues that concerned them, or that they were not conscious of a range of unrelated pressures as they sat around the Cabinet table. The crisis demanded their attention. But it also interrupted their normal business. And while the ministers assembled round the Cabinet table on that Friday evening had the Falklands in the front of their minds, it is important not to forget what must have been at the back of them. No one foresaw at this stage how serious the conflict would become or the extent to which it would affect other aspects of government policy. Everyone present had a great many other things to think about. Indeed, in the week leading up to the Cabinet meeting the ministers most closely involved in the crisis at this early stage, the Prime Minister, Foreign Secretary, and Defence Secretary all had overseas travel commitments on quite separate issues. Looking at these three, and what they were concerned with in the days immediately preceding 2 April, is a good way of illustrating the complex context against which the Argentine invasion took place.

So much has been written about the personality, achievements, perceived weaknesses, and management style of the Prime Minister, **Margaret Thatcher**, that there seems little need to say much more than she was an intelligent, exceptionally driven, and determined individual who inspired both intense dislike and passionate loyalty.[17] Three years after becoming Britain's first woman Prime Minister in May 1979 at the age of 54, she had almost, but not quite succeeded in securing her dominance, and the dominance of her political philosophy within the government and in the wider Conservative Party. She came into office determined to take radical measures based on a free market economy, break the power of the monopolistic nationalized industries and the trade unions, and restore to the British people a sense of self-discipline and self-worth. In a vivid word picture, Peter (now Lord) Hennessy described her as behaving 'from first to last as if the opening bars of Beethoven's Fifth Symphony were constantly ringing in her ears. She was determined to follow the beat of her own destiny whatever the external or internal circumstances.'[18]

But by no means everyone in her Party, or even in her own Cabinet, shared her views about how this should be done. With the help of trusted lieutenants such as William Whitelaw and Sir Keith Joseph she had to proceed cautiously, often continuing economic policies that had been adopted by her pragmatic Labour predecessor, James Callaghan. Meanwhile, the Prime Minister took steps to remove or sideline opponents and confound the so-called Tory grandees who had thought that she would burn too brightly and too fast, and disappear in a pile of ashes. It was a period of 'establishing hegemony'. Ian Gilmour, who was sacked as Lord Privy Seal in September 1981, said that Mrs Thatcher 'regarded her first Cabinet...not as an aid to good government but as an obstacle to be surmounted'.[19] By early 1982 there were still serious difficulties—in January unemployment in Britain passed the three million mark for the first time—but things were looking up at last, and she had earned the respect, if not always the liking, of most of her ministerial colleagues. Certainly, those assembled round the Cabinet table on the evening of 2 April 1982, whatever their personal opinion of her, recognized that the government was in a better place than it had been the previous year, and that much of the credit was due to her.

Despite this improvement in the government's position, Mrs Thatcher herself was far from complacent. The economy was improving slightly but inflation and unemployment were high, manufacturing industry was struggling, and industrial relations remained troubled. What she saw as the 'rescue' of Britain through the instillation of self-discipline and a free market economy, on which she had embarked in 1979, was by no means complete. And, of course, the British economy did not function in a vacuum. Its trade relations with the EEC, the US, and the rest of the world were crucial to prosperity. In early 1982 the Prime Minster had to deal with two foreign problems that had implications for domestic policy as well: relations with the European Economic Community, and relations with Britain's closest ally, the United States. She had to give attention to both of these in the week leading up to 2 April, attending an EEC heads of government meeting in Brussels from 29 to 30 March, and making an appeal through various channels for American support in trying to persuade General Galtieri to draw back from the brink of invasion.

The Prime Minister herself tended to think of these issues in isolation. Sir Percy Cradock, her foreign affairs adviser from 1984, noted she did not see foreign policy as a continuum, but 'rather as a series of disparate problems with attainable solutions'. Nor was she inclined to give much thought to the sensitivities or intentions of her foreign counterparts (partly because, as Cradock commented, she took 'a poor view of foreigners other than Anglo-Saxons'). Cradock, though an admirer, saw her lack of imagination about other governments as a 'real defect'; she herself tended to regard it as a real strength.[20] The Prime Minister was well known at home and abroad for the way she brought her fierce concentration to bear on the issue at hand in any discussion, and for her refusal to be deflected. Sir Michael Butler, the UK's Permanent Representative to the EEC 1979–85, commented that meetings with her were 'not for the faint-hearted or ill-briefed'.[21] As far as she was concerned, it was a matter of getting the job done, which meant getting her way. But though her single-mindedness had its advantages, it also prevented her from seeing how one issue might well impact on another. Alexander Haig, US Secretary of State in 1982, noted in 1984 how Mrs Thatcher (whom he greatly admired) saw the Falklands issue essentially as a narrow one between Britain and Argentina.[22]

Apart from 'winning the Falklands war', one of the other achievements for which Mrs Thatcher has often been given credit (particularly by her fellow Conservatives) is for 'getting Britain's money back', that is, securing a substantial rebate of Britain's budgetary contribution to the EEC. She took up the baton on this long-running dispute in 1979, and it was not settled until 1984.[23] In 1982, it was a cause of considerable strain between the Prime Minister and her EEC counterparts. Britain had a reasonable case for some form of settlement, since despite being one of the poorer Community members it was the second largest net contributor, and received less in subsidies since its agricultural sector was comparatively small. But the single-minded (again) and strident way in which Mrs Thatcher went about securing the rebate alienated her fellow members, and tended to dominate the proceedings in EEC meetings.

All this was very much a hot topic in early 1982. Talks on Britain's budgetary contribution had broken down at the end of January, and a proposal in early March by the President of the European Commission, Gaston Thorn, for a five-year settlement had been rejected by the French as well as by Mrs Thatcher, who had announced that on the matter of Britain's rebate she was 'not puttable offable'. Britain's insistence on holding up agreement on agricultural prices under the Common Agricultural Policy until the budgetary question was settled had infuriated its EEC partners. France could not, President François Mitterrand warned, allow one government to obstruct the implementation of the fundamental

Community rules.[24] But the Prime Minister was impervious to such warnings, just as she brushed aside the comments of the West German Chancellor, Helmut Schmidt, when he suggested, after talks at Chequers in the middle of March, that there were greater issues at stake than the British contribution to the EEC budget—such as world recession.

The EEC heads of government meeting in the last week of March 1982 was intended to celebrate the twenty-fifth anniversary of the Treaty of Rome. Mrs Thatcher, however, was not in the mood for celebration. According to *The Times*, she arrived 'all in deepest black' and 'would not have looked out of place at a state funeral'.[25] As far as she was concerned, it was important to turn up and to state, yet again, the British case, but little progress was made and she was distracted by anxiety about developments in the South Atlantic. Her obduracy on the budgetary issue was not just a question of single-mindedness, nor based on an opposition to the EEC itself. She accepted that British membership was beneficial, provided that she secured the reforms that she sought. She had no thoughts of leaving the EEC, which would clearly be to Britain's detriment, but she was determined both to secure more equitable terms for membership, and to ensure reform of Community institutions where possible.

In her dealings with the EEC, Mrs Thatcher knew that anything she said or did would be watched closely by Conservative backbenchers and the British press, both of whom were liable to react strongly to anything that implied Britain was not 'standing up to Europe'. Her government was not quite secure enough yet to risk alienating unnecessarily the vocal anti-European lobby (those who today would be called Eurosceptics). These considerations also lay behind her opposition to the proposals put forward in January 1982 by the German Foreign Minister, Hans-Dietrich Genscher, for a greater degree of European political unification. As well as disliking in principle anything that smacked of federalism, she knew that this was just the sort of thing to cause trouble at home. Lord Carrington's view was that these proposals were more hot air than substance, and it was better to go along with them to a limited extent to improve the chances of a budgetary settlement. For Mrs Thatcher, however, it was a political balancing act and, unlike some of her European counterparts, she was not very good at talking the talk without walking the walk.

Britain's relations with its EEC partners were by no means wholly negative. Many years later, William (by then Lord) Waldegrave said of Mrs Thatcher that with her, what you saw was what you got. There was, he said, 'no private agenda or personal priority which was not quite explicitly her view of what the government's priorities also should be'.[26] European leaders, as well as Conservative politicians, recognized this. Although Mrs Thatcher's relations with them were often strained, part of this was for the benefit of their domestic audiences: she was not the only one to have an electorate with strong views on national interests. But over time she had developed a pragmatic, if not warm working relationship with most of her European counterparts, particularly Chancellor Schmidt and President Mitterrand. These relationships were to prove important during the Falklands crisis, but in the first week of April 1982 Mrs Thatcher would probably have said that the Falklands were no business of the European leaders. More problematic was Spain, whose applications to join both the EEC and NATO were supported by Britain. But the status of Gibraltar remained a source of tension between the two governments (Mrs Thatcher had talks with the Prime Minister of Gibraltar, Sir Joshua Hassan, in January 1982), and the precedent of a Latin American country taking direct action to 'repossess' what it regarded as its territory, as Argentina regarded the Falklands, was not a helpful one. Even Mrs Thatcher could see that.

Throughout Mrs Thatcher's discussions in Brussels in the week leading up to the Cabinet meeting on 2 April 1982, she kept in touch with the developing situation in the South Atlantic. It still seemed possible that it might be defused by diplomatic pressure, and the most powerful source of that pressure would be the United States. Contacts had already been made with the US Secretary of State, Alexander Haig, and US military authorities. It was time to turn to President Ronald Reagan, with whom the Prime Minister had formed a good relationship since he took office in 1981. According to Sir Percy Cradock, Mrs Thatcher's basic principles of foreign policy were a belief in the importance of strong defence; a strong aversion to communism; a suspicion of Europe; an instinctive alignment with the United States; and, above all, the 'tireless assertion of British interests'.[27] These principles not only struck a chord with the majority of the general public in Britain, but were a mirror image of those professed by the President. It was one of the reasons that he and Mrs Thatcher—who had paid a very successful visit to the US shortly after his inauguration in 1981—got on well together. Now, with a growing crisis over the Falklands, Mrs Thatcher felt sure that the President would help. But as always, the Anglo-American relationship was rather more complicated than it appeared.

For one thing, it was not easy at this stage to get the Americans to take the Falklands situation seriously. As Haig later put it, in April 1982 the State Department were amused by 'what was perceived as a Gilbert and Sullivan battle over a sheep pasture between a choleric old John Bull and a comic dictator in a gaudy uniform'. They were initially disinclined to take sides, much to Carrington's annoyance.[28] And despite fellow feeling between Prime Minister and President, there were strains in the Anglo-American relationship at this point. The US government's imposition of stringent economic sanctions against the Soviet bloc in response to the declaration of martial law in Poland in December 1981, and their insistence that Western European governments should do the same, had led to serious disagreements in early 1982. In this dispute Mrs Thatcher was on the side of the Europeans, who felt they were being pressured to take measures that would do little damage to the Soviet Union (or to the US) but a lot to their own economies. In particular, US insistence that a contract should be cancelled to supply Soviet gas to Western Europe—a contract that involved equipment from British suppliers—provoked strong resistance from Britain as well as the European powers.[29] It was not unusual for Britain to straddle the Atlantic between its American and European partners: it was less usual for it to come down on the European, rather than the American side.

In respect of the Falklands, the US Administration had reservations about supporting the British case, which some thought smacked of colonialism. And in any case, the Americans were always very wary of British attempts to involve itself with Latin America, which they regarded as firmly in the US sphere of interest. In the early 1980s they were expending large amounts of money and military muscle 'fighting communism' in the region, whether by supporting governments (like the repressive military regime in El Salvador), or by supporting armed revolt against left-wing governments (such as that formed by the Sandinistas in Nicaragua). They were wary of anything that might destabilize the region further, thereby increasing the risk of Soviet influence. They were also concerned that countries that they had been cultivating—like Argentina—would turn against them if they supported the British. Jeane Kirkpatrick, the forceful US Ambassador to the UN (unforgettably described by wicked Alan Clark in his diaries as 'a mixture between Irene Worth and Eleanor Roosevelt'), argued that supporting Britain could lead to 'a hundred years of animosity' towards the Americans in Latin America.[30] Although the British were to receive a good deal of help from the US in the course of the Falklands conflict, they would not, for a variety of reasons, receive wholehearted support.

Relations with the EEC and with the US were the basis of British foreign policy, and it was natural that they would be high on the Prime Minister's agenda. But of course, she was not directing British foreign policy single-handed. Mrs Thatcher relied heavily on her Foreign Secretary, and on expert briefing from the Foreign Office itself, as well as her advisers in No. 10. This may seem like stating the obvious for any Prime Minister, but in her case it is worth emphasizing because of the impression that she gave (usually deliberately), of looking down on her professional advisers in the Foreign Office. It would be wrong to take this too much at face value. Although she famously entertained a disdain for the Foreign Office as an institution, regarding it as defeatist and weak, she had great respect for individual officials, and for the intellect and professionalism of British diplomats such as Sir Nicholas Henderson and Sir Anthony Parsons, HM Ambassadors in Washington and at the UN who were key players in the Falklands crisis. As George Walden wrote later, the idea that she despised and disregarded the Foreign Office was largely a myth, encouraged and exploited by her for her own purposes. It gave her someone to blame when things went wrong, and enabled her to maintain what Walden calls Britain's make-believe view of itself, 'cultivating the illusion that if only we had real men running our affairs rather than Foreign Office types, Britain could regain its lost grandeur and show the world a thing or two'.[31] This was very much the Thatcher style.

Peter Carrington, who had succeeded as 6th Baron Carrington in 1938 and had served as Foreign Secretary since 1979, understood Mrs Thatcher's style well, and knew how to deal with it. According to her biographer John Campbell, she 'had a curious weakness for a genuine toff, and the sixth Baron Carrington was the real thing'.[32] Certainly the Foreign Secretary's easy charm and teasing manner appealed to her, but it is hard to believe that his hereditary peerage was the chief attraction. Carrington had served in every Conservative government since Macmillan's, including as Defence Secretary under Edward Heath, and so brought a fund of expertise as well as common sense to the role of Foreign Secretary. For the Prime Minister, these qualities, together with his loyalty to her, far outweighed the disadvantage of having a Foreign Secretary in the House of Lords. Another minister would act as FO spokesman in the Commons (Humphrey Atkins, in April 1982, as Lord Privy Seal). Carrington himself was delighted with going to the Foreign Office at the age of 62. It was, he said, a job he had wanted all his life; besides, as he wrote in his memoirs, 'I reckoned I knew more about foreign affairs than any of them by now'.[33]

Unlike most of his colleagues, including the Prime Minister, Carrington had kept a close eye on the Falklands dispute since 1979, although accepting—perhaps too readily, he later admitted—that there seemed no practical solution in prospect. In principle, he supported the idea of leaseback—ceding sovereignty to Argentina while respecting the islanders' wishes to remain British—but was not hopeful, particularly after the Ridley episode in 1980, that it was a viable option given the strength of feeling on all sides. In early 1982, while noting with concern reports of increasing intransigence on the part of the Argentines, he saw 'no particular reason to suppose the situation might not still be contained or defused'. By the last week in March he was fully engaged with the problem, keeping a close eye on the intelligence reports, and urging the Ministry of Defence to engage in contingency planning; but he still felt Argentine military action unlikely, as indeed did the Joint Intelligence Committee. It was for this reason that after accompanying the Prime Minister to Brussels on 29 March, he flew on to Tel Aviv. As he later wrote, he would not have done this if he believed British territory was about to be invaded. And the Middle East was, he said, 'the most dangerous arena in the world and diplomacy there the most urgently required'.[34]

Carrington's approach to deep-seated disputes in foreign policy was consistent, whether it was the Falklands, Rhodesia (on which he had battled valiantly to secure the Lancaster House settlement in 1979),[35] or the Middle East. It was based on trying to understand both sides of the argument, sympathy for those who were suffering as a result of it, and above all believing that a solution must, ultimately, be possible through negotiation rather than confrontation. Though this might mean playing a long game, he believed that it was essential for Britain to be a player in that game if it were to have any chance of securing a favourable outcome, both for the parties to a dispute and for itself. This was particularly true in respect of Britain's role in the Middle East, where its long ties with Arab nations and its involvement with Israel since its foundation in 1948 gave it if not power—only the US really had that—at least a modicum of influence.

It is true that the early 1980s was a period of acute tension in Arab-Israeli relations (although it is hard to find a period from 1948 onwards when that has not been true). But the past few years, since the signature of the Camp David accords in 1978, had seen bitter disagreements not just between Israel and the Arab states but between the Arabs themselves.[36] Those who were willing to at least entertain the prospect of some kind of settlement with Israel, such as Egypt and Saudi Arabia, were bitterly criticized by others. The assassination of Egyptian President Anwar Sadat in October 1981 raised the temperature still higher; the Arab League agreed to support the Lebanon against Israeli aggression, and an Arab summit in November 1981 broke up in disagreement over a Saudi peace plan (supported by Carrington). The Foreign Secretary, who had taken an active interest in the region as Edward Heath's Defence Secretary, felt that while Britain had to try and steer a neutral course, it was important to be involved.

During the 1980 US presidential election campaign, American efforts in respect of a Middle East peace process had, as usual in those circumstances, been put into abeyance. As the Foreign Secretary wrote in his memoirs, it seemed to him that countries in the region, particularly 'moderate' Arabs, 'needed to see that somebody, somewhere was alive to the problem and wanted to help'. But his efforts, including participation in the 1980 Venice Declaration following an EEC summit attended by the Palestine Liberation Organization, incurred criticism for Britain both in Israel and the United States. Carrington certainly did not always agree with US policy in the Middle East, though he was always publicly supportive. For all these reasons the Foreign Secretary felt it important that he honour his commitment to visit Israel at the end of March 1982, to try and put paid to the idea that he was an enemy (with 'two horns and a forked tail', as he put it), and to deny the Israeli government the chance of trying to play London and Washington off against each other. In the event, he had little chance to make much progress.[37] Like Mrs Thatcher in Brussels, Lord Carrington in Tel Aviv was distracted by news from the South Atlantic, and was summoned home early, arriving back late on 31 March in time to attend the meeting with the Prime Minister and Defence Secretary at which Admiral Leach said that a task force could be ready to sail to the Falkland Islands in a few days.

It is worth mentioning that a great deal was going on elsewhere in the world in the first few months of 1982 to cause the Foreign Secretary anxiety, apart from in the Middle East and the Falklands. There was an outbreak of coups, actual (Guatemala, Bangladesh) or threatened (Ghana, Kenya), not to mention political turmoil in Zimbabwe (formerly

Rhodesia), where the two political factions forming the government, led by Robert Mugabe and Joshua Nkomo, had fallen out to such an extent that Mugabe had expelled Nkomo for plotting against him. The status of Hong Kong was under discussion with the Chinese government; the Falklands was to prove an awkward precedent to Mrs Thatcher's visit to China later in the year. And of course, Carrington was also closely involved in EEC affairs, trying to persuade the Prime Minister that a slightly more emollient line might achieve better results, while at the same time reassuring his European counterparts that Britain was seeking only a more equitable budgetary settlement, not to 'get back what she put in' (the so-called *juste retour*).[38] He was also involved in high-level talks in various groupings (EEC, CSCE, NATO) about the menacing situation in Eastern Europe, where a Soviet 'intervention' in Poland (in the same way that it had 'intervened' in Afghanistan in December 1979) was by no means out of the question. Of course, every Foreign Secretary has to have an eye on every corner of the globe, and the episodes described in this book have demonstrated how some, indeed a remarkable number of foreign policy problems never seem to go away. As he himself acknowledged, this is not an excuse for Carrington's taking threatening moves by Argentina insufficiently seriously. But it does show that on 2 April the Falklands was not the only slice on his plate.

While the Prime Minister was busy in Brussels, and the Foreign Secretary in the Middle East, Defence Secretary **John Nott** had just returned from Colorado Springs, where he had attended a meeting of NATO's Nuclear Planning Group. In his memoirs, Nott helpfully included a list of the things he had to do in March 1982: in addition to the NATO meeting, these included a state visit to the Sultan of Oman, to whom Britain was supplying arms; a one-week NATO war game; negotiations on the privatization of the Royal Ordnance factories; negotiations with the Army on the purchase of armoured personnel carriers; attending an Anglo-German summit at Chequers; and finalizing and announcing Britain's purchase of Trident missiles from the United States. And, of course, he had to consult the service chiefs and others about contingency plans in relation to the Argentine threat of invasion. Even allowing for the fact that some of these tasks were ongoing, and some merely the culmination of a long process, it is an impressive list.[39]

Nott had, apparently, told the Prime Minister at the end of 1981 that he wanted to step down as Defence Secretary and to retire from Parliament at the next election.[40] But he was persuaded to carry on, and indeed was to become one of the more recognizable public faces in the Falk-lands conflict. Nott had only served as Defence Secretary since January 1981, when he had been appointed, in the words of Sir Geoffrey Howe, as a 'trustie who could be relied upon to get on top of the brass-hats'.[41] But that year had included overseeing a tough Defence Review, always a testing experience for a Secretary of State. No matter how large the defence budget, there is always a big gap between commitments and spending, tremendous resistance to any reduction in either from the dif-ferent branches of the armed services, and great determination by the Treasury to achieve substantial savings. During the Cold War, the serv-ices could always point to the Soviet threat to support their arguments; on the other side, the Treasury could point to the impossibility of main-taining current levels of defence spending at a time of 15 per cent infla-tion. Nott's job was to square the circle, delivering the savings while maintaining the capability. It was made more difficult by the fact that the Prime Minister took a close personal interest in the process, reinforcing her Defence Secretary's determination if she felt it necessary. At the same time, she had always made great play of the importance of main-taining a strong defence, and indeed had resisted an attempt by Geoffrey Howe to cut back on Britain's commitment to NATO of increasing defence spending by 3 per cent per annum.

Nott was an admirer of the Prime Minister—in his memoirs he noted that he was unusual among his colleagues in also liking her personally, even if in the first few years of the government, when he was Secretary of State for Trade, he found her treatment of those ministers who disagreed with her rather brutal. But he was not 'one of us' in the sense of being a member of the inner circle of her closest allies, though he professed to share her dislike for the 'feeble, appeasing' Foreign Office.[42] The Ministry of Defence was a rather different type of department. Like many of his predecessors, Nott found himself at the centre of inter-service rivalry and competition for resources. He was, he later claimed, 'just another expendable front-line soldier, to be disposed of where nec-essary in the battle for more money', judged by his ability to 'win' against the Treasury.[43] Not surprisingly, the outcome of the Defence Review, announced in June 1981, brought down on his head the combined wrath of senior members of the British military establishment.

In announcing the Review, both Nott and the Prime Minister were at pains to point out that despite the reductions in manpower and capital equipment, defence spending would continue to increase, and Britain's commitments to NATO would be met in full. A telegram sent to British missions overseas, setting out the terms of the Review, was defensive in tone. After listing the cuts, it said that the government wished 'to present its decisions in a positive way…we see no need to put ourselves in the dock'.[44] Although cuts fell across the board, the Navy felt particularly hard done by. The operation of the strategic nuclear submarine force would remain its primary task, but there would be large reductions in the numbers of frigates and destroyers, and fewer aircraft carriers would be required. In practice, this meant getting rid of the aircraft carrier HMS *Hermes*, selling the *Invincible* to Australia, and scrapping the assault ships *Fearless* and *Intrepid*. Crucially, the listening ship HMS *Endurance* was to be withdrawn from the South Atlantic.

These cuts made in the Defence Review were to be of great significance in the run-up to the Falklands conflict, not least in encouraging Argentina to believe that there was no prospect that the British would seek to defend the islands by force. Nott's view that Britain was unlikely to be involved in any major naval battles, and therefore needed fewer aircraft carriers and fighting ships, did not seem unreasonable in 1981, but was to look quite different in April 1982. Luckily, not all of the withdrawals or sales of ships had taken place, so that in the event it was possible to reverse or postpone some of the decisions taken. In particular, the bitterly contested decision to withdraw HMS *Endurance* had not yet been implemented, so that it was still in the area. If the Argentines had waited a few months more to make a move, the ships would not have been available.[45] As it was, the Navy was suddenly the star of the show—a fact of which Admiral Henry Leach, appearing on 31 March in full dress uniform to reassure the Prime Minister of the capability of the Senior Service, was certainly aware. Previously Leach, like other senior military figures, had been actively briefing against the Defence Secretary, and resentful of the Prime Minister's support for him. All this was to be 'swept aside when the bugle sounded'.[46]

The Argentine invasion of the Falklands seemed to vindicate all the warnings given by the armed forces that Britain's defence capability was being reduced to dangerous levels. But in the first months of 1982, it was the Trident programme, not the threat to the Falklands, that preoccupied the Defence Secretary. Ever since British and American scientists had worked on the first nuclear bombs during the Second World War, the Anglo-US relationship in respect of nuclear matters had been both close and difficult. There was close liaison and cooperative working at technical and military levels. But in political terms, the British government had always had to argue its case hard (and dig deep in its pockets) to gain access to the latest generation of nuclear technology. The Americans, like the Russians, were very protective of the programmes on which they had spent so much time and money, and very wary of sharing secrets in case they found their way to the other side. This was a fact of Cold War life, especially at a time when the Soviet Union's military strength and manpower seemed particularly threatening.

Nevertheless, it was in US interests for its British ally to be well defended, both on its own account and as a member of NATO. Britain was, after all, the only European nuclear power apart from France. On 11 March 1982 Nott was able to announce that a deal had been concluded for Britain to buy the American Trident II-D5 submarine-launched ballistic missile system, to replace its own ageing Polaris missiles. Negotiations had been long and difficult, not least because the Americans had upgraded their system along the way, and under the final agreement Britain was to be responsible for 5 per cent of research and development costs. Although the successful conclusion of the Trident deal was a relief to Nott and the British government, it also brought parliamentary and public criticism from the anti-nuclear lobby and those who considered the money would have been better spent in improving Britain's conventional capability.

When Nott attended the meeting of NATO's Nuclear Planning Group at the end of March he also encountered criticism of the Trident deal from some of his European partners. For one thing, it symbolized the Anglo-American nuclear axis that always tended to antagonize countries like France, itself a nuclear power. But some other countries, such as West Germany, Denmark, and the Netherlands, also had strong anti-nuclear lobbies to contend with, and were inclined to think that Trident II represented an unnecessary escalation of the nuclear arms race. Nott had his work cut out to persuade his European colleagues that Trident was vital for the defence of their countries as well as his own. His US counterpart, Caspar Weinberger, supported this argument, but it was a tricky meeting that required sensitive handling.[47] Meanwhile, Nott was in regular touch with the Ministry of Defence about contingency arrangements to meet the growing crisis in the South Atlantic. He returned to London to discuss plans to deploy nuclear submarines to the area, and to put other ships on standby, although the briefing he received on returning to the MOD on 30 March was not encouraging. The more questions he asked about what military response might be possible if there were an Argentine move against the Falkland Islands, the gloomier the prospects seemed. 'Everything that had ever been written about the poverty of Britain's military options in the South Atlantic was being validated.'[48]

By the end of March, the Prime Minister, Foreign Secretary, and Defence Secretary were all back in London and engaged almost full-time in discussions on the developing situation in the South Atlantic. Carrington was in consultation with British representatives in Washington and New York on mustering support for Britain with the US government and in the United Nations. But as the Official History makes clear, everyone concerned still hoped that a diplomatic solution could and would be found and that the Argentine junta would think better of its aggressive posture. And despite arrangements for the deployment of nuclear submarines and other ships, there was an understandable reluctance to do anything in military terms that might escalate the situation rather than defusing it. In any case, the Chiefs of Staff remained cautious about what could be done, stressing the difficulty of mounting any operations in the area, and the time it would take to get there. The idea of assembling a task force and getting it ready to sail if the situation deteriorated was only discussed late on 31 March and on 1 April. Although in retrospect, and with detailed evidence available, the evolution of the crisis has an air of inevitability, it is important to remember that news of the Argentine invasion was only confirmed on the afternoon of 2 April. The ministers who gathered round the Cabinet table at 7.30 p.m. were faced with what was an entirely new situation.

All those present agreed that the British government was faced with an extraordinary challenge that required a firm military response. There was also a rather defensive air to the discussion. Ministers were aware that there was likely to be considerable criticism of the way the Argentine invasion appeared to have caught the government unawares. There would also be criticism, both in Parliament and from the general public, that the cuts made in the 1981 Defence Review meant that the British military were ill-equipped to cope with the threat, because conventional forces had been neglected in favour of the Trident programme. The Cabinet discussed how to respond to these criticisms, pointing out that even if a fleet had been dispatched to the Falklands on the same day that the Argentine salvage vessel had landed on South Georgia, it would still not have arrived in time to prevent the invasion. In addition, sending such a force prematurely would have appeared to be using a sledgehammer to crack a nut, and might well have provided the Argentine junta with an excuse to take action. The government would also argue that the dispute over the Falklands had been going on for many years, and that it would have been disproportionate for British forces to be stationed in the area just in case Argentina launched an invasion.

As they made them, ministers were aware that these arguments, even if reasonable, sounded lame. The government's reputation would have to rest on the success of the task force. Everyone hoped that the situation could still be resolved without actually having to fight, though the Prime Minister at least was clear in her mind that if the islands had really been occupied by the Argentines, they must be taken back, and by force if necessary. There is some question whether everyone in the military appreciated this point. Sir David Omand, then John Nott's Private Secretary, has said that only after the task force had sailed was it fully appreciated in the Ministry of Defence that the Prime Minister intended it not just to deter the Argentines, but to recapture the islands.[49] But if it were necessary to fight, it was also necessary to win, and ministers had received sufficient advice to realize that this would be by no means a foregone conclusion. They agreed that it would be important not to create the impression in the minds of either Parliament or the public that a military solution could be accomplished easily.

Hostilities against Argentina—a war, in fact—naturally had implications for other ministers as well as the Prime Minister and the Foreign and Defence Secretaries. The Chancellor of the Exchequer, **Sir Geoffrey Howe**, has written that the 'least relevant factor' in the decision to send the task force was the likely economic cost of the conflict. It was, he said, 'no part of the Chancellor's duty at such a time to argue against the use of the defence forces for the very purpose for which they had been provided'.[50] The Prime Minister, who regarded the Chancellor as one of her most trusted and loyal ministers, would have expected no less. He and Mrs Thatcher had worked very closely together over the first few years of the government. Although she was inclined to bully him—he said that he felt 'much more menaced than menacing'—he understood that the Prime Minister had a strong 'Treasury instinct', and the fact that the economy was her chief priority made it essential that they operate as a team. This they had done, with Howe fighting his corner successfully on a number of issues. He was, as one newspaper report put it, 'the only man who could work with her at his shoulder'.[51]

The Chancellor had played a major part in the important 1981 budget, and in the gradual turning round of the British economy. His 1982 budget, presented on 9 March, had been relatively upbeat, but he was well aware that there remained many negative economic indicators. If Britain were to embark on armed conflict over the Falklands, it would cost money that had to be found. But on 2 April, Howe knew this was not the time for such a discussion. For the present, his role was to consider the practicalities of taking economic action against Argentina, with whom Britain had a favourable balance of trade, as well as a considerable level of investment there. His first move would be to consult the Governor of the Bank of England about freezing Argentine balances held in the United Kingdom, to deter the junta from taking action against British interests.

The Trade Minister, **John Biffen**, was also concerned about the possible damage to British interests if there were a prolonged conflict with Argentina. His instinct was in favour of a negotiated settlement if at all possible, an argument he made (courageously, in the opinion of both Nott and Cecil Parkinson) on the evening of 2 April. He did not, however, oppose the sending of the task force. Geoffrey Howe noted in his memoirs that during the meeting, when discussing an intelligence report from the Chiefs of Staff that a military operation to recapture the Falklands would be extremely difficult and might fail, he passed a note to Biffen saying that it would be surprising if this were not true; Biffen passed one back, saying 'Absolutely—the bearer of realistic news is rarely welcome! See Cleopatra!'[52] This kind of response was typical of the Trade Minister, and an example of what Mrs Thatcher called 'Biffenry'. Their relationship, though not unfriendly, was not a close one, and Biffen was later to describe her as a 'brilliant tyrant'—or, in another of his snappy phrases, a 'tigress surrounded by hamsters'.[53]

Biffen, together with his fellow ministers **Patrick Jenkin**, Secretary of State for Industry, and **Norman Tebbit**, Secretary of State for Employment (most definitely 'one of us') faced a number of difficult problems in early 1982 that had a direct impact on the British economy. The government's efforts to privatize parts of major nationalized industries were proceeding slowly and in a piecemeal fashion, with adverse effects on industrial relations, unemployment, and Britain's competitiveness with other countries. In addition, in February 1982 both the DeLorean sports car company, into which the Northern Ireland Development Agency had pumped more than £100m, and Laker Airways, run by Mrs

Thatcher's friend Sir Freddie Laker and in receipt of support from the Bank of England, collapsed with high levels of debt. Though not directly related to the Falklands issue, such developments had a bad effect on the prosperity and reputation of British business as a whole, and affected overseas trade relations at a time when the government was likely to need all the support it could get.

Another minister who had particular concerns about the implications of the decision on 2 April was **Cecil Parkinson**, present at the Cabinet meeting in his role as Paymaster-General but who was also chairman of the Conservative Party. In the latter role he was extremely concerned with the possible impact of the Falklands crisis. Self-made, charming, good-looking (Alan Clark wrote that Parkinson was 'underrated just because he is handsome'), Parkinson was very much a man after the Prime Minister's heart. Coming from a background in business, he had been appointed a junior trade minister in 1979 at the age of 47 and rose rapidly in Mrs Thatcher's favour, attending the breakfast policy meetings open only to those who were 'one of us'.[54] Until the news about the invasion of the Falklands, Parkinson thought that things were going rather well for the government in 1982. Despite Roy Jenkins winning the seat of Glasgow Hillhead for the SDP in March, the Conservative Party had pulled ahead of its rivals and economic confidence was returning.

Although he had no hesitation in supporting the decision to send the task force to the Falklands, Parkinson realized how risky the whole enterprise was for the Thatcher government. After the Cabinet meeting, according to his memoirs, he had dinner with **Michael Heseltine**, Secretary of State for the Environment. Both agreed 'that unless we succeeded in ousting the Argentinians this incident could destroy the government'. There were many in the Conservative Party already lining up to dig the Prime Minister's political grave. Heseltine was admired by Parkinson (who had an uneasy relationship with his civil servants) for the way he handled his department. Heseltine's 'constructive and deliberate unreasonableness' was, Parkinson thought, similar to that of Mrs Thatcher. Perhaps that is one reason why the Prime Minister tended to distrust the dynamic and purposeful Heseltine as 'dangerously ambitious as well as ideologically unsound'.[55] On 2 April Heseltine also supported the decision to send the task force, although he was concerned that the wider implications of the crisis had not been considered sufficiently fully. In general, he was concerned by the failure to make enough effort to understand the viewpoint of other countries. In particular, he thought it unwise to rely too heavily on American support. Britain, as he wrote in 1987, had no more right than other Europeans to presume on that support, but it tended to do so. 'At best we are smug; at worst, envious.'[56]

As Home Secretary, **William Whitelaw** had little input into the Falklands discussions, but as Mrs Thatcher's close adviser and, some thought, the 'lynchpin of her authority' his role was crucial. His concerns about the task force decision were based on his own memories of Suez, but he supported it completely. In his memoirs, Whitelaw stated that when Mrs Thatcher was elected Conservative leader in 1975 instead of him, he decided that 'in the interests of the Party' he would serve her 'in any capacity she wanted, and that I would give my undivided loyalty to her'.[57] In fact, it had taken him some time to get to know her well and assess her qualities. But his value to the Prime Minister was far more than that of a devoted supporter, nor was it uncritical. His long experience, including military service during the Second World War, and his ministerial record dating back to the Macmillan government, made him an invaluable source of advice and general wisdom. He knew, as Hugo Young put it, 'what was on and what was not. He could smell it in the wind, feel it through his toes.' In a crisis such as that presented in April 1982, he was someone to rely on. As Hayden Phillips, an Assistant Under-Secretary at the Home Office, put it, 'one of Whitelaw's greatest qualities is that the more serious the crisis he has to deal with, the more frivolous and jokey he becomes'. He was, said Phillips, a 'great defuser', a quality that was certainly in demand in the spring of 1982.[58]

By the time the Cabinet met on the evening of 2 April, the sovereignty of the Falkland Islands was no longer an issue. It was not raised by the Lord Chancellor, **Lord Hailsham**, nor by any other minister. Although it was central to the long-running dispute with Argentina, Mrs Thatcher had not really focused on the issue until discussing it with Carrington (who was certainly aware of the implications) on 28 March. When she realized, on reading the latest reports from Stanley, that sovereignty was the crux of the problem, her first reaction was to submit the issue to the International Court of Justice at The Hague. She was taken aback when the Foreign Secretary told her that if this happened, Britain might not win, though explaining that this was more because of uncertainties about the constitution of the Court than because the British case was not a good one. Now Mrs Thatcher was fully focused. Were the Islands really British? Once Carrington had assured her that the British claim was good ('because', as she told him 'there is no earthly point in sweating blood over it if it's not ours'), she had no doubt that the Falklands must be defended, by force if necessary.[59]

Similarly, once she had been assured by Admiral Sir Henry Leach, First Sea Lord, that 'a fleet able to look after itself', led by HMS *Hermes* and *Invincible*, could be ready to sail the following week and that it would be possible to recapture the Falklands, she was clear this must be done. Previously, she had felt 'outraged and determined': now she felt 'relieved and confident'.[60] But this was written long after the Falklands conflict, in the secure knowledge of military victory. At the time, she was undoubtedly extremely worried about the situation on all fronts: military, diplomatic, and political. Even after the decision was taken on that Friday night, the future remained uncertain: the Argentines might still retreat, or be persuaded to withdraw; there was still scope for a negotiated solution. But if that were not the case, Britain would be ready to fight, as Mrs Thatcher made clear when she addressed the House of Commons, called into emergency session on the morning of Saturday 3 April.

By now the press was full of reports about the events in the South Atlantic, including misleading accounts that the Royal Marines had offered no resistance. There were calls for the resignation of the Defence and Foreign Secretaries, termed by the *Daily Express* 'Thatcher's guilty men'. Despite a calm and reassuring statement by the Prime Minister, the government was given a very rough parliamentary ride, and none of its ministers was left in any doubt that its survival lay in the balance.[61] The announcement of the sending of the task force helped to allay some criticism, but the experience was still bad enough for Nott subsequently to offer his resignation (which was refused). Carrington, however, after a bruising meeting with party members, felt that he had to go, and the Prime Minister accepted his decision. He understood the 'shock and fury' felt throughout Britain at what had happened: the inhabitants of a British colony had been taken over against their will, and nothing had been done to prevent it. 'Someone', he said, 'must take the blame.'[62]

Much has been written about the assumptions that governed the British approach to the Falklands crisis, alleging a sort of self-deceiving post-colonialism and unwillingness to accept declining influence. Certainly a number of Britain's friends, as well as critics, expressed that view overtly or covertly at the time: even its closest ally, the United States, was initially suspicious. Ministers have not dispelled this impression by writing in their memoirs that the crisis reminded them of Suez (and in Margaret Thatcher's case, Munich). But other analogies were current too: General

Galtieri had reckoned that the British government, having agreed a settlement with Rhodesia, would be ready to take a pragmatic approach to the Falklands as well. Lord Carrington reckoned that Britain's reputation for settling difficult issues in Rhodesia and Belize showed up Argentina's fascist dictatorship. On 2 April, however, such considerations remained in the subconscious. The issue at hand was whether Britain was prepared to allow another country to invade its territory unimpeded. For all the ministers present, the answer was in the negative.

In the context of the campaign as a whole, the decision taken by the Cabinet on that Friday night was a preliminary but essential element, the starting point for what was to prove a triumph both for the British armed forces and for Mrs Thatcher's government, whose political fortunes it transformed. The story of the ensuing military campaign to re-establish British control of the Falklands, ending with the surrender of Argentine forces on 15 June, is told in vivid and fascinating detail in the official history by Sir Lawrence Freedman. But on 2 April, most of the Cabinet, even if shocked by the news of the Argentine invasion, did not realize its full implications, or the impact it would have on them personally, on their departments and on the government as a whole. Sending the task force was, in that sense, a shot in the dark. Fortunately for them, the government was to emerge into the light of victory rather than obscurity.

Conclusion

The political landscape of Britain, and of the wider world, changed considerably between the outbreak of the Korean War in 1950 and the Falklands conflict in 1982. The evolution of Britain's global position and influence, of international alliances and alignments, of multilateral institutions and spheres of strategic interest, emerges clearly as we move from turbulent and bruising post-war readjustments, through the forming of new post-colonial relationships and ties with the European continent, to what might be called the beginning of the end of the Cold War. With hindsight, certain trends may seem inevitable, developments ineluctable. That was not how it seemed to the decision-makers at the time.

Nevertheless, the continuities between the six episodes described in this book, and between them and later British foreign policy decisions, are striking. It is not hard to see that British governments have continued to face many of the same problems as their predecessors. Each episode considered here took place against the backdrop of the Cold War, so that every foreign policy problem had implications for the East–West struggle. Throughout the period, Britain wanted to remain an important global power, but its ambitions were constrained by its relative economic weakness. Even after the Cold War, however, many of the continuities persist. It has often been argued that many of Britain's problems since the Second World War have arisen from its inability to understand that it is no longer a world power or to accept the decline in its influence. Nevertheless, it is notable that Britain has always been treated as a world power, and its influence recognized, sometimes unwillingly, by friend and foe alike. At the time of writing this is still the case.

Similar arguments have been adduced to disparage the idea of the so-called 'special relationship' with the United States. While it is certainly possible to argue over whether this is a meaningful or helpful description, the Anglo-American relationship remains unique to each partner in specific but important ways, particularly in respect of security and intelligence. That relationship has always remained central to British policy, while containing innate tensions due partly to imbalances in size and power, and partly to underlying differences in political systems, cultural perceptions, and regional spheres of interest. This seems likely to continue, though shifts in global economic and political power undoubtedly affect the internal and external dynamics.

Britain's relationship with 'Europe'—both inside and outside the European Economic Community, now the European Union—was and remains perennially problematic, even if mutually beneficial, and a divisive issue in British politics. Whatever happens to the European space in the future, the characteristics of the relationship seem likely to persist. Commonwealth ties, though they have evolved, remain relevant, politically, economically, and culturally. In the period covered in this book they exerted a strong pull on British governments, especially in the field of defence and security. NATO, the cornerstone of Western defence since its establishment in 1949, was troubled by disagreements about the way it should adapt to changing circumstances, by the unwillingness of some members to contribute as much as others, and by the fear that the US government, always the dominant military power, would cut back on its commitment and force the Europeans to do more for themselves. These arguments continue. The United Nations Organization was and remains similarly troubled by questions about its funding, its role, its powers, the extent to which it has the right and the ability to intervene in countries' affairs, the composition of the Security Council, and the use of the veto.

Those involved in taking the decisions examined here were aware of some of the continuities at the time. In each case, we see ministers drawing on their earlier political experience to inform their choices. Some of the decision-makers were key players for almost the whole period covered by these six episodes: not just ministers, but advisers, officials, military experts, and parliamentary groupings (not to mention the monarchy). Anthony Eden, taking decisions on Suez as Prime Minister in 1956, looked back on his experiences as Foreign Secretary in the 1930s. Sir Alec Douglas-Home, taking a bold gamble against the Soviet system in 1971, also drew on his pre-war experiences, as well as on the experience of Britain's rejection by Europe not just in 1961, but in 1967 as well. Ministers faced with the Argentine invasion of the Falklands thought about what had happened over Suez. Today, government ministers look back in similar fashion, even if they draw on different and more recent experiences. Analogies are not always helpful, but ministers cannot choose their memories selectively (except when they write their memoirs).

It is important not to take this argument too far. It is unpredictability—not just Harold Macmillan's 'events, dear boy', but the singularities of personality and circumstance, politics and geography—that makes all foreign policy decisions different and difficult. It is a truism to say that history repeats itself, and a dangerous one at that; no two situations are exactly alike. But the factors that affect British foreign policy decisions are remarkably constant, and can provide important insights into other decisions taken at other times. A better understanding of the imperatives and context of past decisions can do greater justice to them, as well as informing decision-making on the challenging foreign policy issues that must be faced now and in the future. There is no doubt that in the realm of foreign policy-making, history can be a constructive tool rather than a misleading guide.

Notes

Introduction

1. Douglas Hurd, *Choose your Weapons: The British Foreign Secretary. 200 Years of Argument, Success and Failure* (London: Weidenfeld and Nicolson, 2010), xvii.
2. Quoted in Richard Crossman's introduction to Walter Bagehot, *The English Constitution*, first published in 1867 (London: Penguin edn, 1963), 20.
3. Tony Blair, *A Journey* (London: Hutchinson, 2010), 405.
4. Peter Hennessy, *The Prime Minister: The Office and its Holders since 1945* (London: Allen Lane/The Penguin Press, 2000; Penguin edn, 2001), 98.
5. Stephen Wall, *A Stranger in Europe: Britain and the EU from Thatcher to Blair* (Oxford: Oxford University Press, 2008), 187.
6. Personal communication.
7. Patrick Gordon Walker, *The Cabinet* (London: Jonathan Cape, 1970), 131.
8. Lord Armstrong's remarks were made at a meeting of the Mile End Group held at Queen Mary College, University of London, on 21 July 2011, during a seminar on the theory and practice of taking Cabinet minutes, chaired by Peter (now Lord) Hennessy with the participation of Sir Gus (now Lord) O'Donnell, who was then Cabinet Secretary.
9. Frank Field (ed.), *Attlee's Great Contemporaries: The Politics of Character* (London: Continuum Books, 2009), 102.
10. Remark made when Professor Hennessy was speaking at a seminar at Corpus Christi College, University of Cambridge, on 5 November 2010.

Chapter 1

1. Present at the meeting were: Clement Attlee (Prime Minister, in the chair); Herbert Morrison (Lord President of the Council); Sir Stafford Cripps (Chancellor of the Exchequer); Hugh Dalton (Minister of Town and Country Planning); Viscount Alexander (Chancellor of the Duchy of Lancaster); Viscount Jowitt (Lord Chancellor); James Chuter Ede (Home Secretary); Emmanuel Shinwell (Minister of Defence); George Isaacs (Minister of Labour and National Service); Aneurin Bevan (Minister of Health); Thomas Williams (Minister of Agriculture and Fisheries); George Tomlinson (Minister of Education); Harold Wilson (President of the Board of Trade); James Griffiths (Secretary of State for the Colonies); Hector McNeil (Secretary of State for Scotland); Kenneth Younger (Minister of State at the Foreign Office); and Lord Ogmore (Under-Secretary of State for Commonwealth Relations). John Wheatley, the Lord Advocate, and William Whiteley, Parliamentary Secretary to the Treasury, were present only for item 5 on the agenda (Interference with Military Supplies). Sir Norman Brook, the Cabinet Secretary, and two Deputy Secretaries, Air Marshal Sir William Elliot and Alexander Johnston, were present throughout. The formal minutes of the meeting, CM(50)50th Conclu-

sions, are in CAB 128/18, TNA. The discussion on item 3, Korea, is printed in H. J. Yasamee and K. A. Hamilton (eds.), *Documents on British Policy Overseas*, Series II, vol. iv: *Korea 1950–1951* (London: HMSO, 1991, hereafter *DBPO Korea*), No. 27. The Cabinet Secretary's notes of the meeting are in CAB 195/8, TNA.

2. The minutes of the Defence Committee on 6 July 1950 are printed in *DBPO Korea*, No. 14.

3. Washington telegram No. 2036 of 23 July 1950, printed in *DBPO Korea*, No. 25.

4. On the Schuman Plan for a European coal and steel organization, in which the British government declined to be involved, see Roger Bullen and M. E. Pelly (eds.), *Documents on British Policy Overseas*, Series II, vol. i: *The Schuman Plan, the Council of Europe and Western European Integration, 1950–52* (hereafter *DBPO Schuman*) (London: HMSO, 1986), chapter I.

5. The Chiefs of Staff's report on 'Defence Policy and Global Strategy', dated 7 June 1950 and circulated as DO(50)45, is printed in *DBPO Korea* as Appendix I (CAB 131/9, TNA).

6. The Defence Committee had met at 5.30 p.m. on 24 July. For a summary of the meeting see *DBPO Korea*, No. 27, especially notes 4 and 5.

7. Kim Il-Sung was to remain in power until succeeded by his son Kim Jong-Il in 1994. The latter died in December 2011 and was succeeded in turn by his son, Kim Jong-un.

8. See Percy Cradock, *Know your Enemy: How the Joint Intelligence Committee Saw the World* (London: John Murray Publishers Ltd, 2002), chapter 5: 'For the first years of communist rule in China the [Joint Intelligence] Committee was ready to assume an identity of interest between Peking and Moscow and tended to treat China almost like a Soviet possession' (84).

9. British intelligence resources in Asia were thin on the ground. They tended to rely on the Americans, who in this case got it wrong. A number of intelligence reports predicting accurately military preparations for the North Korean invasion can be found in Woodrow J. Kuhns (ed.), *Assessing the Soviet Threat: The Early Cold War Years* (Honolulu: Center for the Study of Intelligence (CSI), CIA, University Press of the Pacific, 2005). See also P. K. Rose, 'Two Strategic Intelligence Mistakes in Korea, 1950', CSI, <www.cia.gov>, accessed 28 May 2010. For a superb analysis of common intelligence mistakes, including those made over Korea, see former CIA analyst Cynthia Grabo's *Anticipating Surprise: Analysis for Strategic Warning* (Lanham, MD: University Press of America, 2004). On Anglo-American policy differences and on British intelligence in the region see Christopher Baxter, *The Great Power Struggle in East Asia, 1944–50* (London: Palgrave Macmillan, 2009), chapter 6.

10. At the start of the Korean War, there were apparently more British than US warships in Japanese and Korean waters. The Labour politician Douglas Jay told Peter Hennessy that when Attlee made this statement in the House of Commons Churchill thought it must be wrong, but Jay had received similar information from his brother who was in the Royal Navy. See Peter Hennessy, *Muddling Through: Power, Politics and the Quality of Government in Postwar Britain* (London: Victor Gollancz, 1996), 184–5.

11. For an interesting discussion of party views on Labour foreign policy and on Korea in particular, see R. M. Douglas, *The Labour Party, Nationalism and Internationalism 1939–1951* (London: Routledge, 2004).

12. The Soviet Union had successfully tested an atomic bomb in August 1949, earlier than the UK and US had expected. In 1949 Mao Tse-tung's Chinese People's Liberation Army had defeated Chiang Kai-shek's Nationalist forces and driven them from the mainland to Formosa (now Taiwan). Mainland China was now under communist control.

13. Relations between the Soviet Union and its wartime allies had soured after the end of the Second World War: major points of tension had included Persia (now Iran), in relation to the withdrawal of Soviet troops in 1946, the coup in Czechoslovakia in 1948 that brought a communist government to power, and the Berlin crisis of 1948–9 when the Soviet blockade of links between Berlin and the Western occupation zones had only been broken by a massive airlift operation organized by the British and Americans.

14. See Harry S. Truman, *Memoirs*, ii: *Years of Trial and Hope: 1946–52* (New York: Doubleday & Co., 1956; Signet edn, 1965), 379.

15. See Keith Hamilton, Patrick Salmon, and Stephen Twigge (eds.), *Documents on British Policy Overseas*, Series III, vol. vi: *Berlin in the Cold War 1948–1990* (London: Routledge, 2009), chapter I.

16. See the official history of the Korean War: General Sir Anthony Farrar-Hockley, *The British Part in the Korean War*, i: *A Distant Obligation* (London: HMSO, 1990), 45. Sir Benegal Rau, Governor of the Reserve Bank of India, was President of the UNSC in July 1950.

17. The Chief of the Imperial General Staff, Field-Marshal Sir William Slim, gave this information to the Cabinet at their meeting on 17 July, CM(50) 46th Conclusions, CAB 128/18, TNA.

18. For the Anglo-American staff talks, and General Bradley's speech, see *DBPO Korea*, No. 25.

19. Peter Catterall (ed.), *The Macmillan Diaries: The Cabinet Years, 1950–57* (London: Macmillan, 2003; Pan edn, 2004), entry for 9 August 1950, p. 7.

20. The foundations for many of the Labour government's achievements had, of course, been laid during the war years by the coalition government. Nevertheless, they were striking: see Paul Addison, *No Turning Back: The Peacetime Revolutions of Post-War Britain* (Oxford: Oxford University Press, 2010), part I.

21. The phrase 'intimate, but not exclusive' was used in a memorandum by the FO Permanent Under-Secretaries' Committee on Anglo-American relations, dated 22 April 1950. An extract is printed in Roger Bullen and M. E. Pelly (eds.), *Documents on British Policy Overseas*, Series II, vol. ii: *The London Conferences, Anglo-American Relations and Cold War Strategy January–June 1950* (London: HMSO, 1987, hereafter *DBPO London Conferences*), No. 27.

22. Sir Roderick Barclay, *Ernest Bevin and the Foreign Office 1932–69* (London, 1975), 92.

23. Barclay, *Ernest Bevin*, 30.

24. Geoffrey Warner (ed.), *In the Midst of Events: The Foreign Office Diaries and Papers of Kenneth Younger, February 1950–October 1951* (London: Routledge, 2005, hereafter *Younger Diaries*), entries for 14 and 29 May 1950, pp. 14 and 19. See also

Barclay, *Ernest Bevin*, 49, and Alan Bullock, *Ernest Bevin: Foreign Secretary 1945–51* (London: Heinemann, 1983), 757–8.

25. See Barclay, *Ernest Bevin*, 67, also Farrar-Hockley, *A Distant Obligation*, 29–30.
26. Details of Truman's statement, and of the Cabinet meeting on 27 June 1950 when Bevin's advice was accepted, are given in *DBPO Korea*, No. 2.
27. *Younger Diaries*, entry for 14 May 1950, p. 16.
28. For Bevin's views on this, see *DBPO Schuman*, No. 12. See also Dean Acheson, *Present at the Creation: My Years in the State Department* (New York: W.W. Norton, 1969), chapter 42.
29. See William Manchester, *American Caesar: Douglas MacArthur 1880–1964* (London: Hutchinson, 1979), 536.
30. Minute from Younger to Bevin, 11 July 1950, *DBPO Korea*, No. 17.
31. See Manchester, *American Caesar*, 535; see also Acheson, *Present at the Creation*, and Truman, *Memoirs*.
32. See David Kynaston, *Austerity Britain 1945–51* (London: Bloomsbury, 2007), 340–1. On official measures taken in Britain against communists at this period see Christopher Andrew, *The Defence of the Realm: The Authorized History of MI5* (London: Penguin, 2009), 383–90.
33. Francis Williams, *A Prime Minister Remembers* (London: Heinemann, 1961), 149.
34. Frank Field (ed.), *Attlee's Great Contemporaries: The Politics of Character* (London: Continuum Books, 2009), 112; Nicklaus Thomas-Symonds, *Attlee: A Life in Politics* (London: Tauris, 2010), 142–4. Kenneth Younger, whose appointment as Foreign Office Minister of State in February 1950 brought him into close contact with the Prime Minister because of Bevin's frequent absence, noted in his diary that Attlee had an authority that would surprise outside observers (32).
35. Field, *Attlee's Great Contemporaries*, 151–3. Ministerial knowledge of Korea was certainly imperfect. Sir Alexander Johnston, a member of the Cabinet Secretariat in 1950, later told the official historian of the Korean War that not all government ministers nor their officials had been sure on the outbreak of hostilities where Korea lay. Farrar-Hockley, *A Distant Obligation*, 1.
36. Cabinet Conclusions CM(50)46, 17 July 1950, CAB 128/18, TNA. Menzies had spent a lot of time in Britain during the war, and was greeted by Attlee at the meeting as an old friend whose counsel was 'specially opportune at the present moment, when the situation in the Far East was causing anxiety both here and in Australia'.
37. Attlee had been involved in Indian affairs as a member of the Simon Commission set up in 1927, and as Dominions Secretary 1942–3. As Prime Minister he had been determined to secure Indian self-government: see K. O. Morgan, *Labour in Power 1945–1951* (Oxford: Oxford University Press, 1984), 219–24. India gained independence on 3 June 1947, and was divided into the independent dominions of India and Pakistan on 15 August that year.
38. Conversation between Attlee and the US Ambassador in London on 8 July 1950. See *DBPO Korea*, No. 15, also Nos. 18 and 22; *Younger Diaries*, entry for 6 July 1950, p. 25.
39. Attlee set out his thinking on the impact of the atomic bomb in a letter to President Truman dated 25 September 1945, printed in Roger Bullen and

M. E. Pelly (eds.), *Documents on British Policy Overseas*, Series I, vol. ii: *Conferences and Conversations 1945: London, Washington and Moscow* (London: HMSO, 1985), No. 196.

40. Minute from Sir W. Elliot (Chief of Staff to the Minister of Defence) to the Chiefs of Staff, 10 February 1950, CAB 301/108.

41. See Margaret Gowing and Lorna Arnold, *Independence and Deterrence: Britain and Atomic Energy, 1945–52*, 2 vols. (London: Palgrave Macmillan, 1974).

42. Andrew, *Defence of the Realm*, 388. Chapter 4, 'Vetting, Atom Spies and Protective Security', gives further details of anxieties on the part of both the US and British governments about security problems in the UK at this time.

43. George Mallaby, *From my Level* (London: Hutchinson, 1965), 56–7.

44. The Chiefs of Staff made this admission at the Defence Committee meeting on 6 July, saying that they would require eighteen months' warning before being ready for a war; hardly a practical proposition (*DBPO Korea*, No. 14).

45. Military conscription had ended with the Second World War but was reintroduced in 1947. The system of peacetime conscription embodied in the National Service Act of 1948 stipulated that young men between 17 and 21, if not in an 'essential' occupation, should spend eighteen months in the armed services and then remain on the reserve list for four years. See Kynaston, *Austerity Britain*, 379–80.

46. Relations were particularly strained with Gaitskell, who replaced Shinwell at the Ministry of Fuel and Power in 1947; and with Dalton, who protested to Attlee when Shinwell was appointed as Minister of Defence that he was the one colleague with whom he found it difficult to work, although he later conceded that Shinwell had done a good job. See Ben Pimlott (ed.), *The Political Diary of Hugh Dalton 1918–40, 1945–60* (London: Jonathan Cape, 1986, hereafter *Dalton Diary*), 471 and 480.

47. See G. C. Peden, *Arms, Economics and British Strategy from Dreadnoughts to Hydrogen Bombs* (Cambridge: Cambridge University Press, 2007), 248–9.

48. Cabinet Secretary's notes of the meeting on 25 July, CAB 195/8, TNA.

49. For details of both the 1923 and 1927 incidents, related to the Curzon Memorandum and the Arcos Raid respectively, see Gill Bennett, *Churchill's Man of Mystery: Desmond Morton and the World of Intelligence* (London: Routledge, 2006), chapters 4 and 5. See also chapter 8, on Churchill's access to military information during the 1930s.

50. See Peden, *Arms, Economics and British Strategy*, 232.

51. *Younger Diaries*, entry for 5 August 1950, p. 31.

52. Farrar-Hockley, *A Distant Obligation*, 107–9.

53. CM(50) 46th and 48th Conclusions, CAB 128/18, TNA.

54. CM(50) 50th Conclusions, CAB 128/18, Cabinet Secretary's notes, CAB 195/8, TNA. For Dalton's reaction to Attlee's offer of the Colonial Office see *Dalton Diary*, entry for 28 February 1950, p. 472.

55. See Kynaston, *Austerity Britain*, 343–4. 'The end of the 1940s—decade of war and austerity—signaled no immediate passage into the sunlit uplands' (509).

56. Simon Burgess, *Stafford Cripps: A Political Life* (London: Victor Gollancz, 1999), 257. Details of Cripps's life are taken principally from this work and from the entry in the *Oxford Dictionary of National Biography* by Peter Clarke and Richard Toye. Both works give details of the devaluation episode.

57. Hugh Dalton felt that Cripps's reaction to the devaluation episode, when the decision was taken in Cripps's absence by his three ambitious acolytes, Harold Wilson, Hugh Gaitskell, and Douglas Jay amounted to persecution mania; Attlee, typically, thought him 'rather a silly ass' to take it personally. See Burgess, *Stafford Cripps*, 301–6. Cripps finally resigned in October 1950, and died in April 1952 after a long and painful illness.

58. Record of a meeting of ministers held on 4 May 1950, printed in *DBPO London Conferences*, No. 57.

59. This was the thrust of a paper prepared by the Foreign Office, commented on by the Treasury, and circulated to the Permanent Under-Secretaries' Committee as PUSC(50)79 Final of 27 April 1950, printed in *DBPO London Conferences*, No. 43. See also Nos. 36 and 42 for further exposition of Cripps's views.

60. Bevin to Attlee, PM/50/18, 2 May 1950, printed in *DBPO London Conferences*, No. 55; record of meeting of ministers on 4 May 1950, No. 57.

61. CM(50) 48th Conclusions, 20 July 1950, CAB 128/18, and Cabinet Secretary's notes of that meeting, CAB 195/8, TNA.

62. PREM 8/1409, TNA; see *DBPO Korea*, No. 22.i.

63. Jowitt contested the American argument that they were entitled to come to the aid of South Korea by Article 51 of the UN Charter, which stated that nothing in the Charter impaired the inherent right of individual or collective self-defence against an armed attack on a member of the UN. South Korea was not a member. Although this was discussed on 30 June at a meeting in Younger's room and it was agreed that the point should be submitted to the Law Officers, the Cabinet agreed on 4 July that action taken on behalf of South Korea was 'clearly in accordance with the principle embedded in this Article of the Charter'. See *DBPO Korea*, Nos. 9 and 11.

64. CM(50) 48th and 49th Conclusions, 20 and 24 July 1950, CAB 128/18, TNA.

65. Cabinet Secretary's notes of the Cabinet meeting on 25 July, CAB 195/8, TNA. Reports of sabotage incidents at Portsmouth and elsewhere can be found in *The Times* digital archive.

66. See on this point Baxter, *The Great Power Struggle in East Asia*, 180–1.

67. According to Harold Macmillan, Churchill was dismayed to learn from Attlee that it would take at least two months 'to scrape together 3000 men and their equipment for Korea'. What, Churchill wanted to know, had they done with all the war equipment? 'It would appear that they have thrown it into the sea.' *Macmillan Diaries*, entry for 6 August 1950, p. 4. Similarly, General Dwight D. Eisenhower was dismayed at what he regarded as the lack of urgency in Truman's mobilization plans: see Stephen E Ambrose, *Eisenhower: Soldier and President* (New York: Simon and Schuster, 1997; Pocket Books edn, 2003), 252.

68. For an account of the Defence Committee's precise recommendations, and the military preparations that ensued, see Farrar-Hockley, *A Distant Obligation*, 103 ff.

69. Farrar-Hockley, *A Distant Obligation*, 110.

70. In May 1951 the Defence Committee agreed that National Service should be extended from eighteen months to two years (DO(51)58, 19 May 1951, CAB 131/11, TNA).

71. For an interesting discussion on these issues see Walter Lafeber, 'NATO and the Korean War: A Context', *Diplomatic History*, 13/4 (October 1989), 461–78. On US policy at this time see also John Lamberton Harper, *American Visions of Europe* (Cambridge: Cambridge University Press, 1994), chapter 5.
72. *DBPO Korea*, Appendix I.
73. *Younger Diaries*, entry for 6 July 1950, pp. 27–8.
74. *Younger Diaries*, entry for 5 August 1950, pp. 28–30.
75. Field (ed.), *Attlee's Great Contemporaries*, 156.

Chapter 2

1. In my view the best overall account of the Suez crisis remains Keith Kyle, *Suez* (London: Weidenfeld and Nicolson, 1991; pb edn 1992). The Israeli invasion of Egypt began on 29 October, with the Anglo-French Operation Musketeer launched on the 31st. Following international outcry and pressure from the US Eden announced a ceasefire on 6 November, and Anglo-French troops were withdrawn by 22 December.
2. Present at this meeting were: Anthony Eden (Prime Minister, in the chair); the Marquess of Salisbury (Lord President of the Council); Viscount Kilmuir (Lord Chancellor); James Stuart (Secretary of State for Scotland); Sir Walter Monckton (Minister of Defence); Peter Thorneycroft (President of the Board of Trade); Sir David Eccles (Minister of Education); the Earl of Selkirk (Chancellor of the Duchy of Lancaster); Harold Macmillan (Chancellor of the Exchequer); Selwyn Lloyd (Foreign Secretary); the Earl of Home (Secretary of State for Commonwealth Relations); Duncan Sandys (Minister of Housing and Local Government); David Heathcoat Amory (Minister of Agriculture, Fisheries, and Food); Iain Macleod (Minister of Labour and National Service); Patrick Buchan-Hepburn (Minister of Works); Aubrey Jones (Minister of Fuel and Power); Edward Heath (Parliamentary Secretary, Treasury); General Sir Gerald Templer (Chief of the Imperial General Staff); Admiral Earl Mountbatten (First Sea Lord and Chief of the Naval Staff); Air Chief Marshal Sir Dermot Boyle (Chief of the Air Staff); Cabinet Secretary Sir Norman Brook and two other members of the Cabinet Secretariat. R. A. Butler, the Lord Privy Seal, was absent through illness. The minutes of the meeting, CM(56) 54th Conclusions, can be found in CAB 128/30, TNA.
3. The second of these objectives is not mentioned in the formal Cabinet minutes, but is spelled out in the Cabinet Secretary's notes of the meeting. The relevant Cabinet Secretary's notebook is in CAB 195/15, TNA.
4. A concession to construct a canal linking the Mediterranean and Red Sea was granted to Frenchman Ferdinand de Lesseps by the Ottoman government in 1854, and it opened in 1869. At first Britain opposed the project, particularly because it did not want the route to India being controlled by any other country, but when the enterprise got into financial difficulties the British government bought 44 per cent of the shares in 1875. From 1882 British forces occupied Egypt, and the Convention of Constantinople, signed by the European powers in 1888, laid down that the canal should be open in peace and war to all countries. Britain's position in relation to the canal was set out in the Anglo-Egyptian Treaty of 1936, recognizing the Canal as an integral

part of Egypt as well as an international waterway, and providing for British forces to be stationed in the Canal Zone until Egypt could ensure its security and freedom of navigation with its own forces. See W. N. Medlicott, Douglas Dakin, and M. E. Pelly (eds.), *Documents on British Foreign Policy 1919–1939*, Second Series, vol. xvi: *The Rhineland Crisis and the Ending of Sanctions March–July 1936* (London: HMSO, 1977), *passim* and Appendix V. The Canal Base Agreement of October 1954 entrusted security and free passage entirely to the Egyptian government and provided for the withdrawal of British forces, although they could return in the event of a threat to any of the Arab states or Turkey.

5. Following the overthrow of the Egyptian monarchy in the Free Officers' coup of 1952, Nasser, at the age of 34, became Deputy to Mohammad Naguib as Prime Minister, but forced the latter to stand down in 1954 and became PM himself. He was elected President of Egypt in January 1956. For details of his career and political philosophy see Laura M. James, *Nasser at War: Arab Images of the Enemy* (Basingstoke: Palgrave Macmillan, 2006).

6. JIC(56)20 of 4 April 1956, 'Factors Affecting Egypt's Policy in the Middle East and North Africa', CAB 158/23, TNA. On the significance of this paper see Peter Hennessy, *Having it so Good: Britain in the Fifties* (London: Penguin, 2006), 415. See also Kyle, *Suez*, 78. On Nasser's intelligence links with the West see also Miles Copeland (former CIA officer), *The Game Player* (London: Aurum Press, 1989), and Yaacov Caroz, *The Arab Secret Services* (London: Corgi Books, 1978).

7. Robert Murphy, the US diplomat then serving as Under-Secretary for Political Affairs, considered that 'the effects of summarily withdrawing the Aswan offer had not been weighed carefully in advance': *Diplomat among Warriors* (London: Collins, 1964), 459. Nasser may well have planned to nationalize the Suez Canal Company anyway, but the withdrawal of the dam funding provided a good opportunity. As Harold Macmillan said in his memoirs, it was 'the occasion not the cause of Nasser's illegal action': Harold Macmillan, *Riding the Storm: 1956–59* (London: Macmillan, 1971), 100.

8. See on this point John Darwin, *Britain and Decolonisation: The Retreat from Empire in the Postwar World* (London: Macmillan, 1988).

9. D. C. Watt, 'Britain and the Suez Canal', Royal Institute of International Affairs pamphlet, August 1956; see also the essays by Steve Morwood and Michael T. Thornhill in Simon C. Smith (ed.), *Reassessing Suez 1956: New Perspectives on the Crisis and its Aftermath* (Aldershot: Ashgate Publishing Ltd, 2008), chapters 1 and 2.

10. Sir Anthony Eden, *Full Circle* (London: Cassell & Co., 1960), 424.

11. Though seized on by the British press and critics of the government's Middle East policy as symbolic of the decline of British influence, the root causes of Glubb's dismissal lie more in Jordanian domestic politics. Sir Alec Kirkbride, a former British Ambassador in Amman, told the Cabinet on 9 March 1956 that according to the King of Jordan the 'move against Glubb was personal' and that he wanted the traditional friendship between Jordan and Britain to continue (CM(56) 21st Conclusions, CAB 128/30, TNA).

12. Papers on this review, in the 'PR' series, can be found in CAB 134/1315, TNA. The review was coordinated by the Cabinet Secretary, Sir Norman

Brook: participating ministers were the Prime Minister, Lord President, Lord Privy Seal, Chancellor of the Exchequer, Foreign Secretary, and Minister of Defence. This group held ten meetings between June and December 1956 and produced forty-two memoranda. For further detail see George C. Peden, 'Suez and Britain's Decline as a World Power', *Historical Journal*, 55, 4 (2012).

13. On the negotiation of these loans, see Roger Bullen and M. E. Pelly (eds.), *Documents on British Policy Overseas*, Series I, vol. iii: *Britain and America: Negotiation of the United States Loan, 3 August–7 December 1945* (London: HMSO, 1986). Repayments were due to begin in 1957.

14. Peter Catterall (ed.), *The Macmillan Diaries: The Cabinet Years, 1950–57* (London: Macmillan, 2003; Pan edn, 2004), entry for 21 July 1956, p. 576.

15. Anthony Sampson, *Macmillan: A Study in Ambiguity* (London: Simon and Schuster, 1967), 112.

16. Brian Harrison, *Seeking a Role: The United Kingdom 1951–1970* (Oxford: Clarendon Press, 2009), 435–47.

17. See Michael Thornhill, 'Eden, Churchill and the Battle of the Canal Zone 1951–54', in Smith (ed.), *Reassessing Suez*. Lord Hankey had been Cabinet Secretary 1916–40 and later became a Director of the Suez Canal Company. His comment, made in a note to Eden of 11 February 1953, is in FO 371/102763 E 1052/68, TNA.

18. The Baghdad Pact, signed in 1955 between Turkey, Iran, Iraq, Pakistan, and Britain, was intended to prevent the spread of communism and promote Middle Eastern peace. For succinct accounts of both Baghdad Pact and Project Alpha, together with an analysis of their incompatibility, see Kyle, *Suez*.

19. A report by the Joint Intelligence Committee dated 21 March 1956 described Soviet objectives in the Middle East as the destruction of the Baghdad Pact, denial of bases and oil supplies to the Western powers, and the undermining of Western, particularly British, influence in the region: JIC(56)36 (Final), 'Probable Soviet Attitude to an Arab/Israel War', CAB 158/24, TNA.

20. Shuckburgh to Kirkpatrick, 10 March 1956, V 1054/84, FO 371/121235, TNA.

21. See Sue Onslow, 'The Suez Group', in *Oxford Dictionary of National Biography* (Oxford: Oxford University Press, 2005).

22. See, for example, Churchill's remark to his Principal Private Secretary and close friend Jock Colville, the night before offering his resignation: 'I don't believe Anthony can do it.' John Colville, *The Fringes of Power: Downing Street Diaries 1939–55* (London: Hodder and Stoughton, 1985), 708.

23. For a detailed analysis of Eden's medical condition and its possible effects on his abilities and behaviour see David Owen, *In Sickness and in Power: Illness in Heads of Government during the Last 100 Years* (London: Methuen, 2008), chapter 3, 'Prime Minister Eden's Illness and Suez'.

24. On 26 July 1956, the day before the Cabinet meeting, Eden had asked a few ministers to meet and discuss his position in relation to the Conservative Party, and the hostile campaign being waged against him by sections of the press. *Macmillan Diaries*, 578.

25. Evelyn Shuckburgh, *Descent to Suez: Diaries 1951–56* (London: Weidenfeld and Nicolson, 1986), 148 and 340–5. Anthony Nutting, *No End of a Lesson: The*

Story of Suez (London: Constable, 1996 edn), 32. Nutting's verdict was retrospective, so may have been influenced by later developments in the Suez crisis. But clearly something was amiss.

26. CAB(56) 54th Conclusions, CAB 128/30, TNA.

27. Notes by Cabinet Secretary, CAB 195/15. TNA. In 1953 Mossadegh had been deposed by covert action planned by British and American intelligence agencies. In the light of close ongoing intelligence liaison with the US, Eden may, as Keith Kyle puts it, have 'counted on receiving the degree of partnership in covert action that produced the Iranian countercoup' (*Suez*, 150). Eden might have done better to cast his mind back to 1951, when Britain suffered a major policy reverse with the nationalization of Iranian oil refineries at Abadan. On the implications of Abadan for Suez see Peter J. Beck, 'Britain and the Suez Crisis: The Abadan Dimension', in Smith (ed.), *Reassessing Suez*.

28. Robert Gascoyne-Cecil, as Viscount Cranborne, had been Eden's Parliamentary Under-Secretary from August 1935 until he resigned with the Foreign Secretary in February 1938. He succeeded as 5th Marquess in 1947.

29. Notes by Cabinet Secretary, CAB 195/15, TNA.

30. There has been considerable speculation regarding Eden's desire for the forcible removal of Nasser by covert means, but there is a great difference between wanting Nasser out of the way and the requisite resources, coordination, and political will.

31. Selwyn Lloyd, *Suez* (London: Jonathan Cape, 1978; Coronet edn, 1980), 4. Lloyd's full name was John Selwyn Brooke Lloyd, but he was always known as Selwyn Lloyd and was ennobled in 1976 as Lord Selwyn-Lloyd of Wirral.

32. Shuckburgh, *Descent to Suez*, 338.

33. CM(56) 24th Conclusions, 21 March 1956, CAB 128/30, TNA.

34. Copeland, *The Game Player*, 198.

35. CM(56) 47th Conclusions, 5 July 1956, CAB 128/30, TNA. For British military preparations to meet the commitment to Jordan see Eric Grove, 'Who to Fight in 1956, Egypt or Israel? Operation Musketeer versus Operation Cordage', in Smith (ed.), *Reassessing Suez*.

36. Eden and Lloyd reported on their visit to North America at a Cabinet meeting on 9 February, CM(56) 10th Conclusions, CAB 128/30, TNA. Although the Americans had been less 'forceful' on the question of Arab–Israeli settlement, and had given moral support to the Baghdad Pact rather than joining it, Lloyd and Eden had been pleasantly surprised to find the US government willing to take a firm line over restricting the supply of arms to Israel, 'despite the importance of the Jewish vote in an election year'.

37. Lloyd, *Suez*, 78.

38. The British intelligence establishment had suffered a series of disclosures and scandals in 1956, including the resurfacing of the Soviet agents Guy Burgess and Donald Maclean in Moscow, the disappearance of Commander 'Buster' Crabb in Portsmouth Harbour, and the discovery by Soviet and East German technicians of the Anglo-US tunnel under Berlin. On the state of British intelligence in 1956, particularly in relation to the Middle East, see Gill Bennett, 'Suez and the Threat to UK Interests Overseas', in M. Goodman and R. Dover (eds.), *Learning from the Secret Past: Cases in British Intelligence History* (Washington, DC: Georgetown University Press, 2011), chapter 8. British intelligence had

close links with their US, French, and Israeli counterparts, though it does not appear that the British were aware of how close the links were between the CIA and Nasser as described by Copeland in *The Game Player*.

39. Copeland, *The Game Player*, 200.
40. Notes by Cabinet Secretary, CAB 195/15, TNA. The Earl of Home, formerly Lord Dunglass, was to renounce his peerage in 1963 to become Prime Minister as Sir Alec Douglas-Home. Home had extensive experience in foreign affairs dating back to serving as Principal Private Secretary to Prime Minister Neville Chamberlain between 1937 and 1940.
41. See Keith Kyle, 'Britain and the Crisis, 1955–56', in W. Roger Louis and Roger Owen (eds.), *Suez 1956* (Oxford: Oxford University Press, 1989), 113–15.
42. Memorandum by the Lord Chancellor of 31 July 1956, CAB 21/4112, TNA.
43. CM(56) 3rd Conclusions, 11 January 1956, CAB 128/30, TNA.
44. Notes by Cabinet Secretary, CAB 195/15, TNA. *Macmillan Diaries*, entry for 27 July 1956, pp. 578–9.
45. *Macmillan Diaries*, entries for 9 and 13 December 1955, p. 516. See also Charles Williams, *Harold Macmillan* (London: Weidenfeld and Nicolson, 2009), 235–6.
46. Quoted in David Carlton, *Anthony Eden* (London: Allen Lane, 1989), 389. Carlton also comments that becoming Chancellor put Macmillan in a position of 'immense strength . . . Eden, having discarded one Chancellor, could not possibly discard another'.
47. Williams, *Harold Macmillan*, 224. Murphy, *Diplomat among Warriors*, 462.
48. Macmillan claimed that although he naturally shared responsibility, as a Cabinet minister, for all decisions taken on Suez, he had been 'fully employed with my own problems from the financial point of view' and so could have only a 'general knowledge of the issue'. He admitted, however, that he had expressed his views on the character and target of any military operations, although the matter was 'outside my sphere'. Macmillan, *Riding the Storm*, 106 and 111.
49. *Macmillan Diaries*, entries for 12 and 28 January 1956, pp. 524 and 531.
50. On British policy towards the development of the European Communities at this period see Alan S. Milward, *The United Kingdom and the European Community*, i: *The Rise and Fall of a National Strategy, 1945–63* (London: Frank Cass Publishers, 2002), chapters 7–9.
51. *Macmillan Diaries*, entries for 15 February and 4 May 1956, pp. 537 and 556.
52. *Macmillan Diaries*, entries for 5 and 21 July 1956, pp. 572 and 576.
53. Macmillan, *Riding the Storm*, 112.
54. *Macmillan Diaries*, entry for 20 December 1955, pp. 518–19.
55. Murphy, *Diplomat among Warriors*, 462–8; *Macmillan Diaries*, entries for 30 July–1 August 1956, pp. 579–80.
56. Sampson, *Macmillan*, 110–15.
57. Letter from Lloyd to Eden, 13 July 1955, PREM 11/1778, TNA. For Treasury views on defence spending during this period see George C. Peden, *Arms, Economics and British Strategy: From Dreadnoughts to Hydrogen Bombs* (Cambridge: Cambridge University Press, 2007), chapters 5 and 6.
58. In Cabinet on 19 June 1956, Macmillan said that proposed defence savings would 'do little to meet the major problem of easing the economic situation by

relieving the pressure on industrial resources in men and equipment', and took no account of the long-term changes required in the size and shape of the armed forces (CM(56) 44th Conclusions, CAB 128/30, TNA).

59. 'Defence policy', PR(56)2, 20 March 1956, CAB 134/1315, TNA.
60. *Macmillan Diaries*, entry for 28 May 1956, p. 562.
61. CM(56) 42nd, 44th, and 46th Conclusions, 14, 19, and 28 June 1956, CAB 128/30, TNA.
62. A popular uprising in Hungary against Soviet rule began on 23 October 1956, but was crushed brutally by Soviet troops in early November.
63. DO(56) 6th meeting, 10 July 1956, CAB 131/17, TNA. The Defence Committee did not meet again until 2 October 1956.
64. Detailed responses taken from the Cabinet Secretary's notes, CAB 195/15; CM(56) 54th Conclusions, CAB 128/30, TNA.
65. 'Internal Security in the Colonies', CAB 21/2925; the proceedings of an official committee set up to consider this report can be found in CAB 130/11, TNA.
66. The minutes of the Egypt Committee can be found in CAB 134/1216, TNA.

Chapter 3

1. Present at the meeting were: Harold Macmillan (Prime Minister, in the chair); R. A. Butler (Home Secretary); Lord Home (Foreign Secretary); John Maclay (Secretary of State for Scotland); Iain Macleod (Colonial Secretary); Henry Brooke (Minister of Housing and Local Government, and for Welsh Affairs); Peter Thorneycroft (Minister of Aviation); Reginald Maudling (President of the Board of Trade); Edward Heath (Lord Privy Seal); Ernest Marples (Minister of Transport); Viscount Kilmuir (Lord Chancellor); Duncan Sandys (Commonwealth Relations Secretary); Harold Watkinson (Minister of Defence); Sir David Eccles (Minister of Education); Lord Mills (Paymaster-General); John Hare (Minister of Labour); Dr Charles Hill (Chancellor of the Duchy of Lancaster); Christopher Soames (Minister of Agriculture, Fisheries, and Food); Martin Redmayne (Parliamentary Secretary to the Treasury); Anthony Barber (Economic Secretary to the Treasury); Sir Norman Brook (Cabinet Secretary) and two other members of the Cabinet Secretariat.
2. Minutes of the meeting on 21 July and other Cabinet meetings held during that period can be found in CAB 128/35, TNA.
3. The Commonwealth (formerly known since 1931 as the British Commonwealth of Nations) took its present form in 1949 when India became a republic: in 1961 there were fourteen members, three of whom joined in that year (while South Africa was to withdraw). The six countries in the European Economic Community were France, the Federal Republic of Germany (West Germany, FRG), Italy, Belgium, the Netherlands, and Luxembourg.
4. Alistair Horne, *Macmillan 1957–86* (London: Macmillan, 1989), 266–7. Horne notes that the 'Garden Girls', the No. 10 secretarial staff, were also unhappy in Admiralty House, while Dorothy Macmillan missed her garden. They did not move back into Downing Street until the summer of 1963.

Notes to pages 69–70

5. *The Times* political correspondent commented, when reporting proceedings in the House on 20 July, that 'part of the significance of the exchanges, both when Mr Macmillan was at the dispatch box and when Mr Butler succeeded him, was the hard commitment of sections on the Government side before the Prime Minister's statement has been heard, or, on good evidence, before the Cabinet decision has been taken'. *The Times*, 21 July 1961.

6. Eden had himself set out these priorities on becoming Foreign Secretary in 1951: 'We wish to cultivate the idea of an Atlantic Community based on the three pillars of the United States, United Kingdom (including the Commonwealth) and Continental Europe.' See Robert Rhodes James, *Anthony Eden* (London: Weidenfeld and Nicolson, 1986), 350–1.

7. See Chapter 1, pp. 12 and 19.

8. The Treaty of Rome came into effect on 1 January 1958, bringing the EEC into formal existence. A detailed account of these developments can be found in the Cabinet Office official history by Alan S. Milward, *The United Kingdom and the European Community*, i: *The Rise and Fall of a National Strategy 1945–63* (London: Frank Cass Publishers, 2002).

9. View of Sir Peter Smithers, former Conservative politician and secretary of the European Council, quoted in Sue Onslow, *Backbench Debate within the Conservative Party and its Influence on British Foreign Policy, 1948–57* (London: Macmillan Press Ltd, 1997), 27. Opinion in the Labour Party on Europe was confused, and subordinate to the internal battles on Clause 4 and unilateral nuclear disarmament. For an interesting analysis see R. M. Douglas, *The Labour Party, Nationalism and Internationalism 1939–1951* (London: Routledge, 2004); see also Hugo Young, *This Blessed Plot: Britain and Europe from Churchill to Blair* (New York: The Overlook Press, 1999), 148–9, describing the approach of Labour leader Hugh Gaitskell as 'an elaborate public agnosticism' towards Europe.

10. Macmillan's speech, delivered at Bedford on 20 July 1957, was in fact intended as a warning that the country was living beyond its means and that 'sacrifices could be needed to maintain prosperity': see John Ramsden, *The Winds of Change: Macmillan to Heath 1957–1975* (London: Longman Group, 1996), 2–3, also Peter Catterall (ed.), *The Macmillan Diaries*, ii: *Prime Minister and After, 1957–1966* (London: Macmillan, 2011), entry for 26 July 1957, pp. 50–1 and n. 79. On the question of British growth see Alec Cairncross (ed.), *The Robert Hall Diaries 1954–1961* (London: Unwin Hyman, 1991), 254. Hall, who retired as Economic Adviser to the government in April 1961, noted in his diary on 20 October 1960 that it was hard to disentangle the possible causes of poor British economic performance but that 'we are still left with an element which suggests that there is something wrong with the UK'.

11. A detailed account of the negotiations for the formation of the EFTA and its subsequent fortunes is given in Milward, *Rise and Fall of a National Strategy*, chapters 9 and 10. The founding members were Austria, Denmark, Norway, Portugal, Sweden, Switzerland, and the UK. In his report on 'The Six and the Seven: Long-Term Arrangements', dated 25 May 1960, Sir Frank Lee, Permanent Secretary to the Treasury, wrote that although the Seven (i.e. EFTA) was 'not a despicable grouping in economic terms', it was 'doubtful whether a heterogeneous and scattered grouping—brought together by ties of common funk, rather than

by any deeper purpose or by geographical contiguity—can develop a real cohesion or even continuity' (EQ(60)27, CAB 134/1852, TNA).

12. General Charles de Gaulle, wartime leader of the Free French Forces (when he and Macmillan had known each other well) and head of the first French postwar government, had retired in 1953 but returned to politics and became President of France in 1958 during the Algerian revolt. Konrad Adenauer was the first Chancellor of the Federal Republic of Germany (West Germany) formed in 1949.

13. American confidence in the British intelligence services had been shaken by the 'Cambridge spies', and was only partly mitigated by the arrest in January 1961 of the Lonsdale spy ring and the confession of George Blake. On these matters, and the relationship more generally of the Macmillan government with the intelligence services, see Christopher Andrew, *The Defence of the Realm: The Authorized History of MI5* (London: Penguin, 2009), 483–93.

14. See on this point John Newhouse, *De Gaulle and the Anglo-Saxons* (London: André Deutsch, 1970), 123: 'Every American administration has strongly favored Britain's involvement with the EEC, but Washington's views have never been decisive on this issue, and sometimes not even significant.'

15. Nigel Lawson has written that there is no evidence to suggest that the 1960 reshuffle was intended to bring in pro-European Ministers, and that the key personnel change was Selwyn Lloyd becoming Chancellor of the Exchequer (Jock Bruce-Gardyne and Nigel Lawson, *The Power Game: An Examination of Decision-Making in Government* (London: The Macmillan Press, 1976), 52). Whatever Macmillan's intention, however, there is no doubt that the reshuffled Cabinet contained several avowedly pro-European Ministers, in particular Edward Heath, and marked an evolution if not a change in attitude that was mirrored by civil service changes too. See Milward, *Rise and Fall of a National Strategy*, chapter 11, particularly 330–5.

16. On the increasing tension over the status of Berlin in the late 1950s and leading up to the crisis in August 1961 see Keith Hamilton, Patrick Salmon, and Stephen Twigge (eds.), *Documents on British Policy Overseas*, Series III, vol. vi: *Berlin in the Cold War 1948–1990* (hereafter *DBPO Berlin*) (London: Routledge 2009), chapter II.

17. CC(61) 23rd and 24th Conclusions, 25 and 26 April 1961, CAB 128/35, TNA. Macmillan visited General de Gaulle at Rambouillet 28–9 January 1961, where he found de Gaulle 'relaxed; friendly and seemed genuinely attracted by my themes—Europe to be united, politically and economically; but France and Britain to be something more than European powers, and to be so recognised by U.S.' Macmillan thought that 'everything now depends on (a) whether we really can put forward a formula for 6s and 7s wh[ich] both Commonwealth and British agriculture will wear, (b) whether the Americans can be got to accept France's nuclear achievements and ambitions' (*Macmillan Diaries*, 358). See Milward, *Rise and Fall of a National Strategy*, 337–8 on the shaky basis for these hopes; and on the relationship between Macmillan and de Gaulle, who had known one another during the Second World War, see Peter Mangold, *The Almost Impossible Ally: Harold Macmillan and Charles de Gaulle* (London; IB Tauris, 2006).

18. CC(61) 42nd Conclusions, CAB 128/35, TNA. The Cabinet Secretary's note-book covering the meeting is in CAB 195/19.

19. Edward Heath, *The Course of my Life: My Autobiography* (London: Hodder and Stoughton, 1998), 182.

20. *Macmillan Diaries*, entries for 15–22 June 1961, pp. 392–6.

21. Ramsden, *Winds of Change*, 130.

22. This aspect of Macmillan is conveyed convincingly by his biographer Alistair Horne, who had considerable personal contact with Macmillan as well as access to his diaries and papers. See Horne, *Macmillan 1957–86* (London: Macmillan, 1989).

23. Harold Evans, *Downing Street Diary: The Macmillan Years 1957–63* (London: Hodder and Stoughton, 1981), 151.

24. F. A. (later Sir Freddy) Bishop had been Principal Private Secretary to Eden as Prime Minister, and continued in that role with Macmillan. It was generally agreed, as his entry in the *Oxford Dictionary of National Biography* put it, that he exercised influence over Macmillan 'out of all proportion to his formal responsibilities'. Philip (later Sir Philip) de Zulueta, who had joined the Foreign Office in 1949, moved to No. 10 as a private secretary to Eden and remained there under both Macmillan and his successor Sir Alec Douglas-Home. Macmillan tried out his ideas on both Bishop and de Zulueta regularly, as he did on Cabinet Secretary Sir Norman Brook.

25. Young, *This Blessed Plot*, 98; Milward, *Rise and Fall of a National Strategy*, 310.

26. See Jacqueline Tratt, *The Macmillan Government and Europe: A Study in the Process of Policy Development* (London: Macmillan, 1996), 169.

27. Memorandum by the Prime Minister, written between 29 December 1960 and 3 January 1961, 'The Grand Design', PREM 11/3325, TNA.

28. *Macmillan Diaries*, entry for 8 April 1961, p. 372; *Robert Hall Diaries*, entry for 9 April 1961, pp. 264–5.

29. For an interesting analysis of Kennedy's decision to support the disastrous and unsuccessful attack on Cuba by US-trained anti-Castro exiles on 17 April 1961, see David Owen, *In Sickness and in Power: Illness in Heads of Government during the Last 100 Years* (London: Methuen Publishing Ltd, 2008), chapter 4.

30. *Macmillan Diaries*, entry for 11 June 1961, p. 389.

31. See *The Times*, 21 July 1961.

32. CC(61) 37th and 41st Conclusions, 30 June and 20 July 1961, CAB 128/35, TNA.

33. *The Times*, 21 July 1961. The diplomatic correspondent's view was that when Macmillan addressed the House on 31 July 'the tide will be seen to be flowing strongly towards Europe'.

34. Hare was not originally on the list for the Commonwealth consultations, but was asked to go when Reginald Maudling, President of the Board of Trade, refused to do so. In addition to Sandys, Thorneycroft, and Hare, Lord Perth, Minister of State for the Colonial Office, went to the West Indies, while Edward Heath visited Cyprus. On the detail of the consultations and Commonwealth considerations see Milward, *Rise and Fall of a National Strategy*, 349–51 and chapter 12, *passim*.

35. *Macmillan Diaries*, entry for 30 May 1961, p. 385; CC(61) 29th Conclusions, 30 May 1961, CAB 128/35, TNA.
36. Lord Orr-Ewing in an interview with Sue Onslow, quoted in her *Backbench Debate within the Conservative Party*, 18. Sandys's marriage to Winston Churchill's daughter Diana broke down in some acrimony in the late 1950s, and they were divorced in 1960: Diana committed suicide in 1963. Whatever Macmillan's views on Sandys's private affairs may have been, he described him in his diary as 'cool as a cucumber, methodical, very strong in character', and 'most loyal to me and absolutely tireless' (*Macmillan Diaries*, entries for 4 and 22 June 1961, pp. 389 and 396).
37. Onslow, *Backbench Debate within the Conservative Party*, chapter 2.
38. Macmillan noted in his diary that Thorneycroft, arguing that expenditure for 1958–9 should be kept to its 1957–8 levels, had 'behaved in such a rude and *cassant* way that I had difficulty in preventing some of the Cabinet bursting out in their indignation'; the Chancellor's letter of resignation, he thought, was 'calculated . . . to do the maximum injury to sterling' (*Macmillan Diaries*, entries for 6 and 7 January 1958, pp. 85–9). In July 1960, however, he recorded that 'after much reflection' he had offered the Ministry of Aviation to Thorneycroft who 'seemed reconciled' to the post even though it was not one of the key departments (*Macmillan Diaries*, entry for 17 July 1960, p. 315). The other two ministers to resign in 1958 were Enoch Powell and Nigel Birch.
39. CC(61) 42nd Conclusions, 21 July 1961, CAB 128/35, TNA.
40. CC(61) 24th Conclusions, 26 April 1961, CAB 128/35, TNA.
41. Halifax's remarks, made at a dinner in 1958, were noted by the diarist and political commentator Harold Nicolson: *Diaries and Letters 1945–1962* (London: Collins, 1968), entry for 15 May 1958, p. 349. See also Andrew, *Defence of the Realm*, 451–8, on the role of the Security Service (MI5) in supporting colonies during their progress towards independence.
42. Ramsden, *Winds of Change*, 6; *Macmillan Diaries*, entry for 19 May 1961, p. 383.
43. Milward, *Rise and Fall of a National Strategy*, 333: Milward comments in general, Eccles 'did not seem to think them a very desirable bunch to be flirting with anyway'.
44. Born Alexander Douglas-Home in 1903, he became Lord Dunglass in 1918 until he succeeded as the 14th Earl of Home in 1951. In 1963 he renounced his peerage, and served as Prime Minister, leader of the Opposition, and Foreign Secretary as Sir Alec Douglas-Home. He was created Baron Home of the Hirsel in 1974.
45. Evans, *Downing Street Diary*, 116–18; *Macmillan Diaries*, 306; Ramsden, *Winds of Change*, 132.
46. CC(61) 23rd Conclusions, 25 April 1961, CAB 128/35, TNA.
47. See *DBPO Berlin*, Nos. 231 ff.
48. CC(61) 36th Conclusions, 29 June 1961, CAB 128/35, TNA. On 19 June 1961 Edward Heath, on behalf of the British government, had announced the abrogation of the Anglo-Kuwaiti agreement of 1899, thereby recognizing Kuwait as an independent state. The Iraqi statement was issued on 25 June, and British troops began arriving in Kuwait from 2 July. In September they were withdrawn to be replaced by Arab League forces.

49. His speech was reported in *The Times*, 24 July 1961.
50. Lord Home, *The Way the Wind Blows: An Autobiography* (London: Collins, 1976), 173–4.
51. During a visit to London in late February 1961 with a group of senior French diplomats to discuss a possible association between the EFTA and the EEC, Wormser had rejected the idea of half-membership, and pointed out in a note of 1 June the impossibility of free Commonwealth entry to the EEC, the incompatibility of Britain's agricultural support system with the Common Agricultural Policy, and that there could be no guarantees for Britain's partners in the EFTA. This note, and Maudling's submission to Macmillan of 15 June, are in M 615/151, FO 371/158177, TNA.
52. See Bruce-Gardyne and Lawson, *The Power Game*, 43–6 and 53–7.
53. In John Ramsden's view, by 1961 Butler was 'like Macmillan to an extent acting out a self-parody of his earlier career in which he was "safe" rather than "dynamic" ': *Winds of Change*, 134. See also *Macmillan Diaries*, 17 and 28 June, 5 July 1961, pp. 308 and 311–12. Macmillan claimed that he had offered Butler the posts of Chancellor of the Exchequer and Foreign Secretary, though Butler subsequently disputed the latter claim. In 1963, when Macmillan resigned, Butler again lost out, this time to Lord Home (Sir Alec Douglas-Home).
54. Bruce-Gardyne and Lawson, *The Power Game*, 58.
55. See Milward, *Rise and Fall of a National Strategy*, 341–2.
56. CC(61) 24th Conclusions, 26 April 1961, CAB 128/35, TNA.
57. Anthony Howard, *RAB: The Life of R. A. Butler* (London: Jonathan Cape, 1987), 249. Butler had been Leader of the House since 1955, becoming Home Secretary in 1957, adding the chairmanship of the Party in 1959. In October 1961 his parliamentary and party roles were given to Iain Macleod.
58. According to Macmillan's press secretary, Butler was much exercised about the takeover of Odhams by Cecil King, chairman of the *Daily Mirror* group, regarding it as 'abuse of capitalism'. Macmillan declined to intervene, arguing that it was less a political than an economic issue, Evans, *Downing Street Diary*, 136.
59. Butler embarked on a programme of penal reform and refused to reintroduce capital punishment despite the 'flogging and birching' lobby, but was less successful in moving towards the decriminalization of homosexuality. He also opposed Tony Benn's (ultimately successful) campaign not to succeed to the title of Viscount Stansgate when his father died.
60. For Heath's own account of the evolution of his views on Europe see *The Course of my Life*, chapter 8. See also Philip Ziegler, *Edward Heath* (London: HarperCollins, 2010), chapter 7.
61. Horne, *Macmillan 1957–86*, 242.
62. Heath to Kilmuir, 30 November 1960, printed in David Gowland and Arthur Turner (eds.), *Britain and European Integration 1945–1998* (London: Routledge, 2000), document 5.7A. Both Denmark and Norway, EFTA members, had expressed the intention of applying to the EEC.
63. See Chapter 2, p. 50.
64. Kilmuir to Heath, 14 December 1960, printed in Gowland and Turner, document 5.7B. The issue of sovereignty is explored fully in Milward, *Rise and Fall of a National Strategy*, chapter 13.

65. Milward, *Rise and Fall of a National Strategy*, 345.

66. Cabinet Secretary's notebook, CAB 195/19, TNA.

67. Ziegler, *Edward Heath*, 118; *HC Deb.*, vol. 644, 2 August 1961, cols. 1490–1.

68. Young, *This Blessed Plot*, 77. Young went on to note that if politicians were faced with something they did not like or want to do, the strategy was to 'let it be stigmatized as an insupportable assault on the British way of life'.

69. *Macmillan Diaries*, entry for 22 July 1961, p. 399.

70. CC(61) 43rd Conclusions, 24 July 1961, CAB 128/35, TNA.

71. Young, *This Blessed Plot*, 139.

Chapter 4

1. Tony Benn, *Office without Power: Diaries 1968–72* (London: Hutchinson, 1988; Arrow edn, 1989, hereafter *Benn Diaries*), entry for 11 January 1968, p. 11.

2. Roy Jenkins, *A Life at the Centre* (London: Methuen, 1991; Politico's edn, 2006), 223.

3. David Owen, *The Politics of Defence* (London: Jonathan Cape, 1972), 97. David (later Lord) Owen was at that time a Labour MP, and was to serve as Parliamentary Under-Secretary for the Navy 1968–70.

4. The minutes of all the Cabinet meetings in January 1968 can be found in CAB 128/43, TNA. All senior ministers attended all the meetings unless overseas, and every meeting was well attended. With some variation, those present were: Harold Wilson (Prime Minister, in the chair); George Brown (Foreign Secretary); James Callaghan (Home Secretary); Roy Jenkins (Chancellor of the Exchequer); Denis Healey (Secretary of State for Defence); Patrick Gordon Walker (Secretary of State for Education and Science); George Thomson (Secretary of State for Commonwealth Affairs); Anthony Greenwood (Minister of Housing and Local Government); Ray Gunter (Minister of Labour); Barbara Castle (Minister of Transport); Richard Marsh (Minister of Power); Michael Stewart (First Secretary of State); Lord Gardiner (Lord Chancellor); Richard Crossman (Lord President of the Council); William Ross (Secretary of State for Scotland); Anthony Crosland (President of the Board of Trade); Peter Shore (Secretary of State for Economic Affairs); Lord Longford (Lord Privy Seal); Fred Peart (Minister of Agriculture, Fisheries and Food); Cledwyn Hughes (Secretary of State for Wales); Anthony Wedgwood Benn (Minister of Technology); Reginald Prentice (Minister of Overseas Development); John Diamond (Chief Secretary to the Treasury); John Silkin (Parliamentary Secretary to the Treasury); Sir Burke Trend (Cabinet Secretary) and members of the Cabinet Secretariat. On 12 January Goronwy Roberts (Minister of State for Foreign Affairs) and George Thomas (Minister of State for Commonwealth Affairs) were also present. On 15 January, Kenneth Robinson (Minister of Health), Edward Short (Postmaster-General), and Robert Mellish (Minister of Public Building and Works) were present.

5. On the Treasury angle see G. C. Peden, *Arms, Economics and British Strategy from Dreadnoughts to Hydrogen Bombs* (Cambridge: Cambridge University Press, 2007),

331–2. Detailed accounts of the development of British policy East of Suez and the run-up to the Cabinet decision can be found in a number of works, including Saki Dockrill, *Britain's Retreat from East of Suez: The Choice between Europe and the World?* (Basingstoke: Palgrave Macmillan, 2002). See also in particular Matthew Jones, 'A Decision Delayed: Britain's Withdrawal from South East Asia Reconsidered, 1961–68', in *English Historical Review*, 117/472 (June 2002), 569–95.

6. The South East Asia Treaty Organization, established formally in 1955, comprised Australia, New Zealand, Pakistan, the Philippines, Thailand, France, and the USA as well as Britain. Its aim was collective resistance to armed attack and the prevention of counter-subversion directed against its members. Other agreements to which Britain was party included the Central Treaty Organization (CENTO, formerly known as the Baghdad Pact), and the Anglo-Malaysian Defence Treaty of 1963.

7. The US had been involved in active military operations in support of South Vietnam's struggle against North Vietnam since 1965, although the conflict dated back to the division of the country in 1954 after the communist Ho Chi Minh defeated the French colonial power.

8. McGeorge Bundy to Johnson, quoted in Clive Ponting, *Breach of Promise: Labour in Power 1964–70* (London: Hamish Hamilton, 1989; Penguin edn, 1990), 50, n. 10. Ponting cites a number of documents from the Johnson Presidential Library in support of his thesis.

9. On this see Ponting, *Breach of Promise*, chapter 3. The title of his book gives the flavour of what Ponting thought about Labour's perpetuation of Britain's world role and deference to the Americans.

10. Harold Wilson's remark about being an 'East of Suez man' was apparently made to the journalist Chapman Pincher in 1964. See Chapman Pincher, *Inside Story: A Documentary of the Pursuit of Power* (London: Sidgwick and Jackson, 1978), 227. For Wilson's parliamentary statement on 16 December 1964 see *HC Deb. 5s*, vol. 704, cols. 423–4.

11. On Trend's influence see Peden, *Arms, Economics and British Strategy*, 335–6. See also Owen, *The Politics of Defence*, 101–2. Owen also makes the useful point that the British parliamentary system makes governments more susceptible to the pressure of party opinion than in the US where there is separation of powers.

12. This document from the Johnson Library is quoted in Ponting, *Breach of Promise*, 57.

13. The British government had decided in November 1965 to withdraw British forces from Aden in 1968 when the South Arabian Federation became independent. But withdrawal was brought forward to 1967 due to unrest and civil disorder in Aden.

14. Ponting, *Breach of Promise*, 586. For a detailed examination of the decision-making behind devaluation, published less than ten years after the event, see Jock Bruce-Gardyne and Nigel Lawson, *The Power Game: An Examination of Decision-Making in Government* (London: The Macmillan Press Ltd, 1976), chapter 5. Callaghan did not leave the government, but swapped jobs with Home Secretary Roy Jenkins who became Chancellor of the Exchequer on 30 November 1967.

15. Jenkins, *A Life at the Centre*, 224; Patrick Gordon Walker, *The Cabinet* (London: Jonathan Cape, 1970), 129.

16. Jenkins, *A Life at the Centre*, 224.
17. See the editorial, 'From Marshall to Johnson', *The Times*, 3 January 1968, p. 9. On 4 January the paper carried an article by Professor John Dunning, described as 'a leading authority on American investment in Britain', who warned that the US measures might have serious consequences for British industry (*The Times*, 4 January 1968, p. 21).
18. Richard Crossman, *The Diaries of a Cabinet Minister*, ii: *Lord President of the Council and Leader of the House of Commons, 1966–68* (London: Hamish Hamilton and Jonathan Cape, 1976, hereafter *Crossman Diaries*), 641–2.
19. At the first of the Cabinet meetings on 4 January, the Prime Minister informed ministers that Parliament was to be recalled a day early, on 16 January, when the government's measures would be announced. They would then be debated over the following two days, with the debate on foreign affairs postponed until the following week. See CC(68) 1st Conclusions, 4 January 1968, CAB 128/43, TNA.
20. Barbara Castle, *The Castle Diaries, 1964–70* (London: Weidenfeld and Nicolson, 1984, hereafter *Castle Diaries*), entry for 11 January 1968, p. 353.
21. The campaign originated in late December 1967 with five secretaries in Surbiton and spread rapidly. The popular press backed it, and Robert Maxwell started a 'Buy British' campaign of his own. The campaign ran out of steam within a few months, however, particularly after it became known that the tee-shirts bearing the slogan 'I'm backing Britain' had been made in Portugal. See Dominic Sandbrook, *White Heat: A History of Britain in the Swinging Sixties* (London: Little Brown, 2006; Abacus edn, 2007), 608–11.
22. *Crossman Diaries*, entry for 7 January 1968, p. 639.
23. Jenkins, *A Life at the Centre*, 227.
24. For a shrewd analysis of Wilson's character and career, based on personal interviews as well as documentary evidence, see the masterly biography by Ben Pimlott, *Harold Wilson* (London: HarperCollins, 1992).
25. In February 1967 a press story by Chapman Pincher had revealed that commercial cable companies passed an extra copy of overseas cables to British security agencies. The Prime Minister reacted strongly to what he described as a clear breach of the rules of the D-Notice Committee, which regulated the publication of matters relating to national security. It emerged, however, that the secretary of the committee, Colonel Lohan, may have indicated to Pincher that his story would not be a problem. Wilson's handling of the ensuing row, which led to the appointment of an official enquiry under Lord Radcliffe, alienated the press and was widely considered to have inflamed the situation. See Pimlott, *Harold Wilson*, 443–9, and Nicholas Wilkinson, *Secrecy and the Media: The Official History of the United Kingdom's D-Notice System* (London: Routledge, 2009), section 7.
26. Views differed within the Cabinet on the merits of maintaining the embargo on selling arms to South Africa. But it was an issue that aroused strong feelings in the Labour Party, and the suggestion in December 1967 that Wilson might be reconsidering the embargo sparked a major row, inflamed by press leaks from Brown and Callaghan. An interesting account of how Wilson handled the row is given in the *Castle Diaries*, 335–41.
27. On the activities of George Wigg, who as Paymaster-General was accorded a supervisory role in intelligence matters, and on Wilson's anxiety about

conspiracies, see Christopher Andrew, *The Defence of the Realm: The Authorized History of MI5* (London: Penguin, 2009), part D, chapter 11.

28. See Kenneth O. Morgan, *Callaghan: A Life* (Oxford: Oxford University Press, 1997), 208 and 249.

29. For Harold Wilson's meeting with President Johnson in Australia, and visit to Moscow in January 1968, see G. Bennett and K. A. Hamilton (eds.), *Documents on British Policy Overseas*, Series III, vol. i: *Britain and the Soviet Union 1968–1972* (London: The Stationery Office, 1997), 4–32.

30. Resolution 242 was adopted by the UN Security Council in November 1967, with the support of the Soviet Union which shared British interests in an Arab-Israeli settlement. It has never been implemented.

31. Harold Wilson, *The Labour Government 1964–70: A Personal Record* (London: Weidenfeld and Nicolson, 1971; Pelican edn, 1974), 610; Jenkins, *A Life at the Centre*, 217–18.

32. James Callaghan, *Time and Chance* (London: William Collins, 1987; Politico's edn, 2006), 200.

33. Christopher Mayhew, *Britain's Role Tomorrow* (London: Hutchinson & Co, 1967), 14 and 26–9. Mayhew argued that he resigned in 1966 because defence cuts, such as the cancellation of the CVA.01 carrier, were not matched by cuts in commitments. On this see also Denis Healey, *The Time of my Life* (London: Michael Joseph, 1989; Penguin edn, 1990), 275–6. For Brown's remarks to the effect that white forces East of Suez could 'become an embarrassment and a liability' see Jones, 'A Decision Delayed', 587.

34. Wilson, *The Labour Government*, 523. On the second British application to the EEC, and its relevance to British domestic politics, see also Stephen Wall, *The Official History of Britain and the European Community*, vol. ii: *From Rejection to Referendum* (London: Routledge, 2012), chapter 5, 'We shall not take "No" for an answer'.

35. Memorandum for the Cabinet by Sir Burke Trend, 22 December 1967, 'The Approach to Europe', C(67)202, CAB 129/134, TNA.

36. For the protest movement in Britain, and popular perceptions of the government's policy towards Vietnam, see Sandbrook, *White Heat*, chapters 7 and 25.

37. Wilson, *The Labour Government*, 610. Frank Field (ed.), *Attlee's Great Contemporaries: The Politics of Character* (London: Continuum Books, 2009),152.

38. Jenkins, *A Life at the Centre*, 223.

39. Wilson, *The Labour Government*, 610.

40. Jenkins had served as Minister of Aviation from 1964 to 1965, and as Home Secretary from 1965 to 1967.

41. Anthony Howard, 'Roy Jenkins', *Oxford Dictionary of National Biography*.

42. CC(68) 1st Conclusions, CAB 128/43, TNA.

43. George Brown, *In my Way* (London: Victor Gollancz, 1971), 128; Denis Greenhill, *More by Accident* (York: Wilton 65, 1992), 133.

44. Healey, *Time of my Life*, 297.

45. Brown's appointment may also have owed something to Wilson's determination not to give the job to his rival Callaghan, who wanted it. See Pimlott, *Harold Wilson*, 435–6.

46. Brown, *In my Way*, 140.

47. CC(68) 1st Conclusions, CAB 128/43, TNA.

48. *Crossman Diaries*, 634–5 and 639; see also *Benn Diaries*, 2–5. Crossman commented that Brown, Healey, Stewart, and Callaghan formed a 'powerful right-wing junta' in opposition to early withdrawal from East of Suez, and that Callaghan in particular 'opposed with all his old-fashioned Great Britain jingoism the cuts he had been trying to impose as Chancellor'.

49. Healey, *Time of my Life*, 263 and 293.

50. Healey, *Time of my Life*, 289.

51. A number of defence cuts had been announced in 1965–6, including the cancellation of orders for the TSR2 strike reconnaissance aircraft in favour of the cheaper American F-111s, and for a new aircraft carrier, the CVA-01. See Healey, *Time of my Life*, 271–7.

52. *Benn Diaries*, entry for 4 January 1968, pp. 2–5. Benn was 'counting the voices', too, and listed in his diary those in favour and against the East of Suez and F-111 decisions. According to Benn, his was the casting vote in the latter case.

53. CC(68) 1st Conclusions, CAB 128/43, TNA. See also *Castle Diaries*, entry for 4 January 1968, pp. 349–50.

54. *Castle Diaries*, 350, *Benn Diaries*, 6, Jenkins, *A Life at the Centre*, 228. See also Robert Pearce (ed.), *Patrick Gordon Walker, Political Diaries 1932–71* (London: The Historians Press, 1991), 318.

55. *Benn Diaries*, entry for 12 January 1968, p. 12.

56. CC(68) 5th Conclusions, 12 January 1968, CAB 128/43, TNA; *Benn Diaries*, entry for 12 January, p. 12.

57. Susan Crosland, *Tony Crosland* (London: Jonathan Cape, 1982; Coronet edn, 1983), 186–9. Jenkins, *A Life at the Centre*, 217–18.

58. CC(68) 5th Conclusions, 12 January 1968, CAB 128/43, TNA. *Benn Diaries*, entry for 12 January 1968, p. 12.

59. *Castle Diaries*, entry for 12 January 1968, p. 354; CC(68) 6th Conclusions, 12 January 1968, CAB 128/43, TNA. The phrase 'bloody unpleasant' does not appear in the formal Cabinet minutes (where 'disturbing and distasteful' was used), but was attested to by a number of participants.

60. *Castle Diaries*, entry for 12 January 1968, p. 355.

61. *Benn Diaries*, entry for 12 January 1968, p. 15.

62. *Benn Diaries*, entry for 15 January 1968, p. 16.

63. *Castle Diaries*, entry for 15 January 1968, pp. 356–7.

64. CC(68) 7th Conclusions, 15 January 1968, CAB 128/43 TNA.

65. *Castle Diaries*, entry for 15 January 1968, p. 358.

Chapter 5

1. George Walden, then head of the Soviet section of the FCO's Eastern European and Soviet Department (EESD), wrote later that the codename was his idea, 'a thin joke for putting the boot into the Soviet spy machine in London': see Walden's article in the *Evening Standard*, 6 January 1998. For his own account of Operation FOOT see George Walden, *Lucky George: Memoirs of an Anti-Politician* (London: Allen Lane/The Penguin Press, 1999), chapter 6.

2. Notes used by Greenhill in speaking to Ippolitov, printed in G. Bennett and K. A. Hamilton (eds.), *Documents on British Policy Overseas (DBPO)*, Series III, vol. i: *Britain and the Soviet Union 1968–72* (London: The Stationery Office, 1998), Enclosure I in No. 76.

3. In March 2001, following revelations by FBI spy Robert Hanssen, the US government expelled 50 Russian representatives with diplomatic status for engaging in espionage. There have been many smaller-scale episodes, such as the arrest of ten people in the north-eastern US in June 2010.

4. Vasili Mitrokhin, who worked in the archives of the Soviet security service, the KGB, was smuggled out of Russia into Britain in 1992 with detailed notes he had compiled over many years. Material from these papers was published by Mitrokhin with Professor C. M. Andrew as *The Mitrokhin Archive* in two volumes: *The KGB in Europe and the West* (London: Penguin, 1999) and *The KGB and the World* (London: Penguin, 2005).

5. The FCO Historians were permitted to publish intelligence-related material in their documentation of Operation FOOT in *DBPO, Britain and the Soviet Union*. The files from which this material was taken, including the letter from No. 10 to the FCO recording what happened at the meeting on 21 September, have not yet been transferred to The National Archives (TNA). The references in this chapter are, accordingly, principally to documents printed or summarized in *DBPO*. There are, however, files at TNA in the CAB and PREM series containing useful references to Operation FOOT: for details see Geraint Hughes, ' "Giving the Russians a Bloody Nose": Operation FOOT and Soviet Espionage in the United Kingdom, 1964–71', in *Cold War History*, 6/2 (May 2006), 229–49.

6. Anglo-Soviet relations were broken off in 1927 following a raid by British intelligence on the headquarters of ARCOS, the All-Russian Cooperative Society Ltd, which shared premises with the Soviet Trade Delegation: see Gill Bennett, *Churchill's Man of Mystery: Desmond Morton and the World of Intelligence* (London: Routledge, 2006), 94–106. The publication in 1970 of a volume in the FCO's official history of British foreign policy, *Documents on British Foreign Policy 1919–39*, covering the ARCOS raid, stimulated press interest in the STD and it was confirmed in the answer to a Parliamentary Question that four STD officials had been expelled in the second half of 1970.

7. Soviet evidence suggests that Moscow Centre (KGB HQ), unhappy with its penetration of foreign intelligence services, took a conscious decision at this time to improve their operational efficiency in Britain by increasing the size of the residency and 'swamping' MI5. See Christopher Andrew and Oleg Gordievsky, *KGB: The Inside Story of its Foreign Operations from Lenin to Gorbachev* (London: Hodder and Stoughton, 1990; Sceptre edn, 1991), 525.

8. Record of meeting on 25 May 1971, printed in *DBPO, Britain and the Soviet Union*, No. 66.

9. Christopher Andrew, *The Defence of the Realm: The Authorised History of MI5* (London: Penguin, 2009), 491.

10. A BBC News story on 30 September 1971 quoted a police officer, Charles Shearer, who had arrested Lyalin; 'I arrested a KGB superspy.' See also Andrew, *Defence of the Realm*, 569–71.

11. See Andrew, *Defence of the Realm*, 567–71, and *The Mitrokhin Archive: The KGB in Europe and the West*, chapter 23.

12. Details of the meeting are taken from a letter sent later on 21 September by P. J. S. Moon (No. 10) to J. A. N. Graham, Principal Private Secretary to Sir Alec Douglas-Home at the Foreign Office. This letter is not in the public domain, but was made available to the FCO Historians: see n. 6 above.

13. Peter Hennessy, *Muddling Through: Power, Politics and the Quality of Government in Postwar Britain* (London: Victor Gollancz, 1996), 275–6; Edward Heath, *The Course of my Life: The Autobiography of Edward Heath* (London: Hodder and Stoughton, 1998), 473.

14. 'Give our spies cloaks and daggers again', *Daily Express*, 30 July 1970. The article did not, of course, refer to Rennie by name, but to a 'career diplomat' who had been given the top job in the Secret Service while 'the man who should have taken over' (an internal SIS candidate) was overlooked.

15. On the Brooke/Kroger exchange see *DBPO, Britain and the Soviet Union*. Although ministers in the Heath government and some FCO officials were later to condemn the deal (Maudling called it 'culpable neglect' in his memoirs, George Walden 'a squalid transaction'), at the time the reasons for making the exchange, supported by the Americans, were well understood at the highest level.

16. Record of meeting on 15 January 1970, printed in *DBPO, Britain and the Soviet Union*, No. 43.

17. Denis Greenhill, *More by Accident* (York: Wilton 65, 1992), 121.

18. See Andrew, *Defence of the Realm*, section D, chapter 11. During his second administration Wilson's suspicions turned into paranoia: see Andrew, *Defence of the Realm*, section E, chapter 4.

19. See Chapter 4.

20. See Anthony Seldon, 'The Heath Government in History', in Stuart Ball and Anthony Seldon (eds.), *The Heath Government 1970–74* (London: Longman, 1996). In the view of a recent biographer, Heath had prepared rather too thoroughly, and in office imagined 'a future which would roll out smoothly along the lines which he had laid down for it' (Philip Ziegler, *Edward Heath: The Authorised Biography* (London: HarperCollins, 2010)), 202.

21. Lord Carrington, *Reflect on Things Past* (London: William Collins, 1988), 253. In August 1971, a month before the FOOT meeting, the Prime Minister's political secretary, Douglas Hurd, warned Heath that the party thought his government 'less politically conscious than its Conservative predecessor' (Douglas Hurd, quoted in Ball and Seldon, *The Heath Government*, chapter 2). See also Hennessy, *Muddling Through*, chapter 15.

22. See Chapter 3.

23. Christopher Hill and Christopher Lord, 'The Foreign Policy of the Heath Government', in Ball and Seldon, *The Heath Government*, chapter 12.

24. Lord Home, *The Way the Wind Blows: An Autobiography* (London: Collins, 1976), 245.

25. See *DBPO, Britain and the Soviet Union*, No. 63, n. 2.

26. *DBPO, Britain and the Soviet Union*, 376–7.

27. *DBPO, Britain and the Soviet Union*, Nos. 60 and 66.

28. Ziegler, *Edward Heath*, 239.

29. According to Ziegler, it was Carrington, Whitelaw, and the Lord Chancellor, Quintin Hogg, to whom Heath looked for plain speaking after the death of Iain Macleod, Chancellor of the Exchequer, only a few weeks after Heath took office.
30. Reginald Maudling, *Memoirs* (London: Sidgwick and Jackson, 1978), 176.
31. Maudling, *Memoirs*, 156. Not surprisingly, considering the date of publication, his memoirs contain no reference to Operation FOOT.
32. Andrew, *Defence of the Realm*, 602–10; Eunan O'Halpin, *Defending Ireland: The Irish State and its Enemies since 1922* (Oxford: Oxford University Press, 1999), 207.
33. Maudling, *Memoirs*, 168.
34. *DBPO, Britain and the Soviet Union*, No. 66.
35. See Andrew, *Defence of the Realm*, 587–91. According to Security Service archives, Maudling later admitted that he and Heath had been 'a little brash in their approach' to MI5, which had responded by setting out firmly the limits to the service's involvement in industrial intelligence collection.
36. Andrew, *Defence of the Realm*, 571–2. Dame Stella Rimington, DG of MI5 1992–6, noted in her memoirs that her early work in the Soviet section had concentrated on research stemming from the 'Cambridge Five'.
37. Greenhill, *More by Accident*, 158.
38. *DBPO, Britain and the Soviet Union*, No. 70.
39. *DBPO, Britain and the Soviet Union*, Nos. 70 and 73.
40. See Ziegler, *Edward Heath*, 257–8.
41. *DBPO, Britain and the Soviet Union*, No. 66 and n. 2.
42. *DBPO, Britain and the Soviet Union*, No. 73, n. 4; letter from Moon to Graham, 21 September 1971, see n. 12 above.
43. *DBPO, Britain and the Soviet Union*, Nos. 67 and 69.
44. Carrington, *Reflect on Things Past*, 217–19.
45. William Whitelaw, *The Whitelaw Memoirs* (London: Aurum Press Ltd, 1989), 71–2. It was entirely in keeping that there was no mention of Operation FOOT.
46. Moon to Graham, 21 September 1971: see n. 12 above.
47. Heath, *Course of my Life*, 495. The Prime Minister won the Admiral's Cup in 1971.
48. Lewis Baston and Anthony Seldon, 'Number 10 under Edward Heath', in Ball and Seldon, *The Heath Government*, chapter 3; Andrew, *Defence of the Realm*, 588.
49. Details of both Hollis and Blunt can be found in Andrew, *Defence of the Realm*.
50. For example, the arrangement by which, as a result of a 1946 agreement, British military missions in Germany (BRIXMIS) could carry out inspections in Soviet territory, with reciprocal facilities for Soviet military missions (SOXMIS).
51. *DBPO, Britain and the Soviet Union*, No. 66.
52. A series of press articles in the *New York Times* early in 1971 had included reports on Nixon's dissatisfaction with his government's worldwide intelligence operations.
53. Trend to Moon (No. 10), 20 September 1971, PREM 15/1935, TNA.
54. 'Points for decision at ministerial meeting on 21 September', given to the Prime Minister by Moon that morning, PREM 15/1935, TNA.

55. See *DBPO, Britain and the Soviet Union*, No. 75.
56. Tom Bower, *The Perfect English Spy: Sir Dick White and the Secret War 1935–90* (London: Heinemann, 1995), 364. Andrew and Gordievsky, *KGB*, 525.
57. *DBPO, Britain and the Soviet Union*, Nos. 77, 80, and 84.
58. *DBPO, Britain and the Soviet Union*, No. 86.
59. Home, *The Way the Wind Blows*, 248.

Chapter 6

1. Geoffrey Howe, *Conflict of Loyalty* (London: Macmillan, 1994), 245. At the time of writing, the Cabinet minutes for 1982 are not yet in the public domain. However, details of the Cabinet deliberations on the evening of 2 April 1982 (CC(82) 15th Conclusions) are given in a number of published accounts, including the memoirs of a number of ministers present at the meeting, and in Sir Lawrence Freedman, *The Official History of the Falklands Campaign*, vols. i and ii (London: Routledge, 2005). Present at the meeting were: Margaret Thatcher (Prime Minister, in the chair); William Whitelaw (Home Secretary); Lord Carrington (Secretary of State for Foreign and Commonwealth Affairs); Sir Keith Joseph (Secretary of State for Education and Science); John Nott (Secretary of State for Defence); Humphrey Atkins (Lord Privy Seal); John Biffen (Secretary of State for Trade); Norman Fowler (Secretary of State for Social Services); Norman Tebbit (Secretary of State for Employment); Lord Hailsham (Lord Chancellor); Sir Geoffrey Howe (Chancellor of the Exchequer); Francis Pym (Lord President of the Council); Michael Heseltine (Secretary of State for the Environment); Patrick Jenkin (Secretary of State for Industry); David Howell (Secretary of State for Transport); Baroness Young (Chancellor of the Duchy of Lancaster); Cecil Parkinson (Paymaster-General); Michael Jopling (Parliamentary Secretary to the Treasury); Sir Robert Armstrong (Cabinet Secretary), and members of the Cabinet Secretariat. The Chief of the Air Staff, Sir Michael Beetham, and the Chief of the Naval Staff, Sir Henry Leach, were also present.
2. Peter Hennessy, *The Prime Minister: The Office and its Holders since 1945* (London: Allen Lane/The Penguin Press, 2000; Penguin Books edn, 2001), 414.
3. George Walden, *Lucky George: Memoirs of an Anti-Politician* (London: Allen Lane/The Penguin Press, 1999), 209.
4. William Whitelaw said in a television interview some years later that during the Falklands crisis 'all of us who remembered Suez were haunted by Suez': see John Campbell, *Margaret Thatcher*, vol. ii: *The Iron Lady* (London: Jonathan Cape, 2003; Vintage edn, 2008), 133. Suez was also invoked in a number of ministerial memoirs, including those by John Nott and Norman Fowler.
5. Report of a Committee of Privy Counsellors, *Falkland Islands Review*, January 1983, Cmnd 878 (The Franks Report).
6. For a detailed account of the sovereignty issue, covering both the Falkland Islands and the Dependencies, including South Georgia, see Freedman, *Official History of the Falklands Campaign*, vol. i: *The Origins of the Falklands War*, chapter 1.
7. Lord Carrington, *Reflect on Things Past* (London: William Collins, 1988), 357. On the Ridley proposals see Freedman, *Origins of the Falklands War*, chapters 11

and 12. The official history sums up very neatly the position of the British government at the beginning of 1982. The Falklands were, it says, 'in the "too difficult" category for the Government. It was unwilling to face the political costs of pushing forward with a deal in spite of islander and parliamentary opposition or the financial costs of ensuring the prosperity and security of the colony. The result was that the FCO was left pursuing an increasingly fragile middle ground, desperately trying to avoid a major crisis with Argentina but with an increasingly weak hand to play.' Freedman, *Origins of the Falklands War*, 158.

8. Freedman, *Origins of the Falklands War*, chapter 15.
9. Freedman, *Origins of the Falklands War*, 187.
10. For the arrival on South Georgia on 18 March 1982 by an Argentine scrap merchant, and the consequent exchanges between the British and Argentine authorities, see Freedman, *Origins of the Falklands War*, chapter 18. For Mrs Thatcher's assessment of the likelihood of invasion see Margaret Thatcher, *The Downing Street Years* (London: HarperCollins, 1993; pb edn 1995), 179.
11. Freedman, *Official History of the Falklands Campaign*, vol. ii: *War and Diplomacy*, 7. Freedman's two volumes contain a blow-by-blow account of what information was received and when, and of the military arrangements being set in train in consequence.
12. The Social Democratic Party had been founded in March 1981 by four senior members of the Labour party, Roy Jenkins, William (Bill) Rodgers, Shirley Williams, and David Owen (the 'Gang of Four'). A number of other Labour MPs and peers, equally disenchanted with what they considered to be Labour's move towards left-wing extremism, left to join the new party. In September 1981 the SDP agreed an electoral pact with the Liberal Party, thus creating an SDP-Liberal alliance. For an account of the 'annus mirabilis' of the SDP, see Roy Jenkins, *A Life at the Centre* (London: Macmillan, 1991; Politico's edn, 2006), chapter 29.
13. Norman Fowler, *Ministers Decide: A Personal Memoir of the Thatcher Years* (London: Chapmans, 1991), 155.
14. On the exchanges with the US President and State Department, see Carrington, *Reflect on Things Past*, 365–8, Thatcher, *Downing Street Years*, 178–80, and Freedman, *Origins of the Falklands War*, chapter 19.
15. William Whitelaw, *The Whitelaw Memoirs* (London: Aurum Press Ltd, 1989), 203.
16. Howe, *Conflict of Loyalty*, 245.
17. To my mind the most instructive books on Margaret Thatcher's career as a whole are Campbell, *Margaret Thatcher*, and Hugo Young, *One of Us: A Biography of Margaret Thatcher* (London: Macmillan, 1989). But much can also be learned from the various writings of Peter Hennessy and Percy Cradock, from the memoirs of her colleagues, and from her own account of her premiership in *Downing Street Years*.
18. Peter Hennessy, *Muddling Through: Power, Politics and the Quality of Government in Postwar Britain* (London: Victor Gollancz, 1996), 293.
19. Quoted in Hennessy, *Muddling Through*, 400. On 'establishing hegemony' see Anthony Seldon and Daniel Collings, *Britain under Thatcher* (London: Pearson Education Limited, 2000), chapter 2.

20. Percy Cradock, *In Pursuit of British Interests: Reflections on Foreign Policy under Margaret Thatcher and John Major* (London: John Murray, 1997), 19–21.

21. Remark by Butler quoted in Campbell, *Margaret Thatcher*, 16. See also Cradock, *In Pursuit of British Interests*, 22.

22. Alexander M. Haig, Jr. *Caveat: Realism, Reagan and Foreign Policy* (New York: Macmillan Publishing Company, 1984), 267.

23. For a concise and lucid explanation of this issue, see Stephen Wall, *A Stranger in Europe: Britain and the EU from Thatcher to Blair* (Oxford: Oxford University Press, 2008).

24. Wall, *A Stranger in Europe*, 7–12.

25. Quoted in Wall, *A Stranger in Europe*, 9.

26. Waldegrave's view was expressed in a seminar at the Institute of Historical Research in December 1997, and is quoted in Hennessy, *Prime Minister*, 408.

27. Cradock, *In Pursuit of British Interests*, 19.

28. Haig, *Caveat*, 266. See also Carrington, *Reflect on Things Past*, 365 and Freedman, *Origins of the Falklands War*, 190–1.

29. On the issue of sanctions, and on the gas pipeline, see Richard Smith, Patrick Salmon, and Stephen Twigge (eds.), *Documents on British Policy Overseas (DBPO)*, Series III, vol. viii: *The Invasion of Afghanistan and UK-Soviet Relations 1979–82* (London: Routledge, 2012), Nos. 118–27.

30. Haig, *Caveat*, 268. Alan Clark, *Diaries* (London: Weidenfeld and Nicolson, 1993; Phoenix edn, 1994), 70.

31. Walden, *Lucky George*, 208.

32. Campbell, *Margaret Thatcher*, 56.

33. Carrington, *Reflect on Things Past*, 280.

34. Carrington, *Reflect on Things Past*, 367.

35. A settlement of the long-running problem of Rhodesia, and its transition to independence as Zimbabwe, had been drawn up at the Lancaster House conference held from September to December 1979. Lord Carrington's personal impressions are described in *Reflect on Things Past*, chapter 13.

36. The Camp David accords, signed in September 1978 by the leaders of Israel, Egypt, and the United States, were intended to pave the war for an Egyptian-Israeli peace treaty and for a wider Arab-Israeli peace settlement. The treaty was signed in 1979, but the wider peace remains elusive.

37. Carrington, *Reflect on Things Past*, 340 and chapter 15, *passim*.

38. Wall, *A Stranger in Europe*, 9–10.

39. John Nott, *Here Today, Gone Tomorrow: Recollections of an Errant Politician* (London: Politico's Publishing, 2002), 250.

40. Nott, *Here Today, Gone Tomorrow*, 241.

41. Howe, *Conflict of Loyalty*, 223.

42. Nott, *Here Today, Gone Tomorrow*, 186–7.

43. Nott, *Here Today, Gone Tomorrow*, 202–4.

44. FCO Guidance telegram No. 84 of 24 June 1981, EN/081/1 Part A.

45. On the Defence Review, and the decision regarding *Endurance* in particular, see Freedman, *Origins of the Falklands War*, chapter 14. See also Nott, *Here Today, Gone Tomorrow*, 207–13, and Campbell, *Margaret Thatcher*, 128–9.

46. Young, *One of Us*, 275.

47. Nott, *Here Today, Gone Tomorrow*, 251–2.

48. Freedman, *Origins of the Falklands War*, 204–6 and chapter 19, *passim*.

49. Private information.

50. Howe, *Conflict of Loyalty*, 246.

51. *Guardian* report, quoted in Campbell, *Margaret Thatcher*, 10. For Howe's views on his working relationship with Mrs Thatcher at this point see *Conflict of Loyalty*, 144–8 and 211–13.

52. Howe, *Conflict of Loyalty*, 245–6.

53. For comments on Biffen by Ian Gilmour and Mrs Thatcher see Ion Trewin (ed.), *The Hugo Young Papers: A Journalist's Notes from the Heart of Politics* (London: Allen Lane, 2008; Penguin edn, 2009), 144 and 149–51. Biffen's remarks on Mrs Thatcher are quoted in Hennessy, *Prime Minister*, 403.

54. Cecil Parkinson, *Right at the Centre: An Autobiography* (London: Weidenfeld and Nicolson, 1992), 148–9. Clark, *Diaries*, entry for 14 December 1983, p. 57.

55. Parkinson, *Right at the Centre*, 152–3 and 190; Campbell, *Margaret Thatcher*, 9.

56. Michael Heseltine, *Where There's A Will* (London: Hutchinson 1987; Arrow edn, 1990), 278.

57. Whitelaw, *Memoirs*, 143.

58. Young, *One of Us*, 235; *Hugo Young Papers*, 133.

59. Freedman, *Origins of the Falklands War*, 189–90; on the position of the ICJ and earlier consideration of referring the sovereignty question, see Freedman, *Origins of the Falklands War*, chapter 1.

60. Freedman, *Origins of the Falklands War*, 189–90; Thatcher, *Downing Street Years*, 179.

61. For an account of the debate on 3 April see Freedman, *War and Diplomacy*, 16–20.

62. Carrington, *Reflect on Things Past*, 370.

Bibliography

Unpublished Documents

The National Archives, Kew, Surrey (TNA)

Cabinet Office (CAB)
Foreign Office/Foreign and Commonwealth Office (FO/FCO)
Prime Minister's Office (PREM)
Treasury (T)

Published Documents and Official Histories

Documents

Documents on British Foreign Policy 1919–1939 (*DBFP*)
  (London: HMSO)
Second Series, 1931–8 (21 volumes)
Documents on British Policy Overseas (*DBPO*) (London:
  HMSO/TSO/Frank Cass/Routledge)
Series I (1945–50, 9 vols.)
Series II (1950–60, 4 vols.)
Series III (1960–, 8 vols.)
***Gowland, David, and Turner, Arthur (eds.), Britain and
  European Integration 1945–1998*** (London: Routledge, 2000).

Official Histories

Farrar-Hockley, Gen. Sir Anthony, *The British Part in the Korean War*
  (2 vols.) (London: HMSO, 1990).
Freedman, Sir Lawrence, *The Official History of the Falklands Campaign*
  (2 vols.) (London: Routledge, 2005).

Gowing, Margaret, and Arnold, Lorna, *Independence and Deterrence: Britain and Atomic Energy 1945–52* (2 vols.) (London: Palgrave Macmillan, 1974).

Milward, Alan S., *The United Kingdom and the European Community*, vol. i: *The Rise and Fall of a National Strategy, 1945–63* (London: Frank Cass Publishers, 2002).

Wall, Stephen, *The United Kingdom and the European Community*, vol. ii: *From Rejection to Referendum* (London: Routledge, 2012).

Wilkinson, Nicholas, *Secrecy and the Media: The Official History of the United Kingdom's D-Notice System* (London: Routledge, 2009).

Books relevant to decision-making generally

Andrew, Christopher, *The Defence of the Realm: The Authorized History of MI5* (London: Penguin, 2009).

Beck, Peter J., *Using History: Making British Policy* (London: Palgrave Macmillan, 2006).

Bruce-Gardyne, Jock, and Lawson, Nigel, *The Power Game: An Examination of Decision-Making in Government* (London: The Macmillan Press, 1976).

Cradock, Percy, *In Pursuit of British Interests: Reflections on Foreign Policy under Margaret Thatcher and John Major* (London: John Murray, 1997).

—— *Know Your Enemy: How the Joint Intelligence Committee Saw the World* (London: John Murray, 2002).

Dixon, Norman, *On the Psychology of Military Incompetence* (London: Jonathan Cape, 1976).

Field, Frank (ed.), *Attlee's Great Contemporaries: The Politics of Character* (London: Continuum Books, 2009).

Gordon Walker, Patrick, *The Cabinet* (London: Jonathan Cape, 1970).

Grabo, Cynthia, *Anticipating Surprise: Analysis for Strategic Warning* (Lanham, MD: University Press of America Inc., 2004).

Hennessy, Peter, *Whitehall* (London: Martin Secker and Warburg Ltd, 1989).

—— *Muddling Through: Power, Politics and the Quality of Government in Postwar Britain* (London: Victor Gollancz, 1996).

—— *The Prime Minister: The Office and Its Holders since 1945* (London: Penguin Books, 2001).

Hurd, Douglas, *Choose your Weapons: The British Foreign Secretary. 200 Years of Argument, Success and Failure* (London: Weidenfeld and Nicolson, 2010).

Immerman, Richard H., 'Intelligence and Strategy: Historicizing Psychology, Policy and Politics', *Diplomatic History*, 32/1 (January 2008).

Neustadt, Richard E., and May, Ernest R., *Thinking in Time: The Uses of History for Decision Makers* (New York: The Free Press, 1986).

Owen, David, *In Sickness and in Power: Illness in Heads of Government during the Last 100 Years* (London: Methuen Publishing Ltd, 2008).

Peden, G. C., *Arms, Economics and British Strategy from Dreadnoughts to Hydrogen Bombs* (Cambridge: Cambridge University Press, 2007).

Wall, Stephen, *A Stranger in Europe: Britain and the EU from Thatcher to Blair* (Oxford: Oxford University Press, 2008).

Select bibliography for individual chapters

Introduction

Blair, Tony, *A Journey* (London: Hutchinson, 2010).

Crossman, Richard, Introduction to Walter Bagehot, *The English Constitution* (first published 1867; London: Penguin edn, 1963).

Chapter 1

Acheson, Dean, *Present at the Creation: My Years in the State Department* (New York: W.W. Norton, 1969).

Addison, Paul, *No Turning Back: The Peacetime Revolutions of Post-War Britain* (Oxford: Oxford University Press, 2010).

Ambrose, Stephen E., *Eisenhower: Soldier and President* (New York: Simon and Schuster, 1997).

Barclay, Sir Roderick, *Ernest Bevin and the Foreign Office* (London, 1975).

Baxter, Christopher, *The Great Power Struggle in East Asia, 1944–50* (London: Palgrave Macmillan, 2009).

Bullock, Alan, *Ernest Bevin: Foreign Secretary 1945–51* (London: Heinemann, 1983).

Burgess, Simon, *Stafford Cripps: A Political Life* (London: Victor Gollancz, 1999).

Catterall, Peter (ed.), *The Macmillan Diaries: The Cabinet Years, 1950–57* (London: Macmillan, 2004).

Douglas, R. M., *The Labour Party, Nationalism and Internationalism 1939–51* (London: Routledge, 2004).

Harper, John Lamberton, *American Visions of Europe* (Cambridge: Cambridge University Press, 1994).

Kuhns, Woodrow J. (ed.), *Assessing the Soviet Threat: The Early Cold War Years* (Center for the Study of Intelligence (CSI), CIA, University Press of the Pacific, 2005).

Kynaston, David, *Austerity Britain 1945–51* (London: Bloomsbury, 2007).

Mallaby, George, *From my Level* (London: Hutchinson, 1965).

Manchester, William, *American Caesar: Douglas MacArthur 1880–1964* (London: Hutchinson, 1979).

Morgan, Kenneth O., *Labour in Power 1945–1951* (Oxford: Oxford University Press, 1984).

Pimlott, Ben (ed.), *The Political Diary of Hugh Dalton 1918–40, 1945–60* (London: Jonathan Cape, 1986).

Thomas-Symonds, Nicklaus, *Attlee: A Life in Politics* (London: Tauris, 2010).

Truman, Harry S., *Memoirs*, vol. ii: *Years of Trial and Hope: 1946–52* (New York: Doubleday & Co., 1956).

Warner, Geoffrey (ed.), *In the Midst of Events: The Foreign Office Diaries and Papers of Kenneth Younger, February 1950–October 1951* (London: Routledge, 2005).

Williams, Francis, *A Prime Minister Remembers* (London: Heinemann, 1961).

Chapter 2

Bennett, Gill, 'Suez and the Threat to UK Interests Overseas', in M. Goodman and R. Dover (eds.), *Learning from the Secret Past: Cases in British Intelligence History* (Washington, DC: Georgetown University Press, 2011).

Carlton, David, *Anthony Eden* (London: Allen Lane, 1989).

Caroz, Yaacov, *The Arab Secret Services* (London: Corgi Books, 1978).

Catterall, Peter (ed.), *The Macmillan Diaries: The Cabinet Years, 1950–57* (London: Macmillan, 2004).

Colville, John, *The Fringes of Power: Downing Street Diaries 1939–55* (London: Hodder and Stoughton, 1985).

Cooper, Chester L., *The Lion's Last Roar: Suez, 1956* (New York: Harper and Row, 1978).

Copeland, Miles, *The Game Player* (London: Aurum Press, 1989).

Darwin, John, *Britain and Decolonisation: The Retreat from Empire in the Postwar World* (London: Macmillan, 1988).

Eden, Sir Anthony, *Full Circle* (London: Cassell & Co., 1960).

Harrison, Brian, *Seeking a Role: The United Kingdom 1951–70* (Oxford: Clarendon Press, 2009).

Hennessy, Peter, *Having it so Good: Britain in the Fifties* (London: Penguin, 2006).

James, Laura, *Nasser at War: Arab Images of the Enemy* (London: Palgrave Macmillan, 2006).

Kelly, Saul, and Gorst, Anthony (eds.), *Whitehall and the Suez Crisis* (London: Frank Cass Publishers, 2000).

Kyle, Keith, *Suez* (London: Weidenfeld and Nicolson, 1991).

Lloyd, Selwyn, *Suez* (London: Jonathan Cape, 1978).

Louis, W. Roger, and Owen, Roger (eds.), *Suez 1956* (Oxford: Oxford University Press, 1989).

Lucas, W. Scott, *Divided We Stand: Britain, the US and the Suez Crisis* (London: Hodder and Stoughton, 1991).

Macmillan, Harold, *Riding the Storm: 1956–59* (London: Macmillan, 1971).

Murphy, Robert, *Diplomat among Warriors* (London: Collins, 1964).

Nutting, Anthony, *No End of a Lesson: The Story of Suez* (London: Constable, 1967).

Peden G. C., 'Suez and Britain's Decline as a World Power', *Historical Journal*, 55, 4 (2012).

Sampson, Anthony, *Macmillan: A Study in Ambiguity* (London: Simon and Schuster, 1967).

Shuckburgh, Evelyn, *Descent to Suez: Diaries 1951–56* (London: Weidenfeld and Nicolson, 1986).

Smith, Simon C. (ed.), *Reassessing Suez 1956: New Perspectives on the Crisis and its Aftermath* (Aldershot: Ashgate Publishing Ltd, 2008).

Williams, Charles, *Harold Macmillan* (London: Weidenfeld and Nicolson, 2009).

Chapter 3

Cairncross, Alec (ed.), *The Robert Hall Diaries 1954–61* (London: Unwin Hyman, 1991).

Catterall, Peter (ed.), *The Macmillan Diaries*, vol. ii: *Prime Minister and After, 1957–1966* (London: Macmillan, 2011).

Evans, Harold, *Downing Street Diary: The Macmillan Years 1957–63* (London: Hodder and Stoughton, 1981).

Heath, Edward, *The Course of my Life: My Autobiography* (London: Hodder and Stoughton, 1998).

Home, Lord, *The Way the Wind Blows: An Autobiography* (London: Collins, 1976).

Horne, Alistair, *Macmillan 1957–86* (London: Macmillan, 1989).

Howard, Anthony, *RAB: The Life of R. A. Butler* (London: Jonathan Cape, 1987).

James, Robert Rhodes, *Anthony Eden* (London: Weidenfeld and Nicolson, 1986).

Mangold, Peter, *The Almost Impossible Ally: Harold Macmillan and Charles de Gaulle* (London: IB Tauris, 2006).

Newhouse, John, *De Gaulle and the Anglo-Saxons* (London: André Deutsch, 1970).

Nicolson, Harold, *Diaries and Letters 1945–62* (London: Collins, 1968).

Onslow, Sue, *Backbench Debate within the Conservative Party and its Influence on British Foreign Policy, 1948–57* (London: Macmillan Press Ltd, 1997).

Ramsden, John, *The Winds of Change: Macmillan to Heath 1957–1975* (London: Longman Group, 1996).

Tratt, Jacqueline, *The Macmillan Government and Europe: A Study in the Process of Policy Development* (London: Macmillan, 1996).

Young, Hugo, *This Blessed Plot: Britain and Europe from Churchill to Blair* (New York: The Overlook Press, 1999).

Ziegler, Philip, *Edward Heath* (London: HarperCollins, 2010).

Chapter 4

Benn, Tony, *Office without Power: Diaries 1968–72* (London: Hutchinson, 1988).

Brown, George, *In my Way* (London: Victor Gollancz, 1971).

Callaghan, James, *Time and Chance* (London: William Collins, 1987).

Castle, Barbara, *The Castle Diaries, 1964–70* (London: Weidenfeld and Nicolson, 1984).

Crosland, Susan, *Tony Crosland* (London: Jonathan Cape, 1982).

Crossman, Richard, *The Diaries of a Cabinet Minister*, vol. ii: *Lord President of the Council and Leader of the House of Commons, 1966–68* (London: Hamish Hamilton and Jonathan Cape, 1976).

Dockrill, Saki, *Britain's Retreat from East of Suez: The Choice between Europe and the World?* (London: Palgrave Macmillan, 2002).

Greenhill, Denis, *More by Accident* (York: Wilton 65, 1992).

Healey, Denis, *The Time of my Life* (London: Michael Joseph, 1989).

Jenkins, Roy, *A Life at the Centre* (London: Macmillan, 1991).

Jones, Matthew, 'A Decision Delayed: Britain's Withdrawal from South East Asia Reconsidered, 1961–68', *English Historical Review*, 117 (June 2002).

Khong, Yuen Foong, *Analogies at War: Korea, Munich, Dien Bien Phu, and the Vietnam Decisions of 1965* (Princeton: Princeton University Press, 1992).

Mayhew, Christopher, *Britain's Role Tomorrow* (London: Hutchinson & Co., 1967).

Morgan, Kenneth O., *Callaghan: A Life* (Oxford: Oxford University Press, 1997).

Owen, David, *The Politics of Defence* (London: Jonathan Cape, 1972).

Pearce, Robert (ed.), *Patrick Gordon Walker, Political Diaries 1932–71* (London: The Historians Press, 1991).

Pimlott, Ben, *Harold Wilson* (London: HarperCollins, 1992).

Pincher, Chapman, *Inside Story: A Documentary of the Pursuit of Power* (London: Sidgwick and Jackson, 1978).

Ponting, Clive, *Breach of Promise: Labour in Power 1964–70* (London: Hamish Hamilton, 1989).

Sandbrook, Dominic, *White Heat: A History of Britain in the Swinging Sixties* (London: Little Brown, 2006).

Wilson, Harold, *The Labour Government 1964–70: A Personal Record* (London: Weidenfeld and Nicolson, 1971).

Chapter 5

Andrew, Christopher, and Gordievsky, Oleg, *KGB: The Inside Story of its Foreign Operations from Lenin to Gorbachev* (London: Hodder and Stoughton, 1990).

Andrew, C. M., with Mitrokhin, Vasili, *The Mitrokhin Archive*, 2 vols.: *The KGB in Europe and the West* (London: Penguin, 1999); *The KGB and the World* (London: Penguin, 2005).

Ball, Stuart, and Seldon, Anthony (eds.), *The Heath Government 1970–74* (London: Longman, 1996).

Bower, Tom, *The Perfect English Spy: Sir Dick White and the Secret War 1935–90* (London: Heinemann, 1995).

Carrington, Lord, *Reflect on Things Past* (London: William Collins, 1988).

Greenhill, Denis, *More by Accident* (York: Wilton 65, 1992).

Heath, Edward, *The Course of my Life: My Autobiography* (London: Hodder and Stoughton, 1998).

Home, Lord, *The Way the Wind Blows: An Autobiography* (London: Collins, 1976).

Hughes, Geraint, ' "Giving the Russians a Bloody Nose": Operation FOOT and Soviet Espionage in the United Kingdom, 1964–71', *Cold War History*, 6/2 (May 2006).

Maudling, Reginald, *Memoirs* (London: Sidgwick and Jackson, 1978).

O'Halpin, Eunan, *Defending Ireland: The Irish State and its Enemies since 1922* (Oxford: Oxford University Press, 1999).

Walden, George, *Lucky George: Memoirs of an Anti-Politician* (London: Allen Lane/The Penguin Press, 1999).

Whitelaw, William, *The Whitelaw Memoirs* (London: Aurum Press Ltd, 1989).

Ziegler, Philip, *Edward Heath: The Authorised Biography* (London: HarperCollins, 2010).

Chapter 6

Addison, Paul, *No Turning Back: The Peacetime Revolutions of Post-War Britain* (Oxford: Oxford University Press, 2010).

Campbell, John, *Margaret Thatcher*, vol. ii: *The Iron Lady* (London: Jonathan Cape, 2003).

Carrington, Lord, *Reflect on Things Past* (London: William Collins, 1988).

Clark, Alan, *Diaries* (London: Weidenfeld and Nicolson, 1993).

Danchev, Alex, *Oliver Franks: Founding Father* (Oxford: Oxford University Press, 1993).

Fowler, Norman, *Ministers Decide: A Personal Memoir of the Thatcher Years* (London: Chapmans, 1991).

Haig, Alexander M., Jr., *Caveat: Realism, Reagan and Foreign Policy* (New York: Macmillan Publishing Company, 1984).

Halcrow, Morrison, *Keith Joseph: A Single Mind* (London: Macmillan, 1989).

Heseltine, Michael, *Where There's a Will* (London: Hutchinson, 1987).

Howe, Geoffrey, *Conflict of Loyalty* (London: Macmillan, 1994).

Jenkins, Roy, *A Life at the Centre* (London: Macmillan, 1991).

Nott, John, *Here Today, Gone Tomorrow: Recollections of an Errant Politician* (London: Politico's Publishing, 2002).

Prior, Jim, *A Balance of Power* (London: Hamish Hamilton Ltd, 1986).

Pym, Francis, *The Politics of Consent* (London: Hamish Hamilton Ltd, 1984).

Ranelagh, John, *Thatcher's People: An Insider's Account of the Politics, the Power and the Personalities* (London: HarperCollins, 1991).

Seldon, Anthony, and Collings, Daniel, *Britain under Thatcher* (London: Pearson Education Ltd, 2000).

Thatcher, Margaret, *The Downing Street Years* (London: HarperCollins, 1993).

Trewin, Ion (ed.), *The Hugo Young Papers: A Journalist's Notes from the Heart of Politics* (London: Allen Lane, 2008).

Walden, George, *Lucky George: Memoirs of an Anti-Politician* (London: Allen Lane/The Penguin Press, 1999).

Whitelaw, William, *The Whitelaw Memoirs* (London: Aurum Press Ltd, 1989).

Young, Hugo, *One of Us: A Biography of Margaret Thatcher* (London, Macmillan, 1989).

Index

Index